Louisiana

Its Land and People

Fred B. Kniffen
Sam Bowers Hilliard

Louisiana

Its Land and People

Revised edition

 Louisiana State University Press
Baton Rouge and London

Copyright © 1968, 1988 by Louisiana State University Press

Manufactured in the United States of America

Designer: Laura Roubique Gleason
Typeface: Palatino
Typesetter: The Composing Room of Michigan, Inc.
Printer and Binder: Braun-Brumfield, Inc.

10   9   8   7   6   5   4   3   2   1

Library of Congress Cataloging-in-Publication Data

Kniffen, Fred Bowerman, 1900–
    Louisiana, its land and people.

    Includes index.
    Summary: A geography of Louisiana, covering its
weather, climate, land contours, soils, vegetation
and resources; and investigating the effects man has
had on its landscape, from the prehistoric Indians
through the industries and urbanization of the present.
        1.   Louisiana—Description and travel.   [1. Louisiana—
Geography]   I. Hilliard, Sam Bowers.   II. Title.
F369.K7   1987   917.63   87-2859
ISBN 0-8071-1369-7
ISBN 0-8071-1448-0 (text)

Contents

Preface / xi
Preface to the Revised Edition / xiii

1 Introduction / 1
2 A Geographic Ramble / 5
3 Orientation and Space Relations / 11
4 Weather and Climate: *Introduction* / 17
5 Weather and Climate: *Temperature and Moisture* / 21
6 Weather and Climate: *Winds* / 29
7 Relief: *Hills* / 34
8 Relief: *Terraces* / 39
9 Relief: *Lowlands: The River* / 44
10 Relief: *Lowlands: Delta and Coast* / 53
11 Relief: *Streams and Lakes* / 58
12 Relief: *Minor Features* / 64
13 Soils / 70
14 Vegetation / 78
15 Resources: *Wildlife and Fisheries* / 86
16 Miscellaneous Resources and Conservation / 95
17 Man in Louisiana / 101
18 Prehistoric Indians / 104

19 Historic Indians / 110
20 Explorers / 115
21 European Settlers and Settlements / 120
22 New Settlers, New Trade, New Crops / 124
23 European Settlement Patterns / 129
24 New Boundaries and New Commercial Crops / 136
25 The Last Hundred Years / 141
26 Steamboats, Railroads, and Modern Transportation / 146
27 Controlling the Mississippi / 154
28 Settlement of the Prairies / 161
29 Industrial Lumbering / 166
30 Mineral Resources / 171
31 Agricultural Shifts / 178
32 Industrial Growth / 186
33 Population and Urbanization / 192
34 Louisiana's Past, Present, and Future / 198

Glossary / 200
Index / 207

Maps

1   Place names / 1
2   Major and minor features / 5
3   Natural regions / 8
4   Louisiana and the world / 11
5   Louisiana and North America / 12
6   Area and size / 13
7   Parishes and boundaries / 14
8   Coastline and shoreline / 15
9   Air masses / 18
10 Average growing season / 22
11 Average annual precipitation / 23
12 Extreme climatic conditions / 27
13 Tropical storms and hurricanes / 33
14 Relief features and regions / 36
15 Extent of glaciation / 39
16 Old drainage course near Baton Rouge / 43
17 Shifting channels / 44
18 Louisiana's rivers / 45
19 False River / 48
20 Modern Mississippi River delta passes / 50
21 Mississippi River delta systems / 54
22 Southern Louisiana / 55
23 Waterways of Louisiana / 63
24 The chenier plain / 65
25 Soils of Louisiana / 72
26 Areas of wind-blown soils / 74
27 Natural vegetation of Louisiana / 79

28 Water from wells / 98
29 Indian economies / 107
30 Indian linguistic groups and tribes / 111
31 The De Soto map, 1544 / 116
32 Iberville's ascent of the Mississippi, 1699 / 117
33 The Gentil map, 1700 / 118
34 Important early sites / 121
35 Linear settlement patterns / 122
36 Early spread of settlers / 125
37 Landholding boundaries / 129
38 Important landmarks / 130
39 Survey and settlement in St. Helena Parish / 133
40 Rural settlement types / 134
41 Plantation settlement pattern / 137
42 The Louisiana Purchase, 1803 / 138
43 Early Louisiana roads / 144
44 Railroads in Louisiana, 1895 / 148
45 Present-day Louisiana railroads / 149
46 Louisiana roadways, 1960 / 150
47 Major highways / 151
48 Pipelines / 152
49 Bonnet Carré spillway / 157
50 Solution to the Atchafalaya problem / 158
51 The Atchafalaya floodway / 159
52 Southwest Louisiana, 1884 / 161
53 Southwest Louisiana, 1917 / 162

54 Oil and gas fields, 1935 / 172

55 Oil and gas fields, 1981 / 173

56 Production along the Tuscaloosa Trend, 1984 / 175

57 Dominant agricultural commodities / 184

58 The Industrial Corridor / 188

59 Black population / 193

60 Population / 194

61 Metropolitan centers / 196

Tables

1 Geologic Time Scale / 40
2 Fur Harvest / 89
3 Alligator Harvest / 91
4 Prehistoric Cultures / 109
5 Indian Population / 114
6 Agricultural Production / 182
7 Urban Growth / 195

Preface

This book is a geography of Louisiana. Its purpose is to describe and understand what we can observe in the landscape about us. We realize that two major forces have created what is called Louisiana. Much the older of the two is nature, whose activities are to be measured in terms of millions of years. The other is man. He has been in Louisiana only a few thousand years, and effectively only 250 years. Nature is comparatively slow in performing its work and is usually submissive to man's treatment and use. Its results are normally predictable. Only now and then nature asserts its latent power in the form of disastrous storm or flood.

Although man has been here only a relatively short time, he is a powerful force for change. He gains power through sheer numbers and an awesome growth of technical capacity. Alterations within a few years or even months transform the landscape into something unrecognizable. Forests are bulldozed away and factories rise in their place. Highways and pipelines crease the marsh. A sea of soybeans blots out swamp and former cotton fields. New lakes appear and the air is hazy with industrial pollution.

There is an established way of treating a region of the earth geographically. It begins with orientation and space relations, then moves on to climate, landforms, vegetation, soils, and other resources. Man is introduced through an account of the region's earliest inhabitants. Changes in the landscape brought about by man are traced through their time sequence. Man's occupance of the region is constantly set against the qualities of nature that mark the area. This book on the geography of Louisiana follows in general the traditional plan. Certain matters may be slighted and others unduly emphasized. These departures largely follow personal interests or disinterests of the author.

In covering such a wide range of materials, it has been necessary to seek the aid of a number of specialists. The assistance of several individuals is gratefully acknowledged: Dr. W. G. McIntire on physical geography; Dr. Thomas Hansbrough and Dr. Norwin Linnartz, vegetation and soils; Dr. Jo Ann Carrigan, history; George Cry, climate; and Robert LaFleur, wildlife and fisheries. These individuals are not responsible for any errors that may have crept into the sections they read.

Many persons have contributed to the large number of illustrations that must be part of the geographical treatment of any region. Philip B. Larimore, Jr., and staff drafted the maps and made the sketches. Both individuals and firms have contributed photographs. Hopefully, they are all acknowledged. Several state agencies generously aided the search for photographs and contributed prints: the Louisiana Section of the State Library; the

Wildlife and Fisheries Commission; the Department of Commerce and Industry; the Forestry Commission; the Louisiana Geological Survey. Apologies are made to any contributor who may have been slighted.

Last to be mentioned but surely most important has been the editorial assistance. The Louisiana State University Press and particularly Mrs. Ruth Hubert have aided in innumerable instances. Special credit must be given Mrs. Irene S. Bass, geographer and primary teacher extraordinary, for her most helpful glossary appearing at the back of this book and for her neverending effort to keep the text comprehensible to the nonprofessional reader.

Fred Kniffen

Preface to the Revised Edition

For sixteen years I have occupied an office two doors from the one in which Fred Kniffen has spent over half a century. In that office he has welcomed, advised, taught, lectured, praised, admonished, and entertained students, faculty, friends, and visitors from all over—from Dry Prong to Timbuktu, from Bogalusa to Kathmandu. And from that office he has sallied forth to study the domain he deemed to be his laboratory—the world. His work has carried him to many parts of the world, and of it he speaks and writes with authority and understanding, but he has always returned to his adopted home, Louisiana, where most of his scholarly studies are focused.

His writings on Louisiana are lucid and loving expressions of an uncluttered mind as it seeks to understand area. He writes of Louisiana as if it were just as important as any other place on the globe (which it is), but he never loses sight of its place in the world. He seems to have that rare gift of seeing both the forest and the trees; he is concerned with things of seemingly small importance, such as the last Spanish moss gin or the outdoor oven, but also delves into the workings of hurricanes or the Mississippi River, both of whose power apparently keep us at their mercy. Not surprisingly, he is known throughout the state and is looked upon as one of the persons who "really know" Louisiana. His book on Louisiana is a classic that has informed a generation of Louisiana students.

Two decades have elapsed since *Louisiana: Its Land and People* was first published. Originally intended as an eighth-grade textbook on the geography of Louisiana, it has served as a reader on the Pelican State for a variety of people. Following the time-tested recipe for a good regional geography, it covers the full range of natural and human topics necessary for gaining an understanding of an area. Fully half the space is devoted to Louisiana's natural condition, leaving the remainder for the study of human occupancy and its resulting landscapes. The book is particularly noteworthy as a geography text, for it brings together a variety of topics into a regional framework that enhances the understanding of the area. For these reasons some have even called it a classic.

Despite its inherent worth, the book is becoming dated. Places and their landscapes are never static. They have a way of changing as events, peoples, and forces assert themselves. Sometimes, such changes take place rapidly and violently but more often slowly and subtly. In either case they have altered the state so profoundly that any book that attempts to describe a region must take them into account. Louisiana in 1988 is quite different from the Louisiana of 1968, as will be the Louisiana of 2008. Thus, it becomes necessary to revise our view of the state in order to more accurately describe its nature. Furthermore, new studies lead to new knowledge, necessitating the revision of existing interpretations.

In undertaking the revision of a book such as *Louisiana: Its Land and People,* I felt a need to preserve as much of the old version as possible. Consequently, I revised only when the need was clear and demonstrable. The reader will find most of the changes in chapters on petroleum, cities, agriculture, and population.

Owing to the nature of a regional book, one is well advised to seek aid from those with specialized knowledge, and a number of persons have been kind enough to help with the revision. Robert A. Muller, state climatologist, read the chapters on weather and climate and provided data for the graphics used. B. J. Miller of the Louisiana State University

Department of Agronomy provided advice on the soils chapter. David Prior, of the Louisiana State University Coastal Studies Institute, read the entire material on relief and pointed out a number of changes necessary owing to more recent interpretations of coastal processes. Charles Groat of the Louisiana Geological Survey opened his office and staff to my efforts, and I am especially grateful to Dianne M. Linstedt for helping me compile data on oil and gas production and to John I. Snead for his help in producing the new maps of petroleum fields and pipelines. My own department has proved a great deal of support, especially Maudrie Monceaux, Joyce Nelson, Mary Lee Eggart, Clifford Duplechin, Linda McQueen, and Philip B. Larimore, Jr.

Sam Hilliard

Louisiana
Its Land and People

1
Introduction

What is geography? The Greek word—*geographia*—from which our English word stems may be translated as "earth description." As is the case with the names of so many fields of study, the literal meaning does not tell us exactly what is included. If we look back over the two thousand years since the word *geography* was first used, we find that geographers have always studied the same

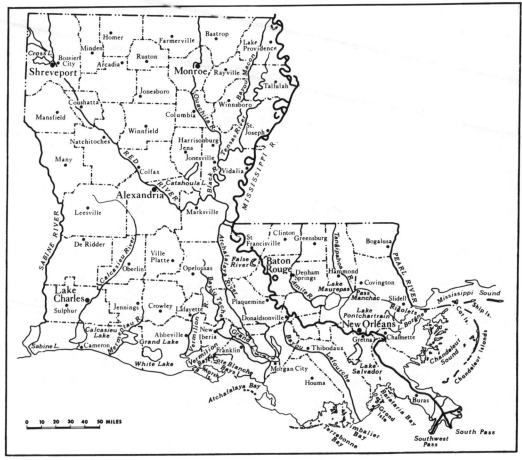

MAP 1
Selected place-names of Louisiana

things in pretty much the same manner. These include things appearing on or near the earth's surface—both the works of nature, such as hills, rivers, trees, clouds, and the works of man, such as houses, fields, roads, and towns. It has been agreed that the geographer must understand as well as describe these objects and that he must see how they are related to each other and how they differ from place to place. Physical, or natural, geography can stand alone, without any reference to man, since nature can hardly be separated from the earth. The works of man, on the other hand, may be studied by students in many fields, quite aside from any reference to the earth's surface. They become truly part of human, or cultural, geogra-

phy only when they are set in a natural framework consisting of space, location, relief, climate, resources, and like elements. As from the beginning of geography, the geographer puts on maps the things he sees and finds out. We may say that the map is the symbol of geography.

What should be learned in a study of Louisiana geography? First comes place geography. We should be able to close our eyes and see a map of Louisiana. In our imagination we must be able to place in proper position and name the rivers, lakes, hills, islands, bays, and other natural features. We should know Louisiana's size and how it compares with the size of other states. Then we must learn Louisiana's location, what its boundaries are,

A natural landscape. Except for the sawed log in the foreground, the photograph shows a cypress swamp as it might have appeared five hundred years ago.

Elemore Morgan

A cultural landscape: New Orleans from the air   Gulf Coast Aerial Mapping Co., Inc., Baton Rouge

and how its position is related to the rest of the United States and to the world. We must do the same for human features—cities, parishes, and other things appearing on a map—for which man is responsible (Map 1). If place geography is not clear in our minds, we have nowhere to put what we learn about Louisiana, and our knowledge will be largely useless.

Once we have constructed a framework of place geography, we can begin to examine nature's contributions to Louisiana. We try to imagine what the state was like for the millions of years before man first appeared here. The hills, the plains, the

rivers, the forests, and the animals all were here long before man's time. We want to know what the country was like then, so that we can measure what man has done to and for it.

After we learn about nature in Louisiana, we will turn to man. The Indians, the first men in the area, appeared here about twelve thousand years ago. This has been determined by the scientific radiocarbon dating technique that we will talk about later in the book. There never were more than a few thousand of these Indians. They were handicapped by the fact that they had little technological capacity; that is, they lacked tools needed to work efficiently. They had no mechanical power of any sort. They had no draft animal. The firstcomers did not even know how to plant food crops. What they did to change the natural conditions they encountered was very limited indeed. You could live in Louisiana all your life without ever becoming aware of anything that the Indians did to alter the landscape. This is not because they were a stupid people; they were surely just as intelligent as any people living today. It was simply that knowledge had not accumulated among them sufficiently to raise them above the primitive level.

We only need look to the Europeans of a few hundred years ago to see how important time and learning are to the way in which people live. The first Europeans in Louisiana had tools and weapons superior to those of the Indians, but, compared to today's people, they lived in a primitive manner and their effect on nature was limited. Despite the settlers' modest technology, all parts of the state, even where natural conditions were very much alike, did not look the same after early European settlement. This is because people from France settled in some areas and people from the British Isles settled in others. Both built houses, barns, and roads, planted fields, and raised cattle, but because of different backgrounds each group did these things in its own manner. We can still observe these differences today, because each group left its own distinctive occupance pattern. Rarely does an individual depart from the way of his group, whether in his religious beliefs or in the kind of house he builds.

We will learn that in the past one hundred and fifty years change has come much more rapidly. Natural forces have remained the same, but man has gained greatly in numbers and in power and is thus able more and more to control nature and subject it to his wishes. Many new works of man have appeared—new kinds of buildings and means of transportation. Man has unlocked and used nature's wealth of timber, petroleum, and sulphur, to mention a few examples. We must remember that when the Indians first appeared nature was unaffected by man. Now, in many places, we can see nothing but what man has done.

There are less obvious, more subtle ways in which European man has changed the landscape. A botanist walking along a ditch bank finds that half the weeds are plants of European origin, probably most of them introduced quite unintentionally. Changes in the plant and animal communities are among man's most profound alterations of natural conditions. Specific references to these changes will be made in the succeeding chapters.

After we have traced all these developments and changes, we must sit back and reflect on the wisdom of our human ways. Have we acted wisely in our use of nature's resources? What of the future? In what kind of Louisiana will the people of A.D. 2000 live? As geographers we must observe, map, learn, judge man's wisdom with regard to nature, and try to see what the future holds.

2

A Geographic Ramble

A good way to begin a geographical study of Louisiana is by means of a map tour of the state. Let it be neither planned nor systematic, but rather a rambling about from one section or feature to another, from large to small, as name suggests name, and by no means inclusive of everything worthy of men-

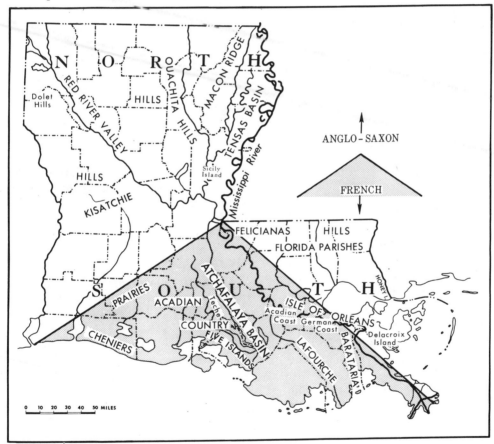

MAP 2
Major and minor features of the state. Shading represents area of most pronounced French influence.

5

tion. You are certainly familiar with nearly all of the names. They must mean something to you. Here will be a chance to see if you have been thinking about them as a geographer does, that is, where they are, what they are, how they are interrelated, and how they came to be the way they are. If this section leaves you with many questions, be assured that most of the matters considered here will be taken up in subsequent chapters. Map 2 provides the basis for our discussion, but you may find it helpful to refer back to Map 1, which contains additional detail.

Suppose that our first glance at the map happens to fall on the name "Kisatchie," appearing in the west-central part of the state. Kisatchie is also applied to a national forest, but we use it here in connection with *wold* or *cuesta*, both terms referring to a ridge of hard sedimentary rock. The Kisatchie Wold is a ridge that reaches from the Texas border to Harrisonburg on the Ouachita River in Catahoula Parish. It is the most conspicuous upland feature in the state. Indeed, we might call it the backbone of Louisiana.

To the northeast is the Tensas Basin, which is actually a trough, for it is open at both ends. The higher sides are Macon Ridge to the west and the high bank, or natural levee, of the Mississippi River to the east. The Tensas River runs south through the basin. You can see that the bends, or meanders, of the small Tensas are the same size as those of the Mississippi. This means the Mississippi once occupied what is now the Tensas channel. On a map you can measure the diameters of Mississippi River meanders and find them to be on the order of three to five miles. Red River meanders measure only a mile to a mile and a half, and those of smaller streams, correspondingly less. We can thus formulate a rule and say that the size of meanders varies directly with the size of streams.

North and east of New Orleans lies a group of eight parishes called the Florida Parishes. In the northwest corner of this section are the Felicianas. These two parishes comprise a distinctive area, because, in spite of a hilly, rolling surface, they have a very productive soil, part of which is known as loess. The Florida Parishes reach westward to the Mississippi and southward along the river past Baton Rouge to a naturally continuous waterway known as Bayou Manchac. In the ancient past it ran out of the Mississippi eastward to join the Amite, eventually flowing into Lake Maurepas. Lake Maurepas empties through Pass Manchac into Lake Pontchartrain, and then through the Rigolets into Mississippi Sound. On the east the Florida Parishes are bounded by Pearl River.

Louisiana has many of the common kind of island, such as Marsh Island, Last Isle, Grand Isle, Wine Island, the Chandeleur Islands, and a number of others. But in the state there are other features called islands that are not bodies of land rising out of open water. There is Honey Island, a low swampy area lying between East and West Pearl rivers. Then there is Sicily Island, a few square miles of high ground in Catahoula Parish, surrounded by low and sometimes flooded country. Somewhat like Sicily Island are the Five Islands of coastal Louisiana, which are domes pushed up by salt to as much as 150 feet above the surrounding, partially inundated lowlands.

The Isle of Orleans includes all the area bounded on the west by the Mississippi, on the south and east by the Gulf of Mexico, and on the north by the connecting water bodies that form the southern boundary of the Florida Parishes. A last example is Delacroix Island, largely swamp and marsh, bounded by the Gulf to the east, Bayou Terre aux Boeufs to the west, and Bayou La Loutre to the north. (*Loutre* is the French word for otter, and the *boeuf* referred to is *boeuf sauvage*, French for buffalo or bison. These were common wild animals at the time of French colonization.)

6

Barataria, Lafourche, and Teche are names of South Louisiana bayous. More important here, their courses are banked on each side by ridges of higher ground, their natural levees, which provide habitable sites and roadways through swamp and marsh. All three bayous flow roughly parallel to the Mississippi River and more or less at right angles to the Gulf coast. In coastal southwest Louisiana is a series of parallel ridges called cheniers. Unlike the levees of the bayous to the east, the cheniers are parallel to the coast. They will be discussed later.

The Atchafalaya Basin is a broad swamp running from the coast to as far north as Lower Red River. It is named for the Atchafalaya River, but contains streams of many names and a large number of lakes. In the lower part of the basin, the Atchafalaya splits into many streams and forms a braided pattern. This means the streams occupy an interlacing network of channels. They rejoin in the Lower Atchafalaya to discharge into the Gulf. This extensive swamp is different from the higher ground around it, and here life, too, is different for its human inhabitants. They are "swampers" cutting timber, moss gatherers, fishermen, oilfield workers, even farmers or cattlemen on higher ground.

To the west of the Atchafalaya and to the north of the marshes are the prairies, broad bands of open grassland lying between narrow bands of woodland. The country is flat, with a gentle slope toward the Gulf. Once this was cattle country, until a flood of settlers arrived to raise prairie rice. Country roads followed section lines to form square patterns. Prairie Louisiana came to look very much like the prairie Midwest from which so many of its settlers came.

Then there are areas named after the original settlers. St. Charles and St. John the Baptist parishes make up the German Coast, so named for the German settlers of 250 years ago. Originally, "coast" meant the natural levees bordering the

Mississippi and not the backswamp. The later-coming Acadians gave their name to the Acadian Coast (St. James and Ascension parishes), upriver from the German Coast. Many of the original Acadians found good land west of the Atchafalaya Basin on the broad levees of Bayou Teche and on the eastern margins of the prairies. They were joined by other Acadians from along the Mississippi, and this section, centering on the city of Lafayette, became known as Acadian Country.

On a much broader scale, everyone knows there is a North Louisiana and a South Louisiana. Suppose we wish to show the two Louisianas on a map. Just where would we draw in the boundary and how would we describe them? If we use terms such as *hills* for North Louisiana and *lowlands* for South Louisiana, we get a division that does not seem at all satisfactory. If we give piney woods to North Louisiana, and other kinds of forests, prairies, and marshes to South Louisiana, the boundary still seems improper. The two sections of the state might be separated on the basis of foods: corn bread, mustard greens, and black-eyed peas for North Louisiana; dark-roast coffee, French wheat bread, and jambalaya for South Louisiana. The food boundary does not agree exactly with any of the others.

Let's look at the differences between people living in North and South Louisiana. The greatest and most basic differences are the ones between those of French descent and those of British, or Anglo-Saxon, descent. The former have the French language in their background and many speak it today; their religious affiliation is largely Roman Catholic. The Anglo-Saxon stock speaks English and largely adheres to Protestant faiths. Even the African peoples brought in as slaves may be so divided, for they adopted the language and religion of their masters.

Such a division can be made, but the boundary is winding and twisting. It is much better to use straight lines showing an approximate division between the two human groups. Such a straight-line boundary is easily described. It begins in the extreme southwestern corner of the state where the Sabine River empties into the Gulf. From this point it runs northeast to the point where the 31st parallel crosses the Mississippi River. The 31st parallel is a boundary between Louisiana and Mississippi. From this point the second straight leg of the boundary runs southeast through the mouth of the Mississippi. North of this boundary is Anglo-Saxon Louisiana; within the triangle is French Louisiana. The area of Anglo-Saxon Louisiana is the larger, but the population of French Louisiana is the greater. Differences in political opinions between North and South Louisiana come out distinctly in many state elections. Maps plotting voters' preferences show that our simple boundary is approximately correct. Remember that this is only one way of separating North from South Louisiana. There are others that may be equally appropriate.

Drawing boundaries on maps has always been and remains a perplexing problem for geographers. In some instances nature provides a precise boundary, for example, where the Mississippi floodplain meets the bluff on its eastern

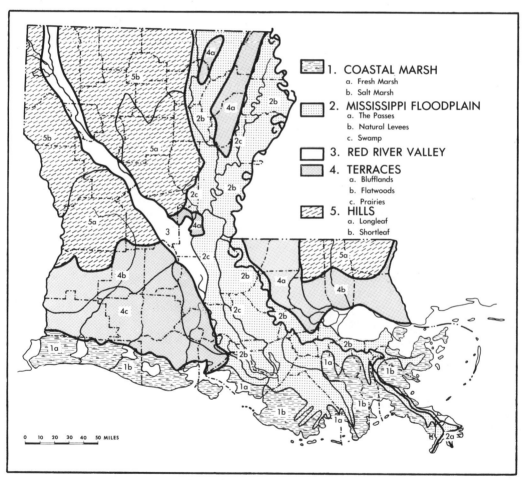

MAP 3
Natural regions of Louisiana. See facing page for explanation of legend.

side. But how can we set boundaries where the ground is perfectly flat? For practical purposes, however, we must put boundaries on maps. Unless they are arbitrary boundaries, such as those established by law, keep in mind that they may be compromises that actually do not mark the abrupt changes their presence may suggest.

There is another, more practical way of dividing Louisiana into unit areas, and that is by natural regions (Map 3). "Natural regions" means that these areas are based on qualities of nature: relief (hills, valleys, etc.), soils, vegetation, and climate, to name the most important. The idea is to find areas or regions that are uniform with respect to those natural qualities, in contrast to other regions about them. You will note that the same kind of natural region can occur in more than one place. It might be better to delay naming the natural regions until the qualities on which they are based are discussed. On the other hand, these divisions are so important and are so much used that they must be described early in our study. The reason they are so important is that we simply cannot talk about every individual hill, valley, tree, and drainage feature in Louisiana. We must be able to say that similar kinds of things prevail over a particular region. Like the map, the natural region provides a kind of cubbyhole in which we can file things that are alike.

Louisiana's Natural Regions

(See Map 3)

Coastal Marsh

Low elevation and relief; longest growing season; abundant rainfall; hurricanes; (a) fresh- and (b) salt-marsh vegetation; muck and peat soils; round and lagoonal lakes; important wildlife and fisheries resources; cheniers; Five Islands.

Mississippi Floodplain

a) Passes: low elevation and relief; maximum growing season; batture vegetation; mudlumps and bars; distributary drainage; interlevee lakes.
b) Natural Levees: moderate relief and slope; second-bottom and batture vegetation; distributary and crevasse channels; cutoff lakes; the lighter (coarser) bottom soils.
c) Swamp: little relief, much standing water; braided channels; bluff lakes; swamp, or first-bottom, forest, Spanish moss abundant; heavy bottom soils.

Red River Valley

Low elevation and relief; drainage unit; raft lakes; red soils; bottom hardwoods.

Terraces

Large percentage tabular surfaces; older alluvium; intermediate elevations and relief.
a) Blufflands: moderate to marked relief; loessial soils; dendritic drainage; bluffland-woodland vegetation.
b) Flatwoods: low relief; mixed longleaf forest; bagols; pimple mounds; dendritic drainage; flatwoods soils.
c) Prairies: low relief; prairie grassland; prairie soils; pimple mounds; dendritic streams; ice-age channels; *platin* and *marais*.

Hills

Maximum elevations and relief; shortest growing season; dendritic and trellis drainage; interior salt domes; wolds or cuestas; ironstone; excellent surface and groundwater resources; mature soils; oldest rocks; forested.
a) Longleaf.
b) Shortleaf.

Dividing Louisiana into natural regions is so useful that it was not left for some student to do. Ever since there were Europeans in Louisiana they have made use of concepts such as marsh, swamp, red hills, flatwoods, prairies, and the like. To the people using them, these terms bring up a picture of a combination of relief, vegetation, drainage features, and lesser qualities. The student uses these concepts. It is his task to define them accurately so that he can draw boundary lines between them and put them on a map. Louisiana scholars have been trying to do this for about 150 years. The best solution was worked out by Samuel Lockett about 1875. This engineer-geographer did such a good job that we can improve very little on it today. Our map and table of natural regions are based largely on Lockett's works. His classification has the great advantage of representing original natural conditions much more closely than we can reconstruct them today. In his day the upland and swamp forests, the prairies, and the marsh were little changed by human activities.

The primary division of Louisiana into natural regions is based on relief. Therefore, we begin with our three great relief regions: hills, terraces, and lowlands. Each of these must be divided into several parts because of differences in location, vegetation, soils, and other natural qualities. The hills, generally the highest and roughest parts of the state, are divided, on the basis of soils and vegetation cover, into longleaf pine and shortleaf pine divisions. The terraces, or flat uplands, are divided into (a) the blufflands along the major streams; (b) the flatwoods covered largely by pine forest; and (c) the prairies, or flat grasslands. The lowlands are divided into marsh and floodplain. The marsh is further divided into saltwater and freshwater divisions, which show marked differences in vegetation cover. Of the floodplains, the Red River Valley is set off as a separate natural region because of minor differences in topography and drainage and its distinctive red soils. The great Mississippi floodplain, or alluvial valley, is divided into (a) the passes, or the "delta" at the mouths of the river; (b) the natural levees, or the frontlands of the riverbanks standing above swamp level; and (c) the backlands, or swamps.

Terms have been introduced here without explaining exactly what they mean. This will all come in due time. Many are explained in the glossary in the back of the book. It is our present task to learn the combinations of conditions that qualify each regional type and to know in what part of the state they exist.

3
Orientation and Space Relations

Louisiana's orientation with respect to local features and distant areas, its physical and cultural setting as compared with other parts of the United States and the world must be established before proceeding to a detailed description of the state itself.

First, Louisiana has a position on the earth's surface that is easy to remember. New Orleans, the state's largest city, is located at 90° West and 30° North. Ninety degrees West means New Orleans is a quarter of the way around the world from the meridian of 0° at Greenwich, England (near London). Translated into time differences, New Orleans is six hours earlier than Greenwich. If it is noon at Greenwich, it is 6 A.M., Central Time, in New Orleans. At the same time it is 7 A.M., Eastern Time, in New York, at 75° W; 5 A.M., Mountain Time, in Denver, 105° W; and 4 A.M., Pacific Time, in Los Angeles, 120° W. All this is true because the 360 degrees of longitude divided by the 24 hours in a day means every 15 degrees equals one hour in time.

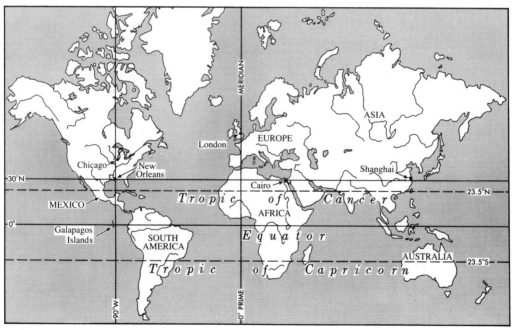

MAP 4
Louisiana in relation to the world

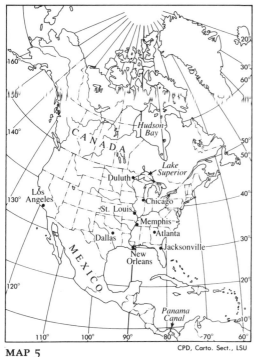

MAP 5
Louisiana in relation to places in North America

Due north on the 90th meridian from New Orleans are Memphis and St. Louis, as you will see on the map of North America. The line passes west of Chicago, east of Duluth across Lake Superior, along the western side of Hudson Bay, and on through the Arctic islands. South of New Orleans the due-south course of the 90th meridian is surprising to most people. It cuts across the Gulf to Yucatan in Mexico, then across Guatemala into the open Pacific, and through the Galapagos Islands that lie about seven hundred miles west of the mainland of South America. This means that New Orleans is well west of any point on the South American continent, even the Panama Canal. Both by sea and air the port of New Orleans has advantages over most other major United States ports in shorter distances to Central America and the west coast of South America. To follow a meridian is to follow a great-circle route, which is the shortest distance between any two points on a sphere.

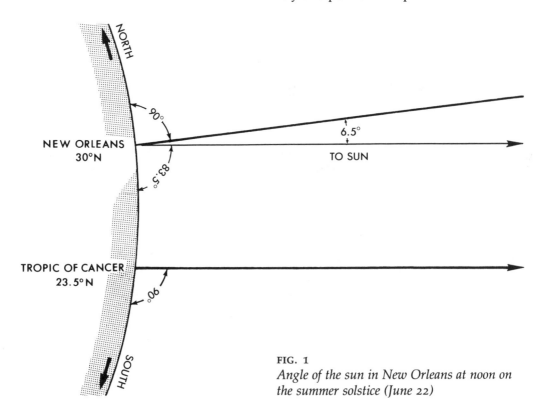

FIG. 1
Angle of the sun in New Orleans at noon on the summer solstice (June 22)

At Latitude 30° N New Orleans lies a third of the way between the Equator and the North Pole. It thus lies north of the Tropic of Cancer at 23½° N. The Tropic of Cancer (a solstice position of the sun) marks the farthest north where the sun ever stands direct over the earth's surface. Thus, it can never be directly overhead in New Orleans. This means that all of Louisiana is outside the tropics, and that on noon of the longest day of the year, June 22, the sun at New Orleans is 83½° above the horizon instead of 90° (directly overhead, Figure 1). Louisiana's latitudinal position means that while there is a noticeable difference in length between days and nights at different times of the year, the range is less than in other more northerly parts of the United States.

If we compare our latitude with that of other places, we can see how far south Louisiana is. In the continental United States only Florida and Texas extend farther south. If we follow the 30th parallel westward across North America, we see that it runs nearly through Houston, Austin, and Big Bend in Texas, then crosses northern Mexico to enter the Pacific almost two hundred miles south of the southern boundary of California. Eastward, the 30th parallel cuts across northern Florida into the Atlantic south of Jacksonville. Across Africa it lies everywhere south of the Mediterranean Sea and runs through Cairo, Egypt, on the Nile River. Every point in Europe lies north of New Orleans.

Eastward from Cairo the 30th parallel cuts across northern Arabia and northern India to reach the Pacific slightly south of Shanghai in China. All of Japan and Korea lie north of 30°. We know that Spain, Italy, and Greece, at the latitude of New York, can grow citrus fruits, a subtropical crop. We in Louisiana produce citrus with difficulty because of our colder winters. How can this be when Europe is so much farther north? There are several contributing factors that make winters along the Mediterranean Sea milder than

ours. Here we emphasize one major difference: Europe is on the *western* side of the great landmass of Eurasia, while we are on the *eastern* side of North America. Because of the pattern of world air circulation, the western sides of continents in the middle latitudes have milder winters than eastern sides. The summers are generally milder, too. It is important to remember that location at a certain latitude does not ensure a particular climate. Two places at exactly the same latitude but on opposite sides of a continent may have completely different climates.

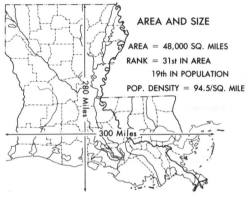

AREA AND SIZE

AREA = 48,000 SQ. MILES
RANK = 31st IN AREA
19th IN POPULATION
POP. DENSITY = 94.5/SQ. MILE

MAP 6
Area and size of the state

Louisiana's approximately 48,000-square-mile area ranks thirty-first in size among the states. Alaska is the largest with 586,000 square miles, and Rhode Island is smallest with a little over 1,000. Our neighbor to the west—Texas, with 267,000 square miles—is over five times as large. Regarding dimensions, we may say that Louisiana is broader than it is tall (Map 6). From its easternmost to its westernmost point, the state measures about 300 miles. Measured in the same way north and south, the distance is about 280 miles. These figures may suggest that Louisiana is about square in shape. Actually it is not. Rather, it resembles a great block "L." The base to the east is formed by the Florida Parishes and the area to the south of them.

The boundaries of Louisiana are of two types, natural and arbitrary. Natural boundaries are formed by natural features such as rivers. Such boundaries are normally irregular in form. Arbitrary boundaries are those that are simply agreed upon. Commonly they are straight lines, such as parallels or meridians, that cut across rivers and other natural features. There are three such arbitrary-boundary segments in Louisiana. One is the parallel of 31° that separates Louisiana from Mississippi north of the Florida Parishes. This boundary is 70 miles due north of New Orleans at 30°, since a degree of latitude is always about 70 land miles in length. (This is not true for a degree of longitude.) Another arbitrary boundary lies between Louisiana and Arkansas. This boundary is just a little north of the 33rd parallel, so that we should speak of it as 33° plus. The third arbitrary boundary

forms the northern portion of Louisiana's contact with Texas. Here the boundary is a meridian, but again not an even-numbered one. We should call it the meridian of 94° plus.

Louisiana has four natural-boundary segments: the Mississippi, Pearl, and Sabine rivers, and the Gulf of Mexico. All this sounds very simple, but these are complicated boundaries. For example, it is the Mississippi River channel of 1812 (the date of Louisiana's admission to the Union) that forms a boundary segment with the state of Mississippi. Since 1812 the Mississippi has shifted its channel so that some parts of Louisiana lie east of the river and small sections of Mississippi lie west of it. We have seen that the lower course of Pearl River forms Honey Island by splitting into East Pearl River and West Pearl River. Honey Island is part of Louisiana because East Pearl River is a bound-

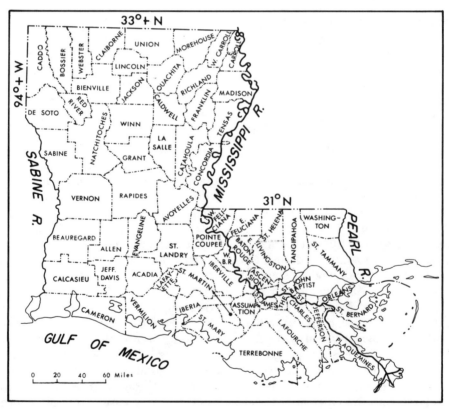

MAP 7
Parishes and boundaries

ary between Louisiana and Mississippi. There has been minor disagreement between Texas and Louisiana as to the precise boundary along the Sabine River. But the main boundary argument, not yet settled, is concerned with just how far Louisiana extends out into the Gulf of Mexico.

The controversy over Louisiana's southern boundary was first regarding the distance out into the Gulf agreed upon at the time of Louisiana's admission as a state in 1812. The boundary was of little importance until very recent times when rich oil fields were discovered on the continental shelf. The federal government insisted that the distance was 3 miles, as is widely the case. Louisiana claimed that, like Texas and Florida, it should extend out a distance of three leagues. A marine league is 3 nautical miles or 3.45 land miles. Three leagues would then be a distance of 10.35 land miles, quite an advantage over 3 land miles. A court decision went against Louisiana, and the boundary was placed 3 miles out. Then another argument arose: from what base line should the 3-mile measurement be made?

Louisiana advocates could point out that except for a few places, chiefly at the mouths of the Mississippi, the shore has retreated inland since 1812. But the main contention involves the contrasting position of shoreline and coastline (Map 8). The shoreline is the actual strand line where land and water meet. Because of numerous bays and points, the shoreline of Louisiana is at least 1,000 miles long. If you will try it, you can see that measuring a constant distance outward at right angles to a highly irregular shoreline leads to utter confusion. It is much easier to measure from the coastline a series of straightline segments that outline Louisiana by extending from point to point and eliminating irregular inlets. In contrast to a 1,000-mile shoreline, such a coastline measures only some 400 miles. Such are the arguments at present regard-

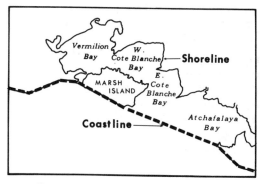

MAP 8
Coastline and shoreline

ing the position of Louisiana's seaward boundary.

With reference to the state's natural setting, it may be said that Louisiana and Florida alone lie entirely in the Gulf Coastal Plain. Louisiana is comparatively young geologically; that means it has existed during only a short period of the total history of the earth. As a plain, it has low local relief, by definition less than 500 feet. This means that local maximum differences in elevation between the highest and lowest points must be less than 500 feet. Possibly the greatest local relief is in the vicinity of Driskill Mountain. The mountain reaches 535 feet, while the lowest point near it is 150 feet, making the local relief only 385 feet. The lowest natural dryland elevation in Louisiana is sea level. Thus, Louisiana's total relief is 535 feet, but locally it is less than 500 feet.

Louisiana lies in the yellow-pine belt, although it also has both bottomland cypress and upland hardwoods. It has a productive climate marked by heavy rainfall, mild winters, and hot summers. But more important than all other qualities combined is the fact that Louisiana encompasses the lower courses and mouths of the Mississippi River. Whether for water supply, rich soils, or transportation, the Mississippi is easily the state's most striking geographical feature and its most valuable geographical asset.

From the human, or cultural, viewpoint

Louisiana is in that section of the United States called the Southeast by most scholars, although when including Louisiana they lose sight of the fact that the state uniquely has strong French population elements not shared with other states of the section. The Southeast would include East Texas if state boundaries could be disregarded. It takes in Arkansas, ranges up to the Ohio River, and encompasses all of the southern states to the east of Louisiana.

Fifty years ago this section, primarily agricultural, with low average education and income and a high birthrate, could have been characterized as backward. Also, fifty years ago few could foresee the modern developments that are transforming Louisiana and other parts of the Southeast into advanced and enterprising sections of the country. New economic developments have been chiefly in the direction of mineral discoveries, industrialization and urbanization, and profound changes in agriculture.

Along with other advances, Louisiana's population has grown from 2.7 million in 1950 and 3.2 million in 1960, to over 4 million at present. Louisiana now ranks nineteenth in population among the fifty states. The average density of population is over 94.5 per square mile, well above the national average of 64 for 1980. And this rapidly increasing population is better educated, better fed, and better off financially than the population of half a century ago.

Early means of transportation. Note that both buggies and automobiles appear in this picture taken in the 1930s.　　Elemore Morgan

Modern four-level highway interchange in Baton Rouge　　Louisiana Department of Transportation

Threshing rice using a belt-powered thresher and mule-drawn wagons　　Elemore Morgan

Harvesting rice in southwestern Louisiana using a modern combine
John Deere Co., Moline, Illinois

4
Weather and Climate
Introduction

Weather and climate are measurable conditions of the atmosphere. That is, whatever is taking place as weather or climate is something that is happening to the gaseous envelope, or atmosphere, that mantles the earth. A number of factors are involved in establishing atmospheric conditions, among them, temperature, moisture, winds, clouds, and solar radiation. In this section we will deal with all aspects of weather but concentrate our efforts on the first three mentioned. When we measure these conditions as of the moment, we are dealing with weather. We say of weather, for example, that it is hot today, or that a rainstorm is coming. Climate, on the other hand, is a synthesis of weather. It deals with both average and extreme conditions over a period of time. We say that Louisiana's climate is characterized by mild winters and warm summers. This is generalized instead of specific as when we speak of weather.

It is hardly necessary to point out how influential weather and climate are. All forms of life are dependent on atmospheric conditions. We perhaps exaggerate the matter of human comfort in saying that a particular day or season is pleasant. Far more important are the aspects of weather and climate that influence plant growth. Often the conditions that are best for the growth of a particular crop are uncomfortable for humans. Another significant aspect of the atmosphere is the production of surplus water, which creates runoff to feed streams and lakes. These, in turn, support aquatic life and may be needed for navigation, industry, and other human activities. Or, excessive rains may produce a destructive flood. Tornadoes and hurricanes are other undesirable atmospheric phenomena from man's viewpoint.

Louisiana's weather and climate are generally like those of the states around it, but in detail they are unique. What factors are responsible? Clearly, the natural location and setting of the state are important. Relief is important, largely in a negative way. Mountainous areas have cooler summers because they are high. For every thousand feet of elevation the temperature is normally 3.3° F. less, as you will see in the illustration of the temperature lapse rate. The highest point in Louisiana, 535 feet, should be about 1.6° cooler than those places at sea level. Obviously this is not important. More significant is the fact that to the north of Louisiana there is no mountain barrier or tempering sea to keep cold Arctic air out of the state in winter. As a result, we tend to experience a climate with a wide range of temperatures, that is, a continental climate.

Another very important locational factor is Louisiana's position on the Gulf of Mexico. Water is slow to gain heat and slow to lose it as compared with land. Since both land and water largely control

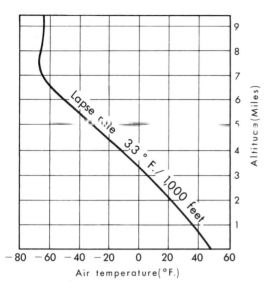

FIG. 2

Lapse rate is defined as the decline in temperature as elevation increases.

the temperatures of the atmosphere above them, areas on the sea have marine climates with less temperature variation than the continental climates inland. The land adjacent to the sea reflects the water temperatures, so that coastal Louisiana is cooler in the summer and warmer in the winter than are interior points in the state. This particular influence of the sea does not extend very far inland, probably less than a hundred miles. Seasonal contrasts in temperature between land and sea are sufficient to produce a monsoon effect felt most strongly near the coast. There the prevailing wind is seaward in winter and landward in summer. Before the days of air conditioning it was good practice to locate sleeping rooms on the south or southeast side of houses to capture the onshore summer breeze. Another ocean-generated wind, the hurricane, is anything but beneficial. More will be said about hurricanes later.

Latitude also is a factor in Louisiana's weather and climate. As was pointed out earlier, we are outside the tropical limit of 23½°. The variation in the length of our day is moderate. Although the sun is

never directly overhead, it approaches that position in summer, which means a greater concentration of solar energy at that period (Figure 1). Equally or more important is the relation between latitude and the domination of our weather by one or the other of two contrasting air masses. An air mass is a great body of the atmosphere that has lain over a particular area long enough to take on its characteristics of temperature and moisture. It then moves as wind and carries its atmospheric conditions with it. Our cold spells in winter come not because the sun suddenly ceases to send down heat energy, but because a cold, dry polar air mass has moved from the far North down over the state. As this air mass moves eastward it is followed by a warm, moist tropical air

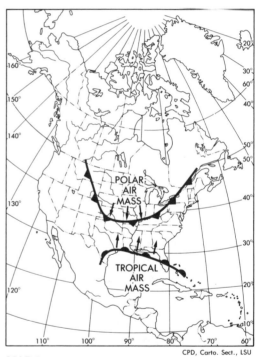

CPD, Carto. Sect., LSU

MAP 9

Idealized map showing the two most important air masses that affect the central United States. When the polar mass moves over the state we experience lower temperatures. When the tropical air mass dominates we can expect warm temperatures and usually some moisture, for it originates over the Gulf of Mexico.

mass coming in off the Gulf. There are other air masses, but these two, polar and tropical, will do for our purposes (Map 9).

As the polar air mass comes rolling in from the northwest, its front is often a squall line of rolling clouds, rain, strong winds, and lightning (Figure 3). When the contrasts between the two meeting air masses, polar and tropical, are sufficient, tornadoes may develop along or near the front, tending to parallel its course from southwest to northeast. In large measure, latitude determines the date when the first big front of a polar air mass arrives in the fall and when the last one appears in the spring. Louisiana really has a two-season climate. Winter begins with the first polar front in the fall and ends with the last in the spring. Between the two lies the summer season. The farther north, the longer the winter and the shorter the summer. Latitude, then, is a primary seasonal determinant.

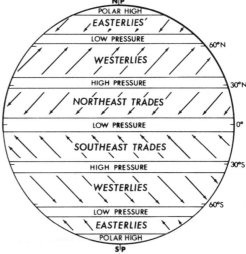

FIG. 4
Ideal planetary wind system

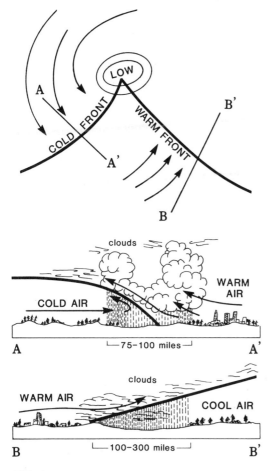

FIG. 3
Air mass and fronts. Note that A–A' represents section across cold front and B–B' represents section across warm front.

Finally, a matter of position already mentioned, Louisiana lies on the east side of a continental mass. East coasts in middle latitudes are on the leeward sides of continents. This means that the general movement of air is from west to east, as is shown in the diagram of wind systems (Figure 4). The west coasts are tempered by winds off the sea. Eastern sides of the landmass are exposed to all the variations and extremes developed in continental interiors. It is the rule, then, that points near the western side are warm for the average of their latitudes, and that locations on the eastern side are correspondingly cold for theirs.

Louisiana has a type of climate commonly called humid subtropical. Humid means that there is abundant precipitation well distributed through the year. Subtropical implies warm summers and mild winters. The latter qualification is

19

the more important of the two. Louisiana summers are at least as hot as those in the tropics. Tropical winter seasons are those in which the temperature never gets low enough to halt plant growth. Normally, a January average temperature of 64.4° F. and above means a tropical condition, or no winter. Louisiana cannot meet this figure, for the state's average January temperatures range between the humid subtropical limits of 64.4° F. and 32° F. There is a period in which plant growth is inhibited, but it does not produce severe freezing and frozen ground. Our winters are "open," which means they are marked by periods of relatively warmer temperatures, in contrast to the "closed" or severe winters of the North.

Of all the states of the Southeast grouped as humid subtropical, Louisiana alone meets the qualifications perfectly. Arkansas, for example, has weather stations that have fallen below a January 32° F. average for some years and hence are colder than subtropical. Florida has stations that sometimes average 64.4° F. or above for January. For those years they qualify as tropical instead of subtropical. Humid subtropical climates appear not only in the southeastern United States but also in other sections of the world having the same latitudinal positions on the east sides of continents. Coastal China, southeastern South Africa, eastern Australia, and the La Plata area of South America all have humid subtropical climates. Check their positions on a globe or world map.

In the following chapters we shall consider some details of Louisiana's weather and climate. A number of figures will be mentioned. They are not all worth remembering precisely, but we should recognize them and remember their import. For North and South Louisiana there will be given figures and descriptions of the three elements of weather and climate— temperature, moisture, and wind. We shall then try to separate Louisiana into meaningful divisions based chiefly on climate's effect on plant growth.

For convenience in the preliminary description of the weather and climate of North and South Louisiana, we divide the state into approximately equal parts by a line drawn a little north of the 31st parallel. This line crosses the state just south of Alexandria.

5
Weather and Climate

Temperature and Moisture

As we have noted, South Louisiana has fewer temperature extremes than North Louisiana, with much milder winters and much longer growing seasons. Also, it has considerably greater precipitation. In short, South Louisiana tends toward a marine climate as opposed to a continental climate for North Louisiana.

The average annual temperature for South Louisiana is 68.5° F. January has the lowest average temperature with 54.2° F. Note how this falls between 32° and 64.4°, the permissible range for a subtropical climate. July is highest with 82.0° F., just about the same as the average at the equator. Bogalusa with 67.4° F. has the lowest average annual temperature and Burrwood, at the mouth of the Mississippi, with 70.5° F., the highest. This does not mean that Burrwood has hotter summers, but that Bogalusa has colder winters. On the immediate coast the temperature rarely climbs to 100° or drops to 32°.

Most important to agriculture is the length of the growing season, that is, the number of days between the last freeze of spring and the first of the fall (Map 10). In general, the coastal Louisiana growing season ranges between February 1 and December 15, and that for the northern part of South Louisiana, between March 10 and November 10. In South Louisiana, Burrwood with an average growing season of 354 days and Clinton with 232

represent the extremes of the season. This range is astonishingly great. In one ten-year period Burrwood had six years with no frost and the other four with only one; thus it is nearly winterless. No weather station outside the extreme Lower Mississippi River area has escaped frost for a year (frost being defined as a temperature below 32° F.). Clinton's season of 232 days is about the same as that of Seattle, Washington, and little more than the average along the Ohio River, hundreds of miles to the north. This contrast means that the tempering effect of the Gulf is quickly lost inland, as shown by the closeness of the isochrones along the coast and their wider spacing inland on the map of growing seasons.

Applications of the temperature factor to agriculture are illustrated by two crops, citrus and sugarcane. Citrus trees are perennial—that is, they are not annual plants that die back every year or are annually harvested whole, like sugarcane. They cannot stand much cold before losing their fruit or even dying. The critical temperature is about 28° for the tenderer species—navel, valencia, and Louisiana sweet oranges. Satsumas, mandarins, and tangerines are tougher, sometimes surviving temperatures as low as 15°. Despite the most favorable circumstances and all possible preventive measures, cold kills the citrus trees about every seven years on the average. The grower must decide if he can afford to replant and wait for the trees to produce. The ready market for Louisiana's premium fruit encourages him to continue.

With a series of good years, commercial growing tends to expand. For example, prior to the great freeze of 1929, Beauregard and St. Tammany parishes were important producers of citrus crops. One bad year put them out of business. The natural levees of the Mississippi below New Orleans have been the traditional producers of the bulk of Louisiana's citrus. In recent years the competition for land and labor between citrus and petroleum has tended to discourage the former. There has been a suggestion that the cheniers of southwestern Louisiana, once producers of prime fruit, might return to this crop.

Actually a perennial, sugarcane is in effect an annual plant, for it is harvested whole each year and generally replanted annually. Like citrus, it is a native of more tropical climates. Also like citrus, it would quickly die out if left to itself. Economically critical for cane is the length of the growing season, rather than the absolute cold of winter. In its native tropics, sugar-

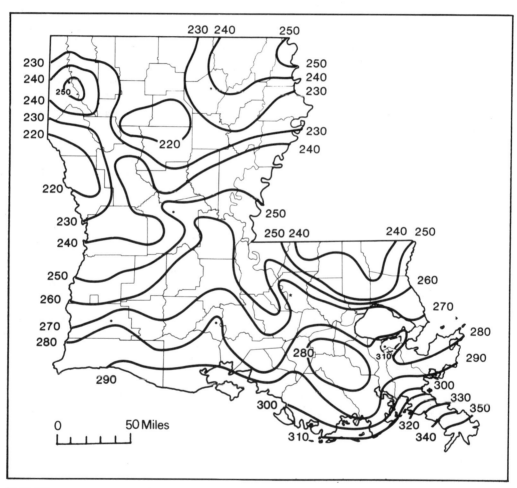

MAP 10

Average growing season. Growing season is defined as the number of days between the last killing frost in spring and the first killing frost in autumn.

cane grows for 15 to 22 months; this is obviously impossible in Louisiana, where 9 to 10 months must suffice. A 250-day growing season is regarded as the minimum time necessary to produce sufficient sugar content to make the crop profitable. This means cane is commercially grown to about the 31st parallel. Beyond that and as far north as the Arkansas line, cane is grown but only as a source of home supplies of ribbon cane syrup. North of Louisiana, sugarcane is replaced by sorghum as a source of syrup.

Other important Louisiana crops require a varied range of growing seasons. Bananas, for example, need more than a year to mature. They were once grown quite extensively in South Louisiana and were covered in winter as protection against frost. Cotton and rice need about 200 days, and corn, 120 days to mature. As far as the growing season is concerned, these three crops can be and are grown far to the north of Louisiana. Strawberries need a growing season of only about 90 days. Louisiana's climatic advantage is that these necessary 90 days come much earlier than in the more

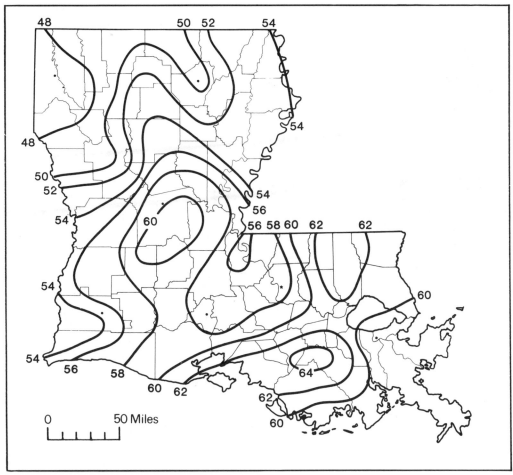

MAP 11
Average annual precipitation. This map, as well as Map 10, is based on forty years of data. Individual years may vary quite markedly from the averages shown.

23

northerly strawberry-growing areas. Louisiana thus has the advantage of an early market. Some root crops, such as beets and Irish potatoes, will grow in Louisiana but do best when grown in winter, for they prefer cooler temperatures.

The second element of weather and climate—moisture—appears in a number of forms: fog, cloud, dew, humidity, rain, snow, sleet, hail, and glaze. We are probably most conscious of precipitation—rain, snow, sleet, hail—that reaches the ground from overlying clouds. Precipitation is also most vital for plant growth. In Louisiana, as well as in the eastern United States, maximum precipitation occurs in the southeast, near the coast, and decreases in a northwesterly direction, as you can see on the annual precipitation map (Map 11). This situation reflects the

fact that the sea is the major source of moisture. With an annual average of 60 inches for South Louisiana, the range is from 65 inches in the southeast to only 54 inches in the northwestern portion of this section.

Although South Louisiana's 60 inches are well distributed through the year, there is a July maximum of some 6.7 inches and an October minimum of about 3.6 inches. To reduce the significance of the difference, it should be pointed out that precipitation is more beneficial in a cool season because less is lost for plant use by evaporation. Severe droughts are uncommon in South Louisiana. However, the high monthly averages of precipitation during the growing season hide a marked tendency toward dry spells of as much as a week or two, followed by rainy

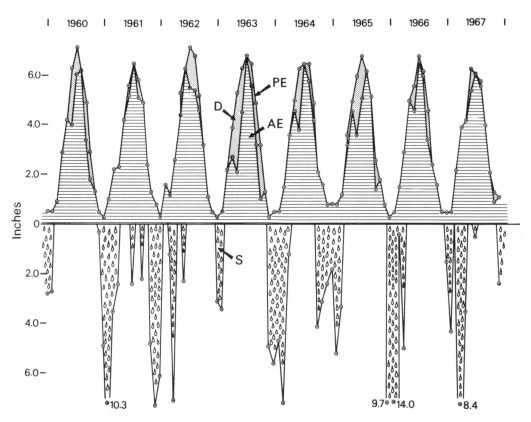

FIG. 5
Water budget for Baton Rouge based on monthly calculations for eight years

Scraping snow off road in central Louisiana
Louisiana Department of Commerce and Industry

spells. Loss of moisture by evaporation is much greater than one expects in an area of generally high humidity. In contrast to our rainfall regime, humid tropical areas of similar seasonal temperatures have daily rainfall. Growing plants suffer during our dry spells; supplemental irrigation would alleviate the situation. A more accurate picture of moisture availability is gained by comparing the moisture received with that lost through evaporation. Figure 5 is based on calculations of precipitation and evaporation, where PE represents potential evapotranspiration, AE represents actual evapotranspiration, S represents moisture surplus, and D represents the moisture deficit. PE, AE, and D are shown above the zero line, and S is plotted below. Note that sizable moisture deficits (D) occurred in 1960, 1962, 1964, and 1965, and a severe deficit occurred in 1963. You should also note that moisture surpluses (S) usually came in winter, a time of low evaporation.

Although rain is the common form of precipitation, snow occurs at infrequent intervals, with an average frequency in Baton Rouge, for example, of about once in ten years. Hail, which accompanies some thunderstorms, appears about twelve times a year in South Louisiana. Fortunately, it is not the crop hazard here that it is in some places. Sleet is a cool-season phenomenon that forms when the air near the ground is below freezing and that of higher strata is above freezing. Allied to sleet is glaze, which is cold rain that is frozen on contact with objects at the surface. Trees and wires may become coated with ice thick and heavy enough to cause severe damage. Glaze is much more common and destructive farther north. Rainfall itself is sometimes of such torrential nature as to cause local flooding and consequent damage to roads, crops, and buildings. Such heavy rainfall often, but not always, is associated with hurricanes.

Humidity is an expression of the invisible water vapor in the atmosphere. All living things are sensitive to its presence. We speak of light air and heavy air, or "mugginess." That Louisiana gets only about 50 percent of possible sunshine because of cloudiness indicates a generally high humidity. High relative humidity keeps evaporation down and so reduces cooling of the human body. We recognize this condition by molding leather and sticking dresser drawers. One of the chief functions of air conditioning is to reduce humidity. Louisiana, especially South Louisiana, has high humidity, notably with tropical summer air. There is an expected decline in humidity north and west away from the coast. There is also a decline in humidity with the coming of polar air masses in winter, when the percentage, even in South Louisiana, may drop as low as 10 to 15. However uncomfortable high humidity may be, it may be quite beneficial for plant growth because of its nightly condensation into dew and its reduction of losses by evaporation.

Some facts bearing on temperature and moisture in South Louisiana may be repeated. There are marked contrasts within the area because of the presence of the Gulf. Along the immediate coast is a narrow strip with little temperature variation, either daily or seasonal. Here 100° temperatures are rare and so is freezing. Continentality increases rapidly inland.

HILL FARM RESEARCH STATION
DAILY CLIMATIC DATA

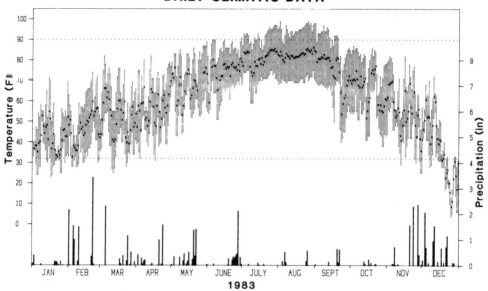

1983

FIG. 6

Precipitation and temperature plotted daily for the Hill Farm (Claiborne Parish) research station in 1983. Daily temperatures are shown by a vertical line. The top of the line indicates the highest temperature of the day and the bottom indicates the low for the day. Daily averages are shown by an X. Precipitation is shown by vertical bars on lower graph.

CITRUS RESEARCH STATION
DAILY CLIMATIC DATA

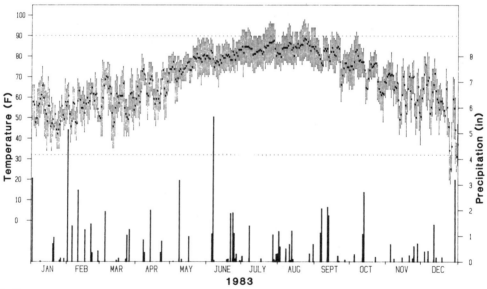

1983

FIG. 7

Precipitation and temperature plotted daily for Citrus research station (downriver from New Orleans) in the year 1983. See Figure 6 caption for detail on how to read the graphs.

26

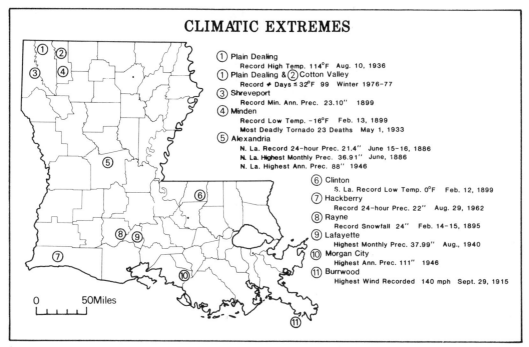

CLIMATIC EXTREMES

① Plain Dealing
   Record High Temp. 114°F Aug. 10, 1936
① Plain Dealing & ② Cotton Valley
   Record ✦ Days ≤ 32°F 99 Winter 1976-77
③ Shreveport
   Record Min. Ann. Prec. 23.10" 1899
④ Minden
   Record Low Temp. -16°F Feb. 13, 1899
   Most Deadly Tornado 23 Deaths May 1, 1933
⑤ Alexandria
   N. La. Record 24-hour Prec. 21.4" June 15-16, 1886
   N. La. Highest Monthly Prec. 36.91" June, 1886
   N. La. Highest Ann. Prec. 88" 1946

⑥ Clinton
   S. La. Record Low Temp. 0°F Feb. 12, 1899
⑦ Hackberry
   Record 24-hour Prec. 22" Aug. 29, 1962
⑧ Rayne
   Record Snowfall 24" Feb. 14-15, 1895
⑨ Lafayette
   Highest Monthly Prec. 37.99" Aug., 1940
⑩ Morgan City
   Highest Ann. Prec. 111" 1946
⑪ Burrwood
   Highest Wind Recorded 140 mph Sept. 29, 1915

0   50Miles

MAP 12

Selected data illustrating extreme conditions in the state

There is abundant precipitation, well distributed seasonally. Humidity is high, especially in summer.

North Louisiana can be discussed much more rapidly since the concepts have now been introduced at some length. Temperatures there are more variable than in South Louisiana. The annual average is 65.9° F. January, the coldest month, has an average of 48.9°, lower than South Louisiana's 54.2°, but still well within the 23° to 64.4° range. Alexandria has, on the average, 32 days annually when temperatures reach 32° or less. An absolute low of −16° F. was recorded in Minden in 1899. July, the warmest month, averages 82.4°, slightly higher than the 82° for South Louisiana. Shreveport temperatures reach 100° in half the years. Plain Dealing has experienced a record high for the state of 114°.

North Louisiana's growing season does not show a great drop from that of the northern section of South Louisiana, but,

in contrast to immediate coastal Louisiana, there is no station that does not record at least two frosts annually. The maximum growing season averages 259 days, and the minimum is 220. The range is such as to qualify the section for cotton, but hardly for commercial sugarcane.

Precipitation is, of course, lighter than in South Louisiana, some 53 inches compared to 60 inches. Within a minimum of 63.28 inches for the southeast, the average annual precipitation decreases in a northwesterly direction to 45.10 inches for Shreveport. Maximum rainfall comes in March and December with frontal storms. The minimum is in September and October, as is the case in South Louisiana. Heavy rainfalls come occasionally, but not as frequently as in South Louisiana. There is average occurrence of snowfall each year near the Arkansas line. There have been as many as 14 inches in a single year; years with no snow are rare. Hailstorms average nine per year, but rarely are they destructive. Glaze storms are more frequent and more damaging than in South Louisiana. Humidity is less and droughts more severe than in South Louisiana.

In summary, and in contrast to South Louisiana, North Louisiana is more continental, with hotter summers and much colder winters and shorter growing seasons. The influence of the Gulf is much reduced. There is less annual precipitation, but relatively greater amounts fall in winter, with its more frequent fronts. Humidity is lower and droughts are more damaging. There are more destructive glaze storms.

6
Weather and Climate
Winds

In the preceding chapter we discussed Louisiana's weather and climate in terms of temperature and moisture. The third atmospheric element—wind—is far more important for weather and climate than generally realized. Contrary to popular opinion, the most important winds are not those in violent storms, but rather the winds of low velocity that move the great polar and tropical air masses. Without the air masses Louisiana's climate would be unlivable, with severely reduced precipitation and seasonal change. On the average, Louisiana's wind velocities are low in comparison with those of other areas of the country. Possibly the strongest evidence of the steady work of winds can be seen along our immediate coast, where live oaks are sheared by onshore winds into striking profiles. Winds up to 50 miles per hour may accompany severe

thunderstorms and the squalls along air-mass fronts. Otherwise, storm velocities are found almost entirely in the series of winds constituting the cyclone family.

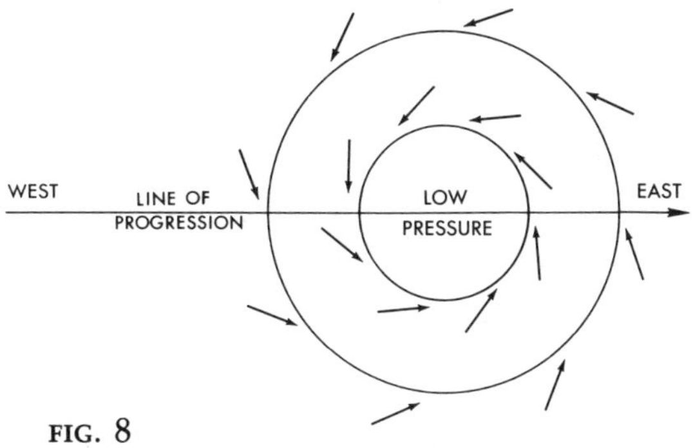

We include in the cyclone family those winds that move in a circular path around a low-pressure cell. Included are dust whirls, waterspouts, extratropical cyclones, tornadoes, and hurricanes. Only the latter two are usually powerful enough to be destructive. The direction of whirl of cyclonic storms in the northern hemisphere is counterclockwise, as you can see in the diagram of cyclonic structure. Only the dust whirl, possibly because of its small size, does not conform to the rule. About as many move one way as the other.

Dust whirls are normally the product of differential summer heating. That is, the air in a limited area becomes much hotter than the air about it, and this air rises. The same process gives rise to waterspouts. According to local tradition, waterspouts occur most frequently in Louisiana along the irregular coast of St. Bernard Parish. Despite a reputation for destructiveness, Louisiana waterspouts are not known to have caused any great damage.

Extratropical cyclones are so large and normally so low in wind velocity that we are hardly aware of their identity. They move in a west-to-east direction, most of them to the north of Louisiana. Nevertheless they are instrumental in bringing

FIG. 8
Ideal cyclonic structure in the northern hemisphere. Movement is from west to east.

through the polar fronts that are so significant, especially for our winter weather.
Another group of extratropical cyclones is
generated in the northern Gulf, many just
to the south of Louisiana. They move
northeastward, bringing precipitation and
increasingly higher wind velocities.

A modern storm cellar   Fred Kniffen

Frontal winds reaching a 50-mile-per-
hour velocity are more common in North
Louisiana because polar air masses reach
that section more often than they do
South Louisiana. Hurricanes are far less
destructive there, although sometimes
they bring heavy precipitation. Tornadoes, an average of three per year, are
as frequent as in South Louisiana, but
they seem to be more destructive. North
Louisiana adjoins the great area of destructive tornadoes that includes Texas,
Arkansas, and other states to the north.
As do those in neighboring states, the
people of northwestern Louisiana frequently build cyclone cellars. Sometimes
they hide their identity by calling them
storehouses. Caddo, Claiborne, Sabine,
Natchitoches, and Winn parishes have
greater than average frequency of tornadoes. No parish is immune.

*Tornado destruction accompanying Hurricane
Hilda, 1964*   Baton Rouge *State-Times*

Tornadoes are the most vicious of the destructive storms and the least predictable. They are small as compared with hurricanes, but they attain wind velocities that are far greater, up to 500 miles per hour. Part of their destructive effect is caused by the extreme low pressure of their centers, which makes buildings in their path burst outward. This type of damage is always good evidence that a storm was of tornadic character. A tornado is on the order of 100 yards wide, and it travels about 50 miles per hour, commonly along a straight course. A tornado is difficult to avoid, because the funnel may touch down at one spot, then skip an area before touching down again. It leaves a swath of devastation through forest and settlement.

Tornadoes are most commonly a product of the contact between two strongly contrasting air masses. These conditions appear most frequently in spring, most often in March, April, and May. November is the only fall month having a tornado frequency as great as that of the spring months. South Louisiana averages three tornadoes a year. They have occurred in every parish, but with more than average frequency in Assumption, Ascension, Tangipahoa, Calcasieu, and Beauregard. There seems to be some evidence to support the common idea that tornadoes are recurrent along the same paths. Why this should be so is not clear.

Of all destructive storms the hurricane is the largest and brings the most widespread damage. It originates in the tropics, and it appears in similar situations under a variety of names over the world. As a member of the cyclone family, it is a great whirl about a low-pressure core, rotating counterclockwise in the northern hemisphere. Wind velocities may reach 150 miles per hour and even more. No storm is officially a hurricane unless its winds have a velocity of 74 miles per hour and above. A major hurricane may pack winds that approach 200 miles per hour. However, the forward progress of the storm may be very slow, only a few miles an hour. This permits ample warning and offers an opportunity to escape the hurricane's course.

The most active portion of a hurricane may be a hundred miles in diameter, but winds of abnormal velocity and heavy rains may extend beyond this area. Tornadoes sometimes occur along the edges of hurricanes. High winds are accompanied by torrential rain. As the storm passes directly over a given point, the area is exposed first to high easterly winds. With the passing of the eye, or calm center (an area 5 to 30 miles in diameter without wind, cloud, or rain), the storm winds resume, this time from a westerly direction.

As long as the storm is over seas it can maintain its vigor. The condensation of the water vapor in moist air releases latent heat and so stimulates upward motion in the atmosphere and keeps the mechanism going. Once the storm moves over land and into air that is low in water vapor, it loses strength. Destructive winds rarely extend far inland. More frequently the dying hurricane brings to inland points an extraordinarily heavy rainfall that may be as destructive as the high winds.

Hurricane damage results from wind and from high water. In the Louisiana coastal marshes the high water is brought by storm surges from the Gulf—locally miscalled "tidal waves." On higher ground inland, high water is a product of the heavy precipitation. It is the low-lying coastal areas that bear the assault of the storm's fury. High winds are followed by an invasion of the sea that may cover the ground to a depth of fifteen feet. Sometimes wind and water come together to batter and destroy. The chief victims are animals, small plants, people and their installations—houses, fences, and the like. Although the immediate shore may suffer considerable alteration through the storm's force, the more protected cheniers are not greatly changed, and the live oaks on them have weathered many storms. There may be even a beneficial result, for the layer of silt deposited over fields by the storm adds to their fertility. The common rules regarding hurricanes are broken by so-called hundred-year storms, when high wind velocities persist inland a matter of two hundred miles. Louisiana had successive hundred-year storms in 1964 and 1965.

For the past century, Louisiana has averaged more than one tropical storm per year. Not all of these reached hurricane force. Hurricanes appear on an average of about once every four years. During one eighty-three-year period, ninety-two storms were unequally distributed among the six months of June through November. Eight came in June, 12 in July, 18 in August, 40 in September, 13 in October, and 1 in November. Clearly, September is the month of major expectancy, and there *is* a hurricane season.

Out of this mass of material emerge certain generalities concerning Louisiana climate. It is humid subtropical, with mild winters and hot summers, with high humidity and abundant, well-distributed precipitation. Winter is a time of alternating air-mass control, tropical then polar, with all the frontal effects and an outward (Gultward) monsoon effect. Summer is a period of continuous hot weather, high humidity, and thunderstorms, sometimes triggered by weak fronts and weak tropical disturbances. The hurricane season begins in earnest in late summer. Spring and fall are poorly developed seasons, because Louisiana has essentially a two-season climate, separated by the absence or presence of polar fronts. The commonly considered fall months are the driest; the spring season shows a maximum number of tornadoes.

The 31st parallel is meaningless as a climatic line. At the same time there are

Damage on Grand Isle from Hurricane Betsy,
1965

Baton Rouge *State-Times*

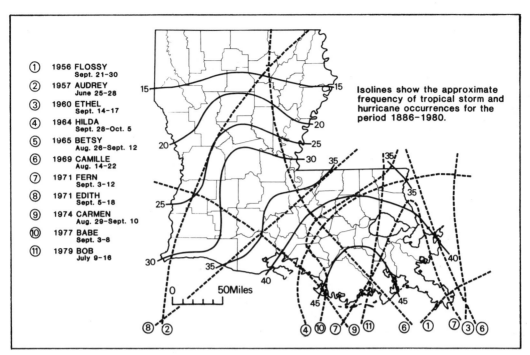

Isolines show the approximate
frequency of tropical storm and
hurricane occurrences for the
period 1886-1980.

MAP 13
*Tropical storms and hurricanes affecting
Louisiana*

important climatic differences in Louisiana, especially in winter. In North Louisiana there is more snow and cold; automobiles must be equipped for winter driving. Crops like peaches and plums fare better there than to the south. Apples and pears prefer even cooler summers. They will grow in North Louisiana, but do far better at latitudes higher than that of Louisiana. South Louisiana grows citrus, palm trees, and sugarcane. Live oaks flourish naturally in the woods. Every traveler has noted the difference in the flowering seasons of North and South Louisiana. Here are a number of significant criteria for dividing the two. The most important distinction must be between a thin marine coastal strip, with little or no winter, and a much larger continental interior. Perhaps this separation might be effected by the January isotherm of 54°, running from Slidell to Cameron, through Lake Pontchartrain and south of Baton Rouge. You can follow this line on the map of growing seasons in Chapter 5. This by no means encompasses all the differences, but as well as any arbitrary line can, it separates a southern area where hardy crops can grow in winter and tropical plants can survive from a northern area of winter plant dormancy.

7

Relief

Hills

Relief, or topography, is concerned with the natural surface form of the land—hills, valleys, plains, ridges, gullies, and similar features. Relief features are of different orders of magnitude. That is, we may say that hills in Louisiana constitute a first-order, or major, division of relief. We may describe the Five Islands as features of far less magnitude and areal extent (see Map 2). We will start by speaking of large divisions and then deal with a number of the smaller relief features of Louisiana. First you will gain an idea of what and where the relief forms of Louisiana are located. For better understanding, and because they are interesting, we will say something of the natural forces that build relief forms. Natural forces act through processes such as erosion (wearing away), deposition (building up), or tectonics (downwarping, tilting, and uplift).

We have already stated that all of Louisiana lies on the Gulf Coastal Plain. The very term "coastal plain" suggests that relief should be relatively slight. At most, the relief features are a series of low ridges and valleys paralleling the coast. Millions of years ago, old land to the

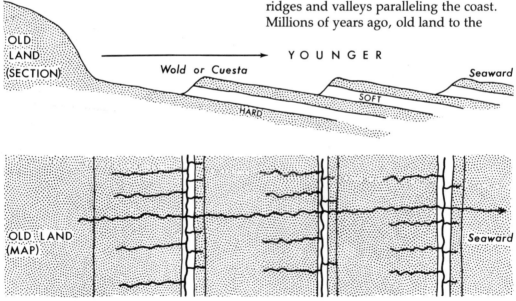

FIG. 9
*Section and map of coastal plain showing
resulting topography and drainage*

north provided sediments that were carried southward by streams and deposited in the sea, gradually extending the shore outward.

The successive layers of sedimentary rocks that were deposited measure from hundreds to thousands of feet in thickness and dip gently toward the sea. They lie like a tilted deck of cards, with younger beds overlying older layers. A glance at the sectional map and sketch will show you that the youngest rock, then, is to be found right along the shore. If we were to drill down, the bit would encounter older and older rocks.

Because these were layers of sediment, they have given rise to sedimentary rocks, clays, shales, sands, sandstones, limestones, gravels, and conglomerates. A basic difference as we classify sedimentary materials is the size of the individual grains that compose them. Clay, at one end of the scale, is very fine grained. Then, in order of increasing coarseness, come silt, sand, and gravel.

Some of these rocks will erode away more rapidly than others. As the land slowly emerges out of the sea through continued deposition and uplift, differential erosion takes place. The harder rocks like sandstone tend to remain as ridges (cuesta or wold), while the less resistant materials are eroded into valleys. An ideal belted coastal plain consists of a series of alternating ridges and valleys running parallel to the coast. Because streams have done the eroding, they occupy the valleys and run down the ridge slopes, all discharging into a master stream that has cut straight across the ridges to the sea. Such a system of drainage is called a trellis pattern, as the streams meet at right angles and form a series of rectangles (Fig. 9).

How well does the coastal plain of Louisiana conform to the ideal? Examination of a surface geological map shows that there are belts of different rock formations, that they lie parallel to the coast, and that they are successively younger

toward the Gulf. Subsurface drilling has shown that younger beds overlie older ones. There are cuesta or wold ridges and suggestions of trellis drainage. Beyond these features that are consistent with the model, however, there are departures from the ideal. For instance, the outcropping beds in the northwestern part of the state bend around northward instead of continuing straight across the state as does the Kisatchie Wold. Also, recent Mississippi River deposits are spread indiscriminately over older rocks throughout its 50-mile-wide alluvial valley. Events have produced features that were not mentioned for the ideal coastal plain, as you will see on the relief map.

Reconstruction of Louisiana's geological history shows that the shoreline has fluctuated as the sea advanced or retreated. As conditions affecting the flow of streams changed, various types of sedimentary rocks were deposited, sometimes in the sea, at other times on the land. At different times and places the earth's crust has been deformed, strongly affecting surface features. One such deformation was the Sabine Uplift in northwestern Louisiana (Fig. 10). There the beds of rock were domed, or pushed upward, perhaps at the same time the top of the dome was being eroded away, leaving the edges of the upturned beds of rock exposed around the center of the dome. This structure explains the north-

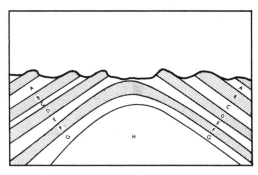

FIG. 10

An eroded dome. Shading shows hard layers that form ridges.

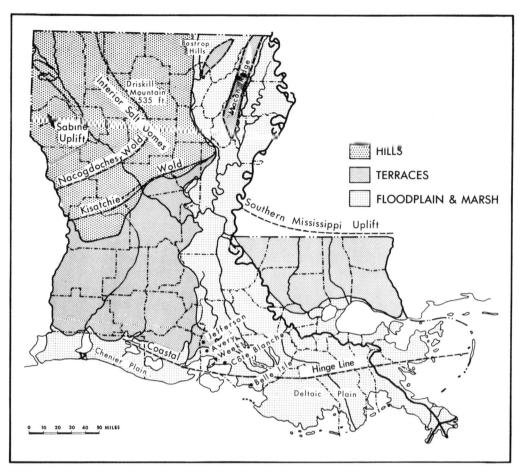

MAP 14
Relief features and regions

ward turn of the beds in northwestern Louisiana.

Along the 31st parallel is the crest of the Southern Mississippi Uplift, which has raised the local beds to some of the highest elevations in the state and introduced a hilly topography. Parallel to and a little north of the coast is the structural feature known as the Coastal Hinge Line (Map 14). South of the line the sediments loaded by the tremendous weights of the annual Mississippi deposits are sinking. North of the line the country is gradually rising. Sinking of the crust in one place and a balancing rise in another is called isostasy. Other structural features—the Five Islands—are caused by the pushing up of salt from depth. The above de-

scribed features are the principal surface evidence of crustal deformation.

If we divide Louisiana into major divisions on the basis of relief, we then have these three: hills, terraces, and lowlands, the last divided into floodplain and marsh. On the relief map we have placed lines around these three divisions. Actually, they are not so clearly separated. The hills include minor sections of floodplain and terraces. The terraces in portions of the northern Florida Parishes are as hilly as some sections of the hills division. The floodplain has some terrace fragments within it. Nevertheless, the division is a practical and useful one.

The hills relief division of Louisiana, composed of the oldest rocks in the state, occupies the northwestern parishes. It is bounded on the south by an irregular line that runs from DeRidder to Harrisonburg. The Ouachita River is the eastern boundary. Within the hills section the highest elevations and the greatest local relief are found. Here is true solid rock, as well as unconsolidated sediments. Aside from the ten-to-fifteen-mile-wide valley of the intrusive Red River, which is a large stream before it ever enters Louisiana, the valleys of local streams tend to be sufficiently narrow so that man's activities, including roads and housing, are on the divides rising between the valleys.

There are few distinguishable local "ranges" in the hills. One exception is the Kisatchie Wold or Cuesta. Here tough sandstone ridges tend to have steep inward faces and gentler slopes seaward, in proper cuesta style. There is a suggestion of trellis drainage. There actually are waterfalls. The Kisatchie is easily the most pronounced and extensive hill section of the state. Less pronounced and less con-

tinuous is the Nacogdoches Wold, whose course is influenced by and encircles the Sabine Uplift. Although Driskill Mountain, the state's highest point, is part of the wold, it is less impressive as a whole than Kisatchie. Around the Sabine Uplift the preservation of ridges is often the result of tough capping layers that defy erosion. Some ridges are gravel capped; others are preserved by the very tough ironstone derived from weathering of greensand or glauconite. The latter provides an iron cement that joins sand grains into highly resistant rock. Ironstone caps Driskill Mountain. It should be kept in mind that where gravel forms capping layers on the higher elevations, this gravel was deposited originally in low stream valleys. Its presence now on ridges affords a measure of the extent of uplift.

Other features of the Sabine Uplift are the Dolet Hills (an eroded upland in De

Kisatchie Wold

Louisiana Office of Forestry Commission

37

Driskill Mountain, the highest point in the state

Soto Parish), the high points in Webster and Claiborne parishes, and the high land near Plain Dealing in Bossier Parish. On the extreme eastern border of the Hills region are the Ouachita Hills, which are neither a part of the Sabine Uplift nor a single, unified system. Ouachita Hills is simply a name given to the higher and rougher country west of the Ouachita River. These hills are higher and rougher as compared with the low, flat floodplain to the east of the Ouachita, and from the floodplain they are quite impressive. At least one segment of the Ouachita Hills—the Bayou Dan Hills of southern Caldwell Parish—is a recognizable unit area of rough country.

In our delimitation of the natural regions of Louisiana (Map 3), we included as longleaf hills a portion of the northeastern Florida Parishes. This section qualifies by elevation, vegetation, and degree of local relief. It does not qualify by age or mode of formation, and hence, among the three relief divisions, it is classed as terrace, to be discussed next.

8
Relief

Terraces

The other two major relief divisions of the state—terraces and lowlands—are largely the products of the Mississippi River and the sea. The relative importance of these two forces has varied in time and place. Terraces and lowlands developed in quite recent times, geologically speaking, perhaps in only two million years. Erosion, deposition, and reworking by both river and sea have taken place in fluctuating climatic conditions. The work of river and sea has been accompanied by local isostatic deformations of the earth's crust and eustatic, or worldwide, changes in sea level.

The Mississippi River of these last two

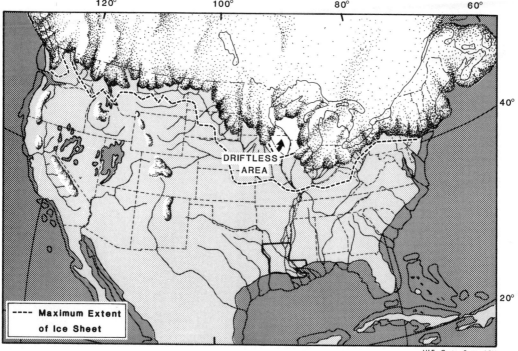

120°　　　　100°　　　　80°　　　　60°

40°

DRIFTLESS AREA

20°

---- Maximum Extent
of Ice Sheet

MLE, Carto. Sect., LSU

MAP 15
Glaciation over North America. The ice sheet is shown as it is diminishing in area. Dashed line indicates the maximum extent the ice sheet reached.

million years is a product of the Ice Age (the Pleistocene period). When the ice covering the northern portion of the continent blocked the preglacial drainage into Hudson Bay and out of the St. Lawrence River, the Mississippi was born. You can see the extent of glaciation on the map of the United States (Map 15). The course of the Ohio River pretty well outlined the southern margin of the ice to the east, and the Missouri River did the same to the west. The two joined to flow south to the Gulf, giving rise to the Mississippi. Even during the cold of glacial advances the river was an active stream. There were seasons then as now. During the glacial summer the meltwater from the ice added great volume to the streams and to the tremendous burden of materials they carried toward the sea. These materials ranged in size from clay to gravel. During the winter season the streams shrank in volume, thus reducing their capacity to carry the coarser sediments. There is evidence in the form of large boulders found in Avoyelles Parish that blocks of ice floated down the river, lodged in shallow water, then melted and deposited the large rocks they carried.

The continental ice sheet advanced and retreated (actually melted back) a number of times. There were at least five major advances and retreats, as shown on the geologic time scale (Table 1). The ice sheet never got within hundreds of miles of Louisiana, but the record of its activities is clearly written in the sediments brought here by the glacier-fed streams. Although the temperature was certainly colder during the glacial advances, it was not bitterly frigid, as commonly pictured. Vegetation grew close to the ice. The greater coolness did, however, push the latitudinal vegetation belts farther south, so that today we have in Louisiana traces of plants that now belong farther north.

Indirectly the sea played an important part in determining how and where the

TABLE 1
Geologic Time Scale, Ice Age and Recent

RECENT	Recent Deposition • formation of floodplain and alluvial valley • rise in sea level
	10,000 years before present

PLEISTOCENE	Late Wisconsin • ice advance • drop in sea level
	40 ft. Prairie Terrace deposition • rise in sea level
	Early Wisconsin • ice advance • drop in sea level
	200 ft. Montgomery Terrace deposition • rise in sea level
	Illinoian • ice advance • drop in sea level
	300 ft. Bentley Terrace deposition • rise in sea level
	Kansan • ice advance • drop in sea level
	350 ft. Williana Terrace deposition • rise in sea level
	Nebraskan • ice advance • drop in sea level
	Two million years before present

Note that, like the layers of the earth, the oldest periods appear at the bottom.

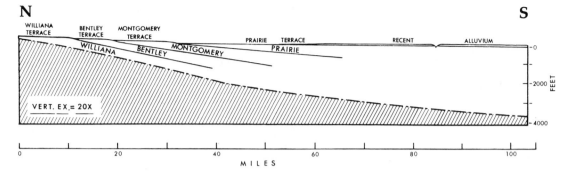

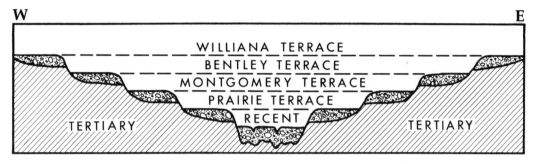

FIG. 11

North-south and east-west sections of terraces

river sediments were deposited. During periods of waxing glaciation, as more and more water was stored on land in the form of ice, its one important source, the sea, was simultaneously shrinking. Sea level was once probably as much as 450 feet lower than it is at present and great river channels and deltas, as well as the coastline, were much farther seaward on what is now the continental shelf. When the ice melted back, the meltwater ran to the sea and raised the level. It has been estimated that if all the water now stored on land as glacial ice should melt and return to the sea, the level would rise by 150 feet, enough to extend the Gulf northward to Memphis.

The terraces are the chief evidence in Louisiana of what was happening during glacial times. Our terraces are former river floodplains or coastal areas that have been raised above present surfaces of deposition. In series they rise above each other like steps. Terrace materials may have been originally deposited by streams in their floodplains, or they may have been

deposited in the shallow waters of the Gulf. If terraces are extensive in area they usually show flat, gently sloping surfaces. They may also have been highly eroded after uplift, leaving small, irregular, remnant knobs.

We can trace the building of terraces, step by step. The ice sheet advances, sea level drops, and the now steeper streams begin to cut. The shoreline retreats and streams extend their courses out onto what had been the sea-covered continental shelf, as much as a hundred miles beyond their present mouths. Since this cutting goes on for thousands of years, its extent becomes great, and there may be little left of the pre-existing surface. As the glacial ice melts back, the sea begins to rise, and the shoreline retreats inland. Streams deposit more than they cut. With increasing reduction in their gradient (degree of slope) the streams in any given spot will, in time, deposit finer and finer materials. The hundreds of feet of terrace deposits commonly have coarse gravels at their bases and range gradually upward through sands to silts and clays. The broad floodplains are buried by the new

*Ancestral Mississippi River meander on the
Prairie Terrace*

deposits, and the beds of the streams move up with them. The older surface that was active floodplain before the glacial advance is now a terrace, lying above the new floodplain.

With the five glacial advances four major terraces have been formed, as noted in the geologic time scale. Now you may well ask why during each period of deposition the new floodplain is not built up to the older one? The reason is that the surfaces inland from the Coastal Hinge Line are being uptilted to counterbalance the sinking of the deltaic area south of the line. This isostatic process results in older terraces having surfaces generally less

continuous but lying higher than the younger ones. Because the older terraces have been subject to isostatic tilting longer, they slope or dip more steeply toward the coast. At the same time, each older terrace dips under all the younger ones. Two cross sections show these relationships, one north and south and the other east and west (Fig 11).

The geological timetable associates the four terraces with the interglacial periods in which they were deposited. The elevations given for the terraces are average rather than absolute, since obviously no dipping surface can have a constant elevation. The oldest terraces are exposed farthest inland, as they should be on a banded or belted coastal plain. The end of the Ice Age, or Pleistocene, is placed at 10,000 years ago. Geologists call the period and deposits since that time the Recent. The present, or Recent, may well be another interglacial period. Perhaps in a few thousand years glaciers will advance again, the sea level will drop, the shoreline will move toward the sea, the Recent floodplains and marshes will be eroded, and what is left will be tilted upward to form another in the series of Louisiana terraces.

The more recently that geologic events have occurred, the clearer is the evidence regarding the steps leading to the formation of terraces and the Recent floodplain. For example, with the appearance of aerial photographs in the 1930s it was possible to see on the Prairie Terrace west of the Teche the unmistakable imprint of previous interglacial Mississippi River channels. Here is indisputable proof that the Prairie Terrace in that area, now at least 20 to 25 feet above the active Mississippi floodplain, was the floodplain before the last glacial advance.

Recently deposited material in the active floodplain in the vicinity of Baton Rouge reaches 300 feet in thickness. This means that during the last glacial advance the bed of the Mississippi was some 300 feet below what is now the surface of the Prairie Terrace. At Baton Rouge the average elevation of the terrace surface is around 40 feet. By present conditions the bed of the Mississippi would have been 260 feet below sea level. This indicates simply that during the glacial advance sea level had dropped at least 260 feet. This deep course of the river has been called the Grand Canyon of the Mississippi.

You can observe today the eroded edges where one terrace meets another on the floodplain. Away from the edges the terrace surfaces are quite flat. The reason for the difference is that the steplike contacts between terraces are steep, thus causing marked erosion. When the bottom of the Grand Canyon of the Mississippi lay some 260 feet lower than the

surface of the adjoining Prairie Terrace in the vicinity of Baton Rouge, a series of short, swift streams developed, creating deep, steep-sided gullies on the terrace edge. In some instances the gullies ate their way back to capture streams that were flowing south and east over the old deltaic surface of the Prairie Terrace (Map 16). They thus diverted the drainage westward into the Mississippi system.

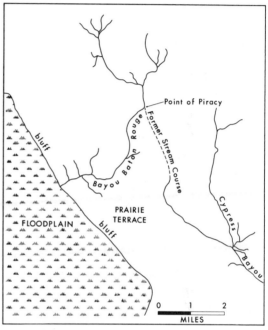

MAP 16
Old drainage course and stream piracy near Baton Rouge

With the reversal of the glacial trend and the rise of sea level, the floodplain began to fill. Gradually the velocity of streams discharging off the terrace was checked. The gullies were actually filled and their bottoms became flat instead of sharp. But they retain their steep walls and show what they once were. With their loss of gradient and power to cut, most of the gullies lost the stream systems they had captured. The latter once more drained to the south and southeast. The gullies became relict, or leftover, features, evidence of an episode of past geologic history.

43

9
Relief

Lowlands: The River

The activities of river and sea, which once built Louisiana's terraces, are presently working primarily in the lowlands—the floodplains and marshes. Here, in the Recent period, rivers have filled the valleys cut during the last ice advance, while the sea has risen to cover older coastal lowlands. Sea level reached a stand about 3,000 years ago, which means that fluctuations in level since then have been slight, perhaps only a few feet. The Mississippi has reached equilibrium, so that it is neither cutting on a major scale nor filling its valley as it did in the past. Instead, it cuts here and deposits there, at the same time carrying a tremendous load of sediments to dump into the sea—some two million tons each day.

The Mississippi is a lowland stream, having low gradient, a big load of sediments to work with, and a wide range between its low-water and high-water stages. Like other streams with these qualities, the Mississippi's pattern of behavior is quite different from that of upland streams. From the Arkansas line to the Gulf, the river's course is 569 miles long; the straight-line distance is about half that figure. The difference in elevation is 115 feet. The average gradient, therefore, is about 2½ inches per mile. Southward to below New Orleans, the Mississippi's course is a series of majestic bends, or meanders, whose diameters are on the order of 3 to 5 miles. These meanders have a natural tendency to

shift, to be cut off, and to build anew, but are presently greatly restrained by the man-made structures built over the past half century. The meander belt within which the Mississippi is presently carry-

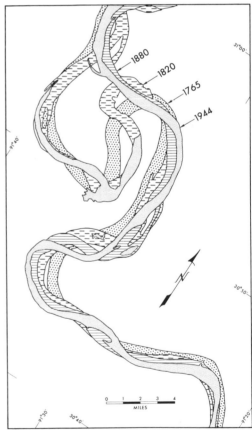

MAP 17
Shifting channels in a meander belt

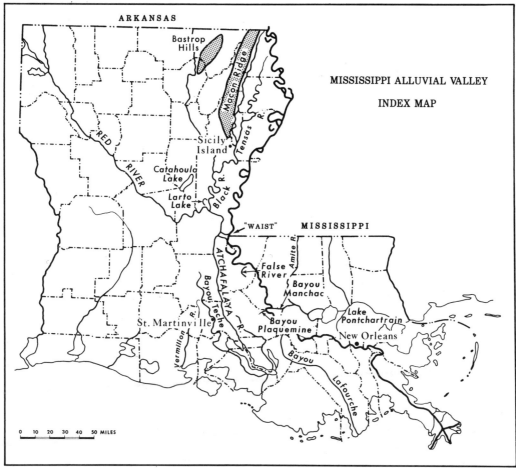

MAP 18

Index map of features associated with Louisiana's rivers

ing on these activities is from 10 to 20 miles wide (Map 17).

Another characteristic of the Mississippi in Louisiana is that it has no normal tributaries. Red River was once a natural tributary, but it no longer is, for both natural and human reasons. There are a few unimportant tributaries along the east bank, but they are tributary only because the river's course is up against the terrace bluff. Instead of tributaries, the Mississippi, in the manner of lowland streams, has *distributaries,* streams that flow out of it. Among the major distributaries are the Atchafalaya River and Bayous Lafourche, Plaquemine, and Manchac. Of these, only the Atchafalaya remains an active dis-

tributary, and its flow is controlled. Under natural conditions the drainage pattern resembled a giant hourglass with the "waist" at about the 31st parallel where the major rivers, the Red, Black, Tensas, and Mississippi, converged. South of that line, Mississippi water flowed into the Gulf through its own channel and through the distributaries mentioned above. You can locate these streams on the Index Map of the Mississippi alluvial valley (Map 18).

To better understand how the Mississippi accomplishes its work, refer to the two sketches, one a profile, or cross section, and the other a map (Fig 12). The section (12A) shows a normal floodplain surface with an elevation of 10 feet. On this surface the river has deposited natural levees 15 feet higher. From levee crests

45

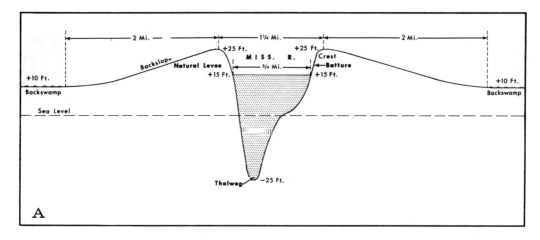

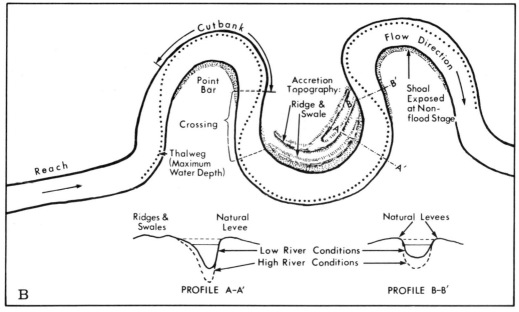

FIG. 12

Ideal section and plan of the Mississippi River channel. A represents section across the river; B represents a part of the channel seen from above.

that are 1¼ miles apart across the channel, the levee backslopes extend some two miles to the backswamp, the deposits composing them becoming finer and finer in texture. The shorter inward slopes, or battures, of the natural levee lead down to the water level, which varies in elevation with the stage of the river. Within its bed the river has scoured out a thalweg (the deepest natural channel) to provide a continuous channel with a minimum depth of about 35 feet southward from Baton Rouge. Note that the river can scour out depths that are far below sea level.

Now let us look above at the map of a meander belt (Fig 12B). The inside, or concave side, of the meander is called a point. Here deposition takes place in the shallow, slack water and builds point bars. As the meander develops, the convex, or cutbank, side advances outward, and the point builds with it. This leaves

A point bar and cutbank on the Amite River

Elemore Morgan

*Ridge-and-swale topography on the inside of a
Mississippi River meander. Actual site is False
River near New Roads in Pointe Coupee
Parish.*

47

behind a low ridge-and-swale topography of old point bars and intervening channels. The cutbank retreats by scour and undercutting in the thalweg and slump of the bank about it. Note how the channel, or thalweg, hugs the cutbanks, crossing from one side of the river to the other in order to do so. Where the river flows in a straight stretch, or reach, the position of the thalweg is not always predictable.

Ordinary overbank flow of floodwaters and crevasses or actual cutting of distributary flood channels take place most effectively on the cutbank side of a meander. As a result you may see here rolling or wavy crevasse topography and find the broadest natural levees, the choice side for agriculture. Where the constricting points of a meander approach each other so closely as to leave between only a narrow *neck*, there is a promising spot for a crevasse and a permanent cutoff. That this has happened many times is shown by the prevalence of the name "Old River" for lakes in Louisiana. The former meander then becomes an *oxbow lake*, of which False River in Pointe Coupee Parish is the best-known example (Map 19).

Finally, there are towheads and islands with chutes lying between them and the near shore. Islands are larger and higher than towheads. Each is the result of the river's effort to bring its width back to the normal distance. That is, where for any reason the width of the river becomes greater than it should be, the current slackens and deposition occurs. Sometimes this takes the form of an island or towhead. The minor channel separating them from the nearest shore is called a chute.

Towhead and chute, terms commonly used along the Mississippi. The writer Mark Twain had Huckleberry Finn and his companion Jim tie their raft to a towhead while on their adventures downriver. James P. Morgan

Aside from the Atchafalaya, a special case, the distributaries of the Lower Mississippi were naturally no more than high-water overflows out of the river. At low-water stages their channels were dry notches in the natural levee of the Mississippi. The channels were shallow and largely unnavigable down the levee backslope of the Mississippi. Only beyond the toe, or edge, of the backslope did the distributaries take on the characteristics of normal channels, with their own natural levees and navigable depths. Bayou Plaquemine was officially severed from the Mississippi in 1770; Bayou Manchac, in 1826; Bayou Lafourche, in 1902.

South of the major distributaries toward the sea, the Mississippi, instead of con-

MAP 19
False River, a cutoff meander in Pointe Coupee Parish.

Abandoned river distributary channel now filled with sediments. Tree growth indicates area of slightly higher ground.

David Prior

tinuing through a series of meanders, flows in a series of reaches. A plausible explanation is that the scouring of the cutbank (convex side of the meander) necessary in the formation of meanders cannot occur in the very tough clays of the lower river. Also, in the lower river the annual fluctuation in height of water is much reduced. As a consequence, the natural levees are reduced in height and size. The many escape routes into the vast Gulf keep the river from building up a high-water stage. Finally, the Mississippi splits into a number of narrow but reasonably deep passes. At the mouths of the passes, however, bars that have been deposited there prevent easy passage for ships.

Looking over the entire alluvial valley in a little more specific detail, we find that its average 50-mile width falls generally between well-defined boundaries. For most of its length each side terminates in the abrupt wall of a higher-lying terrace or other older formation. At the southern end there is no higher ground to bound the floodplain, so its limits must be defined by the marginal streams belonging to the Mississippi system—the Vermilion to the west, and the Manchac-Lower Amite to the east (Map 18). These two streams lie only partly within the alluvial valley, for each begins as a distributary channel in the floodplain, then flows away from it, cutting through the Prairie Terrace to marsh lowland and the sea. The alluvial valley, with its bounding walls, terminates approximately at a line connecting Franklin and Donaldsonville. To the south of this line is the deltaic plain.

The word *delta* is widely and variously applied in the floodplain. It was originally used by Herodotus because the lowland area of distributary channels of the Nile is shaped like the Greek letter Δ (delta). If we apply this original definition, then the Mississippi delta should run southward

49

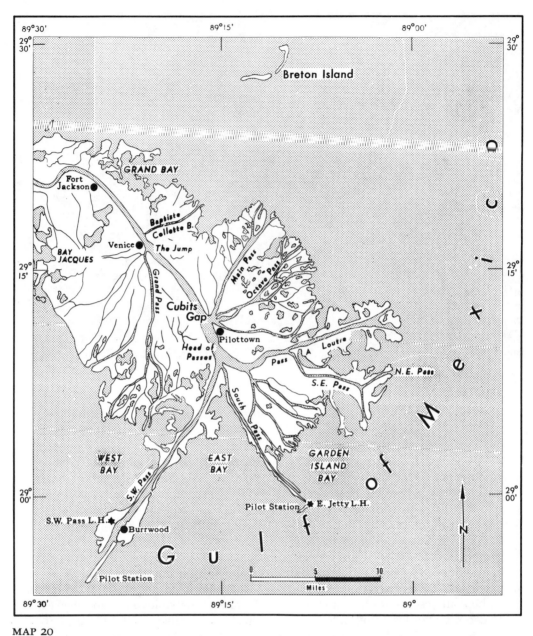

MAP 20

The modern delta of the Mississippi River showing passes. The dynamic nature of the river ensures that such maps do not remain accurate for long, because the river constantly shifts and reworks the outlets.

from the head of the Atchafalaya River. *Delta* is also applied to the small section of distributary passes at the mouths (Map 20). And it is used to include the rich

bottomlands of northeastern Louisiana and western Mississippi. It is impossible to restrict the name to a single feature.

We have already mentioned Macon Ridge and included it with the state's terraces (Maps 2 and 3). It is actually an alluvial cone or fan of the Arkansas River, formed when the latter discharged its sediments onto the Mississippi alluvial valley. On top of the ridge are meander scars of Arkansas River size. The ridge is six to twenty miles wide and extends from the Arkansas line to Sicily Island on the south. Its highest points are forty to fifty feet above the valley floor. Enclosed by Arkansas River sediments are some old Prairie Terrace remnants that project up from the valley floor. The Bastrop Hills are like Macon Ridge, because they are the depositional cone of the Ouachita River and include some Prairie Terrace remnants. The hills reach a width of five miles, are about seventeen miles long, and rise to as much as seventy feet above the lowlands. Similar in origin but wider and lower is the Red River cone. Its distinctive red sediments are deposited over a broad area of the valley in Avoyelles and St. Landry parishes. Red River deposits surround the Prairie Terrace remnant known as Avoyelles, or Marksville, Prairie. This feature, standing abruptly some thirty to thirty-five feet above the floodplain, is clearly of Mis-

sissippi River origin, as proven by its color and the great size of the meander scars on its surface.

Of streams and lakes in the valley, the Tensas-Black channel may be pointed out as an old course of the Mississippi. West of Black River lies Larto Lake, in southern Catahoula Parish. Larto is clearly a Mississippi River cutoff lake. It lacks important silt-bearing tributaries and so has managed to maintain itself for the long period since the Black River channel was occupied by the Mississippi. A similar but more recent cutoff lake is False River in Pointe Coupee Parish, cut off by the Mississippi in 1722 (Map 19). Of quite different character are Catahoula Lake, chiefly in La Salle Parish, and Lake Pontchartrain. The beds of both these lakes are grabens, which are depressed sections of the earth's crust bounded by faults.

The Teche reveals details of a long and interesting history of change (Fig 13). As

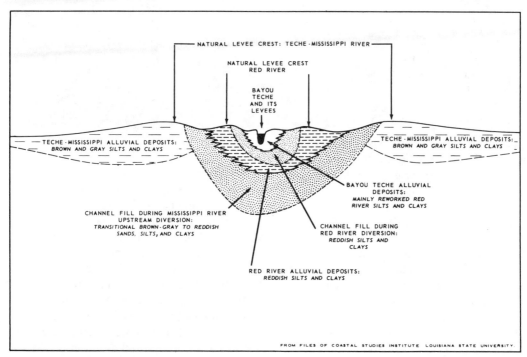

FIG. 13
A section of Bayou Teche indicating its complex history

51

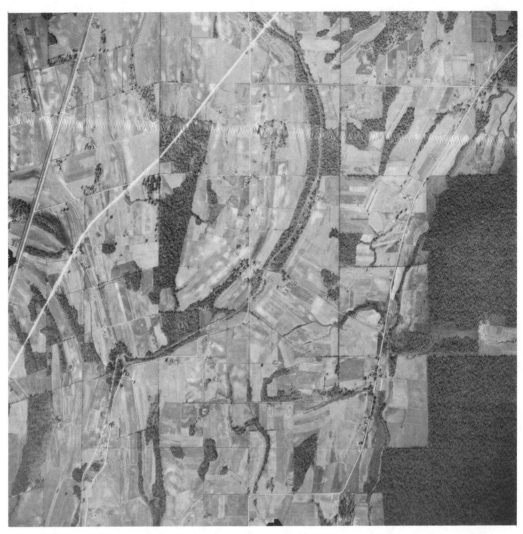

Eastern margin of Macon Ridge in West Carroll Parish. Note the floodplain swamp east of ridge and old Arkansas River meander scar in middle of photograph.

you can see particularly well in the vicinity of St. Martinville, the course of the Teche is bounded outwardly by a set of levees that from composition and size can be said to have once contained the Mississippi. Within these wide levees is first a linear, depressed area occupied by shallow ponds. Next in order inward are levees composed of red soil and of a size commensurate with Red River. In the middle is the small channel of Bayou Teche. The sequence revealed by this series of features is easy to follow. First was the Mississippi with its grayish soils and broad levees. Red River was a tributary of the Mississippi at that time, but when the Mississippi shifted its course to the eastern side of the valley at a point above the confluence with the Red, the latter had no choice but to follow the old course. Within the larger Mississippi levees the Red built its own levees of distinctive red sediments. Finally, the Red abandoned this channel to rejoin the Mississippi. The little Teche thus inherited the channels of two mighty rivers.

10

Relief

Lowlands: Delta and Coast

For the last 10,000 years the Mississippi River has been filling its valley, swinging to one side, then fifty miles away to the other, then down the middle. We have seen evidence of these shifts in the form of long-abandoned meander belts, cutoff lakes, and fragments of old natural levees of Mississippi size. Each system, or group of related channels, had its own delta, a set of distributary channels through which it discharged into the sea. We can reconstruct with reasonable certainty some seven of these old deltas. Much helpful evidence is available on large-scale maps; more comes from aerial photographs.

From maps and photographs we can identify the younger deltaic systems and often can place them in time sequence, that is, in order of relative age. For example, if two systems or meander belts intersect, the one that is continuous and uninterrupted is clearly the younger. Fieldwork can gather excellent evidence, although it is slow business putting down bore holes and examining samples of sediments. By this process it is possible to outline old channels now buried beneath the marsh.

A quite different approach to the relative age of Recent deltaic systems is through a study of the pottery, tools, and other artifacts of the prehistoric Indians who lived along the streams. The use of this approach depends upon two assumptions. The first is that we can, from the study of artifacts, determine the identity of different Indian groups or cultures and separate them into their relative time positions. The second assumption is that as new deltaic systems were developed they were occupied by the Indians. Old deltaic systems abandoned by the main Mississippi River were not necessarily abandoned by their native inhabitants, so that a whole sequence of Indian cultures might occupy a particular site long after the system became inactive. When this is the case, it is important to determine what culture was there first (the oldest culture), for this would establish the time position of the new deltaic system.

On the basis of these avenues of evidence a sequence of seven deltaic systems was set up, as shown in the map of delta systems (Map 21). The absolute time in terms of number of years could only be estimated as perhaps 3,500 years before the present. Although these results satisfied some investigators, they did not convince others. Finally, in the late 1940s, physicists perfected a method of finding the age of the remains of once-living things such as plants, shells, and bones. This method is based on the amount of radiocarbon 14 (C^{14}) found in the organic remains. Live organisms contain C^{14} in a known amount. After death they lose C^{14} at a known rate. It is then possible to measure the remaining C^{14} and determine the age of the object. The method works with considerable accuracy for the past

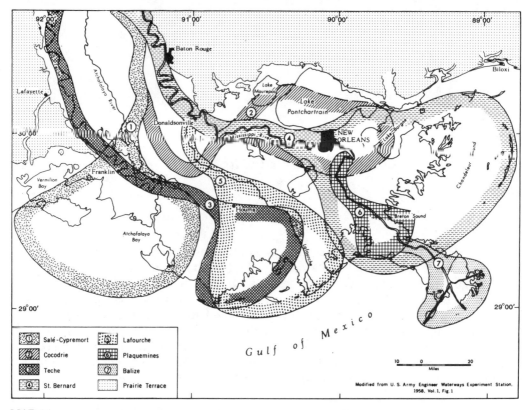

MAP 21

Mississippi River delta systems during recent geologic time. The dates determined for the seven most recent deltas, all shown in years before the present, are: (1) 5,000–4,500; (2) 4,500–3,500; (3) 3,500–2,500; (4) 2,600–1,500; (5) 1,500–700; (6) 1,200–500; (7) 500 to present.

30,000 years or so. It can determine, for example, approximately how many years ago a live clam was pulled from the water to be eaten by an Indian who then discarded the shell. It can show approximately when a tree was cut or an animal killed for human use. The evidence from C[14] confirmed the sequence of deltaic systems based on Indian cultures and provided accurate dating.

The coastal lowland is the meeting place of river and sea. Sometimes one is dominant in the building of characteristic earth features, sometimes the other. They may work together, or they may work in opposition. The area affected in Louisiana is the natural region we have named the marsh, a belt some 20 to 50 miles wide, most of it low, wet, and treeless (Map 3). The river provides the bulk of the material with which river and sea work. The sediments provided by the Mississippi are fine-textured clays, silts, and fine sand. To these sediments have been added organic materials, shells, and plant remains, in varying amounts. In time the fine clays and the organic materials form a tough, resistant material, much harder than the most recent deposits.

We earlier pointed out that the characteristic forms built by the river—levee-bound channels extending out into the sea—create an irregular coast. We also pointed out that the sea tends to build a straight coast. How does it do this? Storm waves erode irregularities and straight coast alike, pushing materials inland over the marsh. As it eats away at the shore the sea performs a winnowing action. It takes into suspension the fine materials, clays and fine silts, and carries them off to

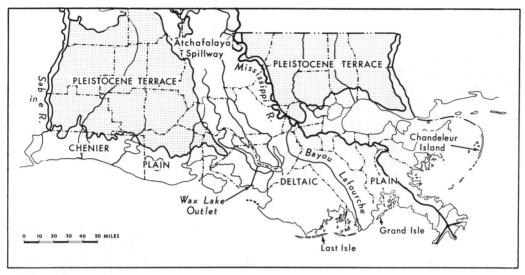

MAP 22
Index map of southern Louisiana

A hooked spit in Chandeleur Sound   David Prior

sea. It pushes onto the shore the coarse materials such as sands and shell fragments. Beaches of coarse material are everywhere the sea has been in command for even a short time. The beach overlies the dark, fine-grained marsh deposits onto which it has been driven.

The lunar tide on the Louisiana coast is so slight as to be a minor agent of alteration. It ranges from only 12 to 18 inches and occurs but once daily. Persistent onshore winds may pile up water to a height of several feet to inundate low-lying areas. More important than the lunar tide is an almost imperceptible long-shore current setting to the westward. Over a period of time this current does a

great deal of work. Evidence of persistence and direction is found in spits of sandy material, attached to the shore at their eastern ends, extending to the west and recurving in a hook back toward the east. Additional sediment is now being supplied from the Atchafalaya Spillway through the Wax Lake outlet (Map 22). The Wax Lake outlet in St. Mary Parish was dug to further the escape of flood-waters from the Atchafalaya Basin. Through the outlet went floods of fine silts and clays, adding to the supplies already present from the Mississippi River outlets to the east. The Gulf current has moved them westward and spread them against the shore to create a broad mud flat seaward from the old beach.

The building of the mud flat is a rare instance of river and sea working together. More common is the sea's activity in tearing down the shore, sorting the materials, and driving long, straight beaches of the coarse sediments inland over fine-grained marsh muds. Beach ridges, straight and lengthwise of the coast, are the mark of control by the sea. If there is open water between the beaches and the shore, these features are known as barrier islands. If they are pushed up tight against the shore, they are called barrier beaches.

Small distributaries in a delta pass   David Prior

The whole coastal area is commonly divided into two sections, extending from either side of Marsh Island: (1) the western portion, called the chenier plain, where beach and ridges parallel to the coast indicate that the sea has been responsible for shaping the area for a long time; and (2) the deltaic plain to the east (Map 22). The latter is marked by several systems of old natural levees striking at right angles to the coast. The present active delta, the Balize, best exhibits the control by the river, with its birds-foot system of passes extending into the sea. Even here in close proximity to areas of active deposition by the river, the sea has taken over to create straight, sandy beaches.

The old St. Bernard delta has been abandoned by the river for some 900

years. Inland are the nonfunctioning remains of old deltaic channels. Against the sea is the arc of the Chandeleurs, barrier islands built by the sea. On the Chandeleur beaches you may see the extrusion through the sand of tough, black marsh deposits, evidence that the beach rests shallowly on the older material into which the sea is cutting. Potsherds (broken pieces of Indian pottery) found on the beaches point to sites now out to sea, eroded and covered as the sea pushed the barrier island inward.

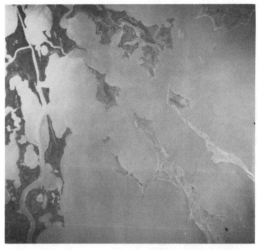

Abandoned but still discernible delta, St. Bernard Parish

The coastal section centered about the mouth of Bayou Lafourche is some 700 years old and is the youngest of the inactive deltas. Here the rate of retreat is greatest, for the youthful sediments are the least resistant to erosion. Barrier islands and beaches such as Last Isle and Grand Isle are being fragmented and moved inland over marsh deposits. Adjoining this section to the west is the chenier plain of present and former beaches, showing no evidence of former great stream channels. The chenier plain is thus the other extreme in configuration from the active Balize delta.

Under the Gulf waters and beyond the land lies the continental shelf, an area of

Mudflat of very soft clay-rich sediments colonized by specialized plants tolerant of the mudflat environment   David Prior

Barrier beach and island   Klaus Meyer-Arendt

outer margin have been detected a number of dome-shaped structures thought to be salt domes. Off the mouth of Bayou Lafourche the continental slope is cut by a submarine canyon, a wide, shallow trough that traverses the slope to the deeper waters of the Gulf. Some have said that such canyons were eroded above the sea and then covered. Such drastic changes in elevation seem an unlikely explanation.

In 1937 the shelf was invaded by fishermen seeking jumbo shrimp. A year later another invasion, this time by oil drillers, took place. Since 1938 the exploitation of the shelf has gone on apace, as described in a later chapter. Continuous mineral discoveries make this offshore area one of the most important in the nation and inspire exploration in like geologic situations elsewhere. Rigs designed for drilling in water up to 1,000 feet deep have been built, and even deeper drilling is possible from floating platforms. Fishermen go ever deeper for large shrimp.

some 17,000 square miles, a third the size of the land surface of Louisiana. As suggested already, where the shoreline is at any particular time and whether any particular point is below or above sea level are conditions dependent on a number of factors; the principal ones are the rising and falling sea level and local changes in the elevation of the land. Most recently the sea has advanced onto the land about four feet in the last 3,300 years—as evidenced by now-submerged river channels and the presence of old Indian sites under water.

The outer edge of the shelf is marked by a steepening of the slope to the deeps of the Gulf. It is a common practice to set the edge at the 100-fathom (600-foot) depth, although the 100-fathom isobathic line often falls on the steep downward slope. The edge of the shelf is about 130 miles at sea off the mouth of Sabine River. It is only 7 miles off South Pass of the Mississippi River.

The surface of the shelf is generally smooth, a boon to shrimp fishermen using bottom-dragging trawls. Along the

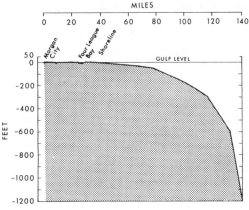

FIG. 14
Profile of the continental shelf off Morgan City

11

Relief

Streams and Lakes

Louisiana contains some 3,500 square miles of water surface, enough to rank it ahead of Michigan and Wisconsin, both noted for their lakes. The beds of Louisiana's lakes have originated in a number of ways. We have spoken already of river cutoff lakes and lakes that occupy grabens, or depressed blocks of the earth's crust. Louisiana's rivers are similarly varied as to size, velocity of current, character of water, and load of sediment. More important as relief features are the patterns of the streams as we observe them on a map or aerial photograph.

Probably the most common stream pattern is the dendritic, meaning treelike, sometimes described as a branch work. A dendritic pattern develops where the material in which a stream flows is uniform throughout. That is, the slope is uniform, the material is all of the same degree of hardness, and there is no geologic struc-

ture to direct the course of the stream. Such conditions are generally found on the terraces and marsh, and commonly in the floodplain. Upland dendritic streams have tributaries, like the branches of a tree. Lowland streams such as the Lower Mississippi may have distributaries that resemble in position the roots of a tree.

Trellis drainage, we have said, tends to develop where there are alternately soft and hard rocks outcropping parallel to each other. Suggestions of a trellis pattern are found in the Kisatchie Cuesta or Wold. Braided channels, mentioned earlier in the book, may be described as networks in which the trunk stream splits into distributaries that may rejoin each other and separate again. A braided pattern is the product of an excessive load of silt and too little current. Excellent examples are found in two swamp areas, the Atchafalaya Basin and Honey Island. Annular and radial patterns are found where

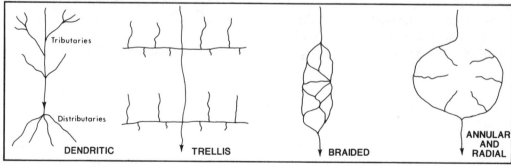

Tributaries

Distributaries

DENDRITIC   TRELLIS   BRAIDED   ANNULAR AND RADIAL

FIG. 15
Drainage patterns

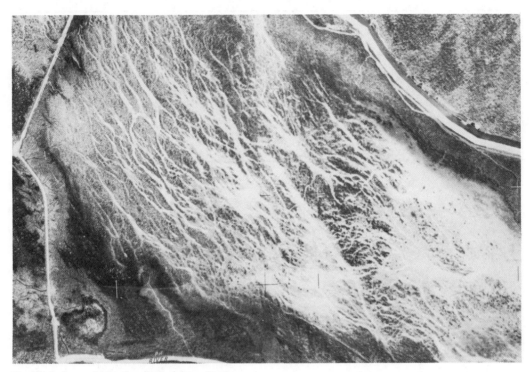

Braided channels in the Atchafalaya Basin

salt domes appear above the surface. Annular refers to the ringlike course of a stream diverted around the base of the dome. Radial refers to the small streams flowing off the dome, like the spokes of a wheel. Avery Island exhibits both annular and radial drainage.

In seeking the origin of the various types of lake beds or basins, our interest is in natural rather than artificial structures. The latter can generally be recognized at once from the map or picture that shows one or more straight sides. Artificial lakes and sawmill ponds have a straight section of shore formed by a dam. In coastal Louisiana there are frequent examples of square or rectangular lakes. Most of these are abandoned reclamation projects, where once-diked fields have been inundated.

Lakes of many types are associated with streams. We have mentioned the cutoff, oxbow, or horseshoe lakes so frequently found along the Mississippi and Red rivers. There are several instances of

bluff lakes, which occupy undrained pockets between levee backslope and the bluff that bounds the floodplain. Of course, the stream channel must be at one side or the other of its alluvial valley. This condition is found near Baton Rouge, and Spanish Lake is the result. Another example is Lake Tasse near New Iberia.

Deltaic lakes occur near the mouths of the Mississippi River. One type occupies what are known as levee-flank depressions. These depressions form where the weight of levee deposits is sufficient to depress the marsh on which they rest. Linear basins are thus formed parallel to and at the outer edge of natural levees. Deposition along an active channel might fill the basins, so they most frequently appear along abandoned channels, such as Bayou La Loutre in St. Bernard Parish. Within the actively depositing delta occurs a second type, the interlevee lake. Where distributary channels extend their levees into the shallow Gulf, they fork off repeatedly into new branches. In some cases the new levees rejoin, or nearly do,

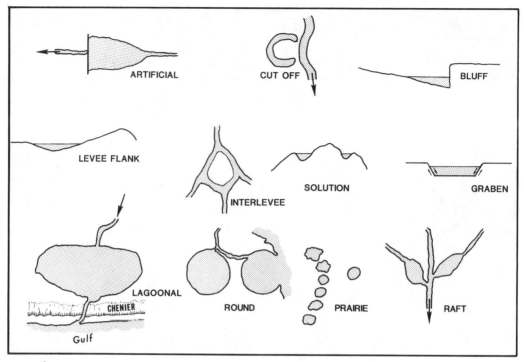

FIG. 16
Lake types

leaving between them interlevee lakes.

Solution lakes or ponds were discussed for the Five Islands. Lake Peigneur, Jefferson Island, is a prominent example. Lake Maurepas occupies a graben, as do Lake Pontchartrain and Catahoula Lake. Especially in southwestern Louisiana there are lagoonal lakes such as White and Grand. Their basins are preserved against the invasion of the sea by chenier bar-riers. Striking features in the coastal marsh are the round lakes, ranging in size from yards to miles across. They are shallow and they develop in uniform deposits that are high in organic materials. Lake Borgne is an example of a large round lake.

In the eastern prairies of southwestern Louisiana there is an abundance of small, shallow ponds, lacking both inlets and outlets. If their form is irregular they are commonly called *marais;* if round, *platin.* These ponds, so important in the old days for watering stock and for growing rice, seem to be the unfilled remnants of old Ice Age river channels. Their alignment in old channels is observable near New Iberia. Probably of similar origin are the bay galls, or bagols, in Anglo-Saxon areas of the state. The term refers to the presence of bay trees and the gallberry, or inkberry, bush, although other types of water-tolerant plants may be present. In the prairie area the term may be applied to the depression filled with trees within the grassland. In the flatwoods it means hardwoods within a pine forest.

Levee flank depression lakes   James P. Morgan

Round marsh lakes   James P. Morgan

A raft of the type that blocked Red River
James P. Morgan

Finally, to conclude our incomplete list of lake types, there are the raft lakes of Red River. We know them today as Caddo, Cross, Edwards, Bodcau, Bistineau, and Black, and we can recognize the dry beds of former lakes in the same area. The raft lakes of today exist because they are dammed. In the past they were lakes without damming, and they bore an uncertain relationship to the Great Raft.

When the first Europeans ascended Red River about 1700 they found above what is now Campti that navigation was impeded by accumulations of trees that had gotten into the river by bank caving and had been carried until they lodged on some obstruction. Somehow the term *raft* was incorrectly applied to what might

better be called a log jam. The length of the affected channel was some 150 miles, and about a third to a half of the stretch was composed of sections of raft with open water between them. The damming effect raised the level of the water, which then escaped by means of outlet channels around the obstruction to the next open water below. The lower portion of the raft was as much as 25 feet thick. It was heavily silted and even supported a growth of willows. The upstream portion was much fresher in appearance.

By 1833 the foot of the raft was at the mouth of Loggy Bayou, some 100 miles by river above Campti. Comparing the years and positions involved, it is evident that the raft was "moving" upstream at the rate of a little less than a mile per year. Of course, the raft could not actually move upstream against the current. The lower end was rotting away at an irregular rate, while the upper end was building up as the annual high water brought more trees.

Where do the raft lakes fit in? They were impounded in sections of the main and tributary valleys, having a relationship to Red River like that of leaves to a branch. It has been argued that the raft caused the lakes, hence the names. On the other hand, it has been pointed out that Red River was building up its floodplain faster than were the tributary streams, hence they could not make their way into the main stream. It seems likely that both factors were needed, that the rafts helped to build up the bed of Red River. The lakes had more water in flood season, less when the Red was low. It is a fact, too, that when the raft was removed the raft lakes drained naturally. Today only those remain that have been dammed artificially.

The raft was a serious impediment to navigation of the Red and the development of the upper river. Hazardous navigation was maintained for some years, through lakes, open sections of the river, and outlet channels. Finally, between

Black Lake, a raft lake

Elemore Morgan

1833 and 1838, Henry Shreve used steam power to clear out the obstruction. His warning that it would form again unless precautions were taken was disregarded. A new raft with its foot near Shreveport formed immediately. The upper river was navigated with difficulty for thirty years until the logs were removed by a federal agency in 1873. Since then constant vigilance has prevented the formation of a new raft.

Louisiana has some 5,000 to 7,500 miles of navigable waterways (Map 23). What constitutes navigability is not accurately defined, because it varies with the type of vessel and with the times. It is hard to believe that some insignificant stream once carried great cargoes of cotton. These streams were used only at high water, and they have deteriorated with cultivation of the surrounding land. Most

of our streams need some kind of improvement to make them fit for navigation today.

A striking feature of the Mississippi's drainage is that the nature of its associated streams changes in Louisiana. Throughout most of its course the Mississippi is fed by numerous *tributaries*, but from about the 31st parallel southward it has *distributaries* instead. In fact, the state's drainage resembles a giant hourglass with all streams converging at its "waist" near Old River. This remarkable arrangement affected east-west transportation routes markedly during earlier times, funneling traffic through the narrow waist. At that point east-west travelers had less difficulty crossing streams than at any other places in the state. Except for the Mississippi, there were few that could not be waded, especially during low water. So important was this area to Indians that villages located nearby served as trading posts.

With a series of tributaries converging at the mouth of Red River and several distributaries below that point, the Mississippi system is well designed to serve all but the southwestern and southeastern parts of the state. These two sections do not lie within Mississippi drainage. The lack of east-west connection in coastal Louisiana has been made up for by the Intracoastal Canal, from which it is possible to reach all other waterways in the state.

Louisiana has no natural deepwater ports. Lake Charles, Baton Rouge, and New Orleans are ports for oceangoing vessels, but only at the expense of maintaining channels to them. Baton Rouge is regarded as the natural head of deepwater navigation on the Mississippi. Nevertheless, it is necessary after long periods of high water to dredge several of the crossings above New Orleans in order to maintain a depth of 35 feet.

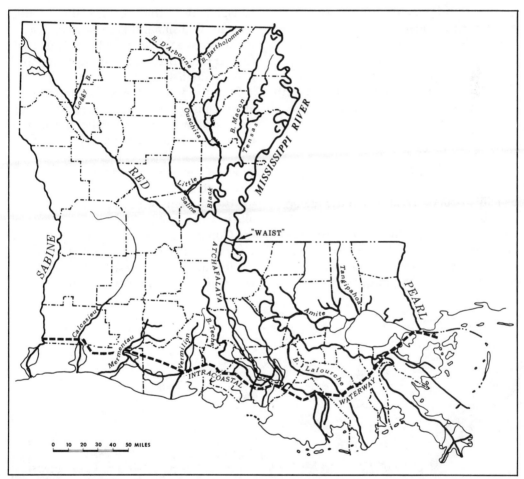

MAP 23
Waterways of Louisiana

12

Relief

Minor Features

There are a number of smaller surface features in Louisiana, among them cheniers, mudlumps, salt domes, and pimple mounds. Possibly only mudlumps are restricted to Louisiana, but in combination the four contribute to the state's distinctive landscape.

Cheniers

Chênière is a French word meaning "place of oaks" or "place where oaks grow." It is usually applied to features in the marsh that, because of their elevation, have a cover of live oaks rather than grass. The name has been given to abandoned natural levees, to Indian mounds and middens, and to the long ridges so conspicuous in the chenier plain of southwestern Louisiana. It is these latter features that we will discuss here. Note that for our references to these ridges we shall use the English form of the word.

In southwestern Louisiana the marsh is about 20 miles wide. The marsh deposit is quite shallow, since the distance down to the sunken Prairie Terrace is only 30 to 50 feet. Lying literally on marsh deposits is a series of cheniers, roughly parallel to each other and to the coast. They are variable in size and length, but they are all shaped like beaches, with a steeper slope toward the Gulf and a longer backslope inland. They reach maximum elevations of about ten feet above the marsh and a maximum width of about a quarter mile. In composi-

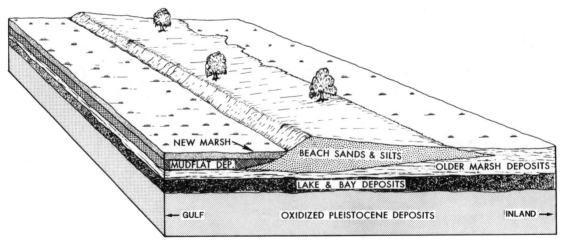

NEW MARSH
MUDFLAT DEP.
BEACH SANDS & SILTS
OLDER MARSH DEPOSITS
LAKE & BAY DEPOSITS
← GULF   OXIDIZED PLEISTOCENE DEPOSITS   INLAND →

FIG. 17
Sections of the chenier plain

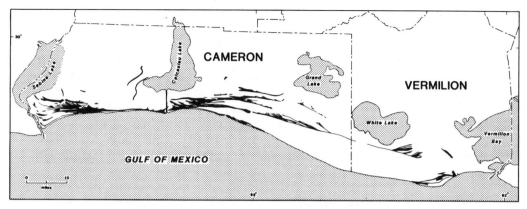

MAP 24
The chenier plain in southwestern Louisiana.
The cheniers are shown in black.

tion they are chiefly shell, most of it
ground into coarse fragments.

An examination of a modern beach
shows how these cheniers were formed.
Cameron Beach reveals some four feet of
shell fragments resting on two feet of
tough, black, fine marsh deposit. That is,
the crest of the beach is about six feet
above Gulf level. A hurricane may drive
the beach deposit several hundred feet
inland, but it will not greatly alter the
marsh deposit. The only coarse materials
that the sea has to work with are shells,
so the beach deposit is shell rather than
sand. Exceptions are beaches near the
mouths of large streams; here fine sands
occur.

Cameron Beach is paralleled successively inland by the seventy-mile-long

Cameron Beach   James P. Morgan

Grand Cheniere-Pecan Island complex,
Cheniere Perdue, and Little Cheniere.
How could beach ridges become set in the
marsh miles from the coast? The explanation is found in what is happening today
where the coast is building seaward off
Cheniere au Tigre by means of mud flat
deposits. A large-scale build-out of the
chenier plain occurred when the Mississippi River was discharging to the
west. This resulted in the construction of
the extensive mud flats and marshes that
presently separate the cheniers. When the
Mississippi was sending its sediments
eastward and the process was reversed
from build-out to retreat, a beach was
formed. Continued retreat resulted in the
gradual enlargement of the beach from
sand and shell derived from the destruction of mud flats and marshes. The cheniers, then, are a decipherable record of

A chenier   James P. Morgan

shifts of the Mississippi's course. The oldest chenier is about 2,750 years old and attests that coastal build-out and retreat have occurred several times since then.

Mudlumps

Mudlumps are curious little islands in the Gulf near the mouths of the Mississippi River passes. Where everything else is at sea level, the mudlumps range up to twelve feet in height. They vary in area from a few square feet to twenty acres. They differ in profile from dome shaped to terraced and steep sided, and in plan from an elongated "S" shape to a more or less round one. In composition they are mostly bowed-up sediments, sandy silts in texture. There may be exposed in the center a tough, plastic clay. The mudlumps may show faults and folds in

A single mudlump island   David Prior

Old mudlumps connected by sands deposited at the mouth of a river and redistributed by waves and currents   David Prior

the bowed sediments, a "raked" or furrowed surface, and mud volcanoes.

The mudlumps are a product of the sorting of fine Mississippi sediments in the Gulf and the gradual movement outward of the bars at the mouths of the passes. Deepest of the sediments, the plastic clay is the finest. The accumulation of coarser sediments above causes movement in the very weak clay, which with favorable circumstances is forced upward. It may emerge through the overlying materials on the seaward slope of the bar, but it breaks the Gulf surface to form mudlump islands only on the bar's landward side. Mudlumps exposed to the sea normally are eroded to extinction within a period of fifteen years, in the process taking on wave-cut features such as cliff faces. The presence of steplike terraces on the eroded sides is evidence that uplift has occurred in more than one stage. The mud volcanoes are caused by escaping marsh gas, a common product of decaying vegetation in coastal Louisiana.

Stories are told that mudlumps have come up so quickly that they have carried a ship above the water's surface. They are likewise said to disappear suddenly beneath the water. There are known instances of a rapid upthrust of as much as four feet in twenty-four hours, but rapid disappearance seems unlikely.

Salt Domes

Salt domes as prominent surface features are rare in proportion to their total numbers. In 1965 there were some 180 known salt domes in Louisiana, but as new domes are being discovered, the total number must be much higher. Many are offshore, and a number are underground with no obvious surface evidence. Of a hundred or so domes on land in South Louisiana, only the Five Islands are truly conspicuous. Of about thirty salt domes known to exist in North Louisiana, half have recognizable surface forms. They are the so-called Interior Salt Domes, which

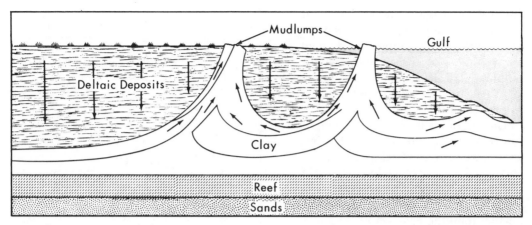

FIG. 18
Section showing how a mudlump is formed

are chiefly in Winn and Bienville parishes, lying on the eastern flank of the Sabine Uplift.

The Five Islands, with the exception of the southernmost, Belle Isle, are spaced at seven- to nine-mile intervals along a line of geologic activity. As surface features the Five Islands are round in plan, with diameters of some two miles. They are the more conspicuous because of the low, flat country around them and because they are heavily wooded areas within low marsh vegetation. Small ponds or lakes, caused by solution of the salt and caving-in of the surface, are characteristic. A salt plug, projecting upward from miles below

Aerial view of Avery Island   Avery Island Inc.

67

the surface, is encountered close to or at the surface. Caprock, deep-seated rock strata composed of impurities derived from solution of the salt, may contain sulphur. Petroleum and natural gas are found in the upturned sediments bordering the salt plug.

The interior salt domes have long been known as licks, sour lakes, and salines; they were sources of salt even for the Indians. They have yielded limestone and gypsum, but only one of them has produced petroleum. The interior domes are smaller than the Five Islands and their common form is different. Like the Five Islands, the interior domes bear proper names, such as Drake's Well, Coochie Brake, Winnfield, Vacherie, Kings.

All the interior domes do not conform to a single surface character, but the majority are marked by an encircling ring of upturned beds. The height of the rimming ridge is on the order of 50 to 70 feet. Within the ridge is the low center of the dome. The rim is not perfectly round but averages about three quarters of a mile in diameter. The normal dendritic, or tree-shaped, drainage pattern of the region is commonly altered by domes. Streams may be diverted around the uplift to form

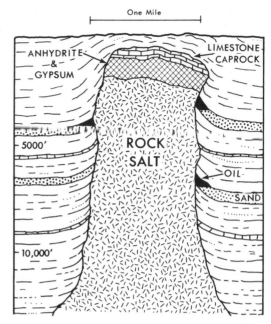

FIG. 19
Section of a salt dome

an annular pattern, and a radial pattern may be developed on the rim. Winnfield dome, abandoned in 1966, had been mined for salt since 1931, but of all the interior domes only Minden has produced petroleum. They clearly are not the economic assets that the Five Islands are.

Saline center of Drake's Well salt dome, Natchitoches and Winn parishes

John Huner

68

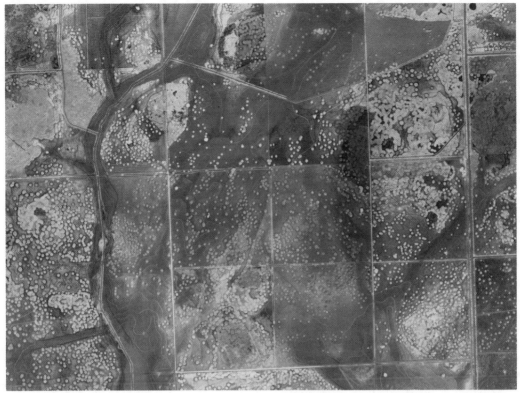

Pimple Mounds

Pimple mounds appear as white dots in rice fields. Note also the small terraces used to impound water in rice fields.

Pimple mounds are widespread, occurring in Iowa, Washington, Texas, and other states. They are given a variety of names, for example, gas mounds, prairie mounds, and hog wallows. They are low, rounded hillocks, circular to elliptical, on the order of a hundred feet in diameter, and up to five or six feet high. They are invariably composed of materials coarser than those around them, sands and silts rather than clay. They occur in treeless and wooded areas. Thousands can be found on the terraces, but they appear less frequently in the hills and on floodplains. They are said not to occur east of the Mississippi River. Seen in cross section there is nothing abnormal about the soil profile. And they do not follow any regular distributional pattern that would suggest deep-seated geological control.

The origin of pimple mounds is by no means clear. They have been attributed to Indians, but gently sloping pimple mounds do not resemble steep-sided Indian mounds. They have been ascribed to burrowing animals, ants, and the wallowing of bison. Perhaps clumps of vegetation held mounds of earth in place while all else around them was eroded away. Gas, artesian water, whirlwinds, overturned trees, deposition on point bars have all been suggested as causes.

The most reasonable explanation seems to be that the mounds are residual features protected by vegetation against erosion. This might explain why they are composed of the coarser material, but it does not explain their absence east of the Mississippi River. Perhaps we should accept the explanation of the Caddo Indians that they were dropped from the aprons of frightened giants!

13

Soils

It has been said that the character of soils is reflected in the character of the people who live on them. This is probably an exaggeration, but, because soils produce the crops that are the primary source of our food and because their qualities vary from poor to highly productive, their character *is* important to those who use them.

The character of soils may also determine whether we have success or failure in numerous uses other than agriculture. For example, soils are used as construction material in earthen dams, highway overpasses, and other earthworks. They provide foundation support for our roads and homes. Our parks, playgrounds, golf courses, and ball fields are built on soils. The character of soils also affects the kinds of natural vegetation and wildlife that live in an area. In Louisiana, soils are even used for crawfish production in many fields following a harvest of rice.

Our first interest in soils is to find how they are related to geologic history, climate, and relief, and how they fit Louisiana's natural regions. We are also interested in soils because they are one of Louisiana's primary natural resources.

Soils form in the outer, weathered crust of the earth to which have been added various organic constituents contributed by plants and animals. Since time is involved in the formation of soils, there is a period before they are soils. During this period they are geologic deposits. The fresh layers of sediment laid down by the Mississippi River are geologic deposits. Each layer may be like or very different from the others above and below it; each represents the deposition of a particular flood. Soils, too, have layers of a sort, but they are quite different from each other. We say of soils that they have horizons (Fig 20). The top or "A" horizon is topsoil. The "E" horizon is beneath the "A" in most upland soils. It is light in color, low in organic matter, and somewhat

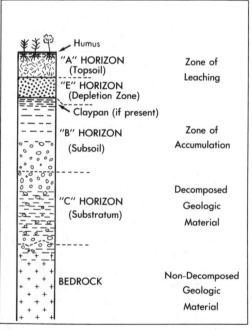

FIG. 20
Soil profile

depleted of clay. Below that is the "B" horizon, or subsoil. Below that is the "C" horizon, which is only partly weathered and altered geologic material. Together they constitute the soil profile, and the three horizons may differ in color, texture, structure, chemical composition, and thickness.

Many things happen to a geologic deposit to convert it to soil horizons. Actually, we usually call fresh geologic deposits young or immature soils, indicating that there has not been enough time to change them to true soils. Water is an important agent in the conversion process. It seeps through soil and carries away the elements that are readily soluble. It removes the fine particles and leaves the coarser ones. Part of what is removed may be deposited in the subsoil, so that topsoil and subsoil become quite different. Humus from decayed plants is added. Roots break up larger lumps. Air gets into the soil and essential living organisms thrive.

The balance of the soil-forming activities varies from place to place to bring about different results. For example, if there is considerable local relief, that is, if the land is hilly, the work of water will be accelerated. It will flow more rapidly over the surface and may penetrate down through the soil more freely. A grass cover adds organic material faster than a pine forest. All factors contribute to different degrees of natural productivity. A productive soil must have a favorable chemical composition to provide plant nutrients. It must have a good structure; that is, the individual grains must be naturally glued together in aggregates, say, the size of small nuts. This is necessary so that water and air can get into the soil. A deep soil is not exhausted as quickly as a shallow one. And there are the matters of flooding and erosion, the first on floodplains, the second in hills. For some types of commercial agriculture, growers prefer soils of very low natural fertility so that fertilizers can be added in

the kind and amount needed to produce desired results in the crop.

The discussion so far demonstrates that soils have characteristics that depend on the kind of environment in which they develop and the length of time they have been there. The kind of soil in a specific area is determined by the combined effects of five factors that soil scientists call factors of soil formation. They are soil climate, organisms, including man, that live in and on the soil, relief and landscape, the kind of geologic material in which the soils form, and the time during which the soil has been forming. The many different combinations of these factors have resulted in nearly 300 different kinds of soil in Louisiana. Each different kind is called a soil series, and areas the size of small farms typically contain several different soil series.

The eight general soil areas in Louisiana are shown on Map 25. Each general soil area contains many different kinds of soils (soil series). The general soil areas each represent unique kinds or combinations of soils that occur in association with one another and are quite different from soils in the other areas.

Natural conditions in Louisiana are such that mature soils like those of the Coastal Plain region are of limited productivity. Much rain combined with high temperatures over long periods of time bring about extensive leaching out of soluble plant foods and removal of fine fragments. The residual soil that results cannot be continuously cropped without the addition of fertilizers. Many areas of mature soils have been abandoned. On the other hand, the immature soils, or geologic deposits, of the major river floodplains are highly productive and constitute one of Louisiana's greatest natural assets. Midway between soils of the Coastal Plain and those of the floodplains are soils intermediate in age and productivity. Note how they fit the natural regions of Louisiana.

Marsh soils are high in organic constitu-

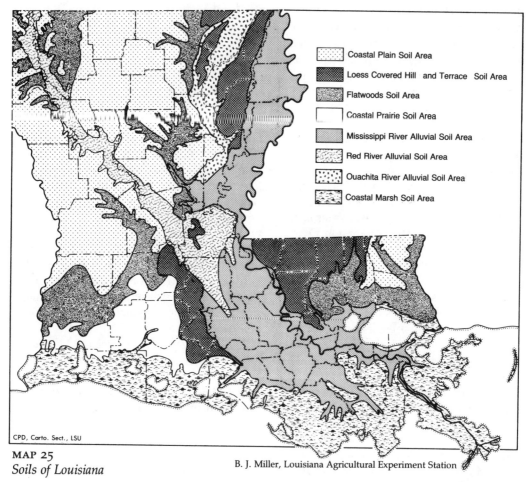

Legend:
- Coastal Plain Soil Area
- Loess Covered Hill and Terrace Soil Area
- Flatwoods Soil Area
- Coastal Prairie Soil Area
- Mississippi River Alluvial Soil Area
- Red River Alluvial Soil Area
- Ouachita River Alluvial Soil Area
- Coastal Marsh Soil Area

CPD, Carto. Sect., LSU

MAP 25
Soils of Louisiana

B. J. Miller, Louisiana Agricultural Experiment Station

ents, particularly decomposed plant remains, and some are very low in inorganic constituents, chiefly river clays and silts. They are young and fresh and can be highly productive. However, their cultivation is expensive and hazardous, for they must be reclaimed by diking and can be flooded by excessive high water of storms. They constitute a reserve of productive soils to be used when the demand is sufficient.

The Mississippi, Red, and Ouachita river bottomland soils have long carried the bulk of Louisiana's commercial agriculture. They are deep, flat lying, and of favorable composition and structure. The Mississippi, with its great natural levees, shows more soil variation horizontally than vertically. That is, on the crests of

the levees, close to the riverbed, the soils are sands and silts. Down the levee backslope the soils become finer. In the backswamp are fine clays, high in organic material. Red River soils are readily distinguishable by their color, derived chiefly from red geologic deposits in Texas and Oklahoma.

Soils of the alluvial area of the Ouachita River are generally less productive than those of the Red and Mississippi rivers. They have a complex history but developed mostly in old sediments the Arkansas River deposited when it flowed through the area until about 3,000 years ago. Therefore, they are older, more highly weathered, and less productive than soils in the Red and Mississippi river alluvial plains.

Until recently agriculture in the alluvial

valley was restricted largely to the natural levees and minor topographic features that rise above the valley floor: point-bar ridges, alluvial cones (Macon Ridge), and terrace remnants (Marksville Prairie). The soils of the valley floor are highly productive but are wet and subject to flooding. The resulting pattern of human use of the valley was distinctive: elongated and sometimes isolated ridges of cultivation, with intervening and much larger areas of forested swampland.

During recent years, however, large areas of clayey backswamp soils have been cleared and are now used mostly for production of row crops. Although clearing these large areas has resulted in considerable increase in agricultural land, much controversy has resulted because of the enormous reduction in bottomland hardwoods and wildlife habitat.

Loess-covered Hill and Terrace soils, in association with the blufflands, occur in several places where there is a consider-

Diked land in southern Louisiana. Land in the extreme lower right corner is still being cultivated, but fields across the stream (shown in dark) have been abandoned.

able amount of local relief and on nearly level terraces, as the natural regions and general soil areas maps show (Maps 3 and 25). These soils are silty in texture and are composed of deposits older than those of the floodplains. They are true soils in that they show a soil profile with well-developed horizons. Especially in a portion of the Felicianas, the soils are developed in relatively unweathered loess.

Loess is a silty windblown deposit that covers large areas of uplands and terraces that adjoin the Mississippi River alluvial plain in Louisiana. The distribution and approximate thickness of the loess are shown in Map 26. These deposits are unique in both origin and characteristics. The loess was deposited thousands of years ago during periods when melting

glaciers in the North Central part of the United States were drained by the Mississippi River and its tributary streams. Sediments were carried southward by the Mississippi River and its tributary streams. The sediments carried southward from the glaciers by the river and redeposited in Louisiana were the source of the loess. Winds blowing in various directions across the river's floodplain dislodged some of the newly deposited sediments and redeposited them on adjoining uplands and terraces. As a result, the thickest loess deposits on both the east and west sides of the river are nearest the floodplain; they become progressively thinner with distance from the river. Two episodes of loess deposition are known to have occurred in Louisiana, one before

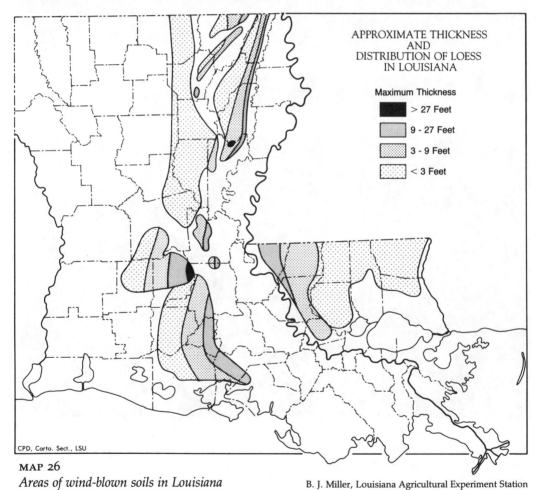

APPROXIMATE THICKNESS
AND
DISTRIBUTION OF LOESS
IN LOUISIANA

Maximum Thickness

> 27 Feet

9 - 27 Feet

3 - 9 Feet

< 3 Feet

CPD, Carto. Sect., LSU

MAP 26
Areas of wind-blown soils in Louisiana

B. J. Miller, Louisiana Agricultural Experiment Station

Bluffs along road in area where loess is unweathered

Elemore Morgan

the time of deposition of the Prairie Terrace and one after the Prairie Terrace was deposited.

Loess, where unweathered, has a distinctive and unmistakable appearance. It is yellowish brown and quite silty with only very small amounts of either sand or clay. Instead of eroding in slopes, it maintains a vertical face, such as may be seen on country roads in the northwestern part of West Feliciana Parish and more readily along Highway 61 south of Natchez in Mississippi. Roads wear down in it in troughlike depressions commonly called "guts." Loess erodes by *spalling off* vertical slabs. It has a high lime content as indicated by snail shells. Ground moss frequently grows on old surfaces. Loess-covered Hill and Terrace soils have been highly productive of commercial crops—

tobacco, cotton, and cane—at various times and places. However, the considerable local relief, notably in West Feliciana Parish, has led to severe erosion and extensive abandonment of agriculture in favor of raising beef cattle and growing pine trees.

In most places where the loess is thin or occupies gently sloping areas, it is somewhat weathered throughout and lacks some of the distinct characteristics of the unweathered loess. In addition, where it is less than about three feet thick the growth of plants and activity of animals over thousands of years have mixed in to varying degrees with the underlying materials. In hilly areas where the deposits were thin they remain only on the ridgetop positions and have been removed from the steeper slopes by erosion over thousands of years since they were deposited.

The silty soils developed in the weathered loess deposits are used mostly for forest production or livestock grazing. They are also important soils for growing cotton, soybeans, and small grains in areas such as the Macon Ridge and on the Prairie Terrace near Lafayette and Baton Rouge.

The Coastal Prairie soils are developed primarily in the prairies of southwestern Louisiana. The parent material was Prairie Terrace deposits, and the natural vegetation cover was grass. There is a well-developed soil profile, the topsoil dark to gray, with good structure. At an average depth of about fourteen inches there is a nearly impervious claypan. It is this impervious layer, which holds water, that makes irrigation work well. The claypan, combined with the general flatness of the prairies, is responsible for the shallow flooding of broad areas after heavy rains.

The soil is quite productive, accounting for nearly all of Louisiana's rice crop.

Flatwoods soils are developed mostly on Prairie Terrace deposits, which are often poorly drained, but the natural vegetation covering is mixed pine and hardwood or hardwood forest. The result is a soil of rather low natural productivity. The profile is quite well developed, the structure fair, the soil horizons rather acid. There is little local relief. Despite a preponderance of unfavorable factors, one flatwoods section, Tangipahoa Parish, is a notable producer of strawberries and vegetables. Strawberries are tolerant of acidity, but the development in the parish is due nearly as much to human factors as it is to natural ones. Strawberries became important commercially only after the decline of lumbering. The first association of growers was formed in 1923. The availability of pine straw as

Harvesting crawfish on flooded prairie soils   Louisiana Department of Commerce and Industry

mulch for the berries, the presence of groves of pine trees for protection against the cold, and high rainfall were favorable natural factors. However, these advantages would have been of no value had it not been for the availability of refrigerated railroad cars, which provided quick access to northern markets.

The remainder of Louisiana's soils may be grouped together as Coastal Plain soils. They vary considerably in character. In general they are old, subject to leaching and erosion, and low in natural productivity. They tend to be reddish in color, the result of long oxidation. They occupy the highest areas and have the maximum local relief. The original shortleaf section (see the natural regions map) in particular was settled in the nineteenth century by farmers whose cash crop was cotton. Much of the old longleaf natural region was never heavily settled. More than in any other part of the state, land use in the areas of Coastal Plain soils trends to forestry and grazing.

It should now be apparent that there are tremendous differences in the character and productivity of Louisiana's soils. Each type of soil is the product of a

Strawberry field in Flatwoods soil area
Louisiana Department of Commerce and Industry

number of factors: geologic history, relief, climate, and vegetative cover. The most productive are those of recent stream deposition. The most deficient are the oldest, the Hill soils. Measured in terms of acreage of good soils, used and potential, Louisiana is one of the best endowed of all states. With its good soils and favorable climate, it has been said that Louisiana alone could feed the nation well. This is likely true, were we to cultivate all our soils as intensively as is done in China.

14
Vegetation

Like soils, natural vegetation is both a major resource and an excellent indicator of the sum of natural conditions existing in any particular region of the state. It is our intent to reconstruct the vegetation as it was before European invaders altered and destroyed it. It is certain that during the several thousand years in which Indians were here before white men, the natural vegetation was altered, principally through the agency of fire. There is no point in speculating regarding changes wrought by the Indians. It is difficult enough to know the changes made by Europeans.

The natural vegetation of the state may be placed in three major divisions: Forest, upland pine and hardwoods, and bottomland hardwoods and bald cypress; Prairie or "dry" grassland; and Marsh or "wet" grassland. A few terms need explanation. Both pine and cypress are conifers, that is, their seeds are borne in cone-shaped husks, and they have needle-shaped leaves. *Hardwood* is a term commonly applied to broadleaved trees. Most broadleaved trees are deciduous, that is, they lose their leaves in winter, but some, like the live oak and magnolia, are evergreen. Pines and cypress differ also, in that the pine is evergreen. The cypress is the state's only example of a needle-leaved tree that is also deciduous. *Swamp* describes a low, wet, forested area; *marsh* is applied to a treeless, grass-covered, low, wet area.

Louisiana's coastal marsh is flat. Probably all of it is inundated at times; some of it is constantly wet. Its waters and vegetation vary from fresh through brackish to salt. The lines dividing them may shift seasonally and locally; an island rim may be salt and its interior fresh. Fresh marsh is seemingly more unstable than salt marsh; that is, it is more difficult to walk on. The reason lies in the fact that in fresh water the fine clay particles remain in suspension, affording no support for weight. In salt water the fine particles flocculate out to form a firmer support for overlying weight. Some of the fresh-marsh plants are quite familiar, such as cattail and iris. There is also three-corner grass, favorite of the muskrat, and two plants introduced by man around the beginning of the century—alligator weed

Batture woods, the tree growth that occurs along the banks of major streams James P. Morgan

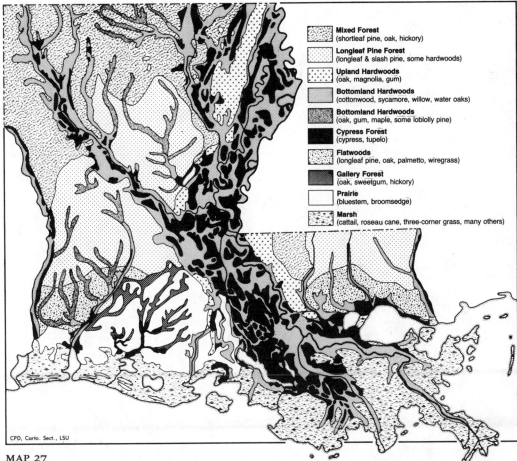

Mixed Forest
(shortleaf pine, oak, hickory)

Longleaf Pine Forest
(longleaf & slash pine, some hardwoods)

Upland Hardwoods
(oak, magnolia, gum)

Bottomland Hardwoods
(cottonwood, sycamore, willow, water oaks)

Bottomland Hardwoods
(oak, gum, maple, some loblolly pine)

Cypress Forest
(cypress, tupelo)

Flatwoods
(longleaf pine, oak, palmetto, wiregrass)

Gallery Forest
(oak, sweetgum, hickory)

Prairie
(bluestem, broomsedge)

Marsh
(cattail, roseau cane, three-corner grass, many others)

CPD, Carto. Sect., LSU

MAP 27
Natural vegetation of Louisiana

and water hyacinth. Hyacinth can exterminate a pond or lake in stages: first, by multiplying into a mat extending from shore to shore; second, as a fixed floating marsh; and then, by further thickening, providing a base on which other plants can grow. Three-corner grass extends into the brackish marsh, but the true salt marsh has its own characteristic species: *spartina*, or salt grass; cord grass; black rush; and mangle bush, or mangrove. Black mangrove is most distinctive, with a root system like the ribs of an umbrella supporting the trunk above the water.

The trees of the bottom hardwoods and cypress association, like the soils of the same bottomlands, vary with elevation. On the sandy batture, wet with floods and dry with low water, is a group of hardwoods with the willow dominant, including cottonwoods, sweet gums, and sycamores. Natural levees, abandoned point bars, high islands, all not subject to long inundation, support a so-called second-bottom hardwood forest. Deciduous and live oaks, the magnolia, hickory, beech, pecan, sweet gum, and canebrakes constitute this magnificent forest. The live oak is apparently a natural component only as far north as a line connecting Opelousas with Baton Rouge. The abundance of mast-producing trees gives the second-bottom forest a richness in all kinds of animal life.

In the first-bottom, or swamp, forest the bald cypress was once dominant, both in size and commercial importance. In-

Second growth in second-bottom forest

Elemore Morgan

cluded with the cypress were the tupelo-gum, the swamp oak, and the swamp red maple. The cypress and the tupelo-gum have swelled butts. The cypress has great buttresses to support its shallow-rooted trunk. It is not a strongly competitive tree but can survive in conditions that other trees cannot tolerate. It can live with its base continuously flooded (see page 2 for photograph of cypress swamp). A popular but false belief is that the cypress sends up its knees to breathe when its roots are water covered. Cypress needs floods to disperse its seeds, but the seeds can germinate only on moist ground, free of standing water. Some cypress forests clearly exist under conditions where the trees cannot propagate.

Louisiana's prairies are tall grasslands interspersed with trees. That is, separately named prairies lie between the woods marking stream courses. The early settlers saw in these areas something reminiscent of the sea, so they called narrow extensions of trees "points"; tree clumps around houses "islands"; and small prairies "coves." The native grasses are wetland plants, including some fresh-marsh species. Principal grasses are the closely related bluestem and broom sedge, water grass, and switch grass. Carpet grass and Johnson grass are introduced species. Native grasses do not afford good year-long grazing, for although they may be tender and nourishing in the spring and early summer, by late summer they are tough and low in nutrition. Since planted groves of pines, catalpas, and other trees grow well in the prairies, the question arises as to why they were not naturally forested. Fires, high summer evaporation, the claypan, and a too-wet-too-dry situation have all been suggested. There is no positive answer.

The longleaf pine hills and flatwoods occur in three areas, as the map of natural regions shows. Every stream of any size that flows through them is bordered by its own hardwood forest strip. The longleaf forest is associated with the lighter, drier soils of the terraces and hills. Some five different species constitute the forest: longleaf, shortleaf, loblolly, spruce, and slash pine. Spruce pine and slash pine occur naturally only east of the Mississippi River. The longleaf flatwoods, notably those of southeastern Louisiana, show the greatest mixture of species and a distinctive understory of wire grass and palmetto. The hill stands were more purely longleaf, and regular burning kept them open, with only a scant covering of

Prairie

Louisiana Department of Commerce and Industry

Longleaf pine forest. The clean, open appearance results from periodic burning or cattle grazing or both.

Elemore Morgan

broom sedge and deciduous oaks. Pure stands of longleaf pine are explained as being fire climaxes. This means that the longleaf survives fires that destroy hardwoods and other pines. With repeated fires, only the longleaf remains, to constitute pure stands. In cutover areas regeneration of the longleaf is impossible in the presence of hogs, for they find its succulent tap root highly edible.

The shortleaf forest grows in the shortleaf hills and somewhat less on the terraces. It is a mixed forest and includes deciduous oaks, hickories, ash, sweet gum, and loblolly pine. The soils of the shortleaf areas perhaps average somewhat better than those of the longleaf belt, but certainly from the standpoint of

Mixed hardwood and pine

Elemore Morgan

Second-growth blufflands forest   Elemore Morgan

commercial importance the shortleaf forests have been of far less value.

Loblolly probably became prominent in shortleaf forests in the days after industrial lumbering took place, for the loblolly has spread greatly because of its ability to seed on denuded ground.

The blufflands forest is also called upland hardwoods. It is associated with the superior soils and considerable local relief of all the blufflands natural regions except the Bastrop Hills. Magnolias, live and deciduous oaks, some pine, yellow poplar, holly, ash, dogwood, small prairies, and canebrakes make up the varied vegetation cover. This is an attractive woodland because of the species represented, but it has lacked the commercial importance of some of the other forest types.

The history and problems of industrial lumbering and regrowth are discussed elsewhere. Relative to natural factors associated with forest growth, we may repeat here that Louisiana's climate is favorable to rapid growth, so that the annual gain well exceeds the annual cut. Despite rapid growth, trees like longleaf

pine and cypress make heartwood slowly. The outside sapwood is inferior for some purposes, for it is heartwood lumber that is strongest and most durable. Only to a limited extent have creosoting and other methods of preservation made up for the lack of heartwood.

Vegetation, more than any other aspect of nature, is an expression of a variety of factors: climate, relief, soils, and other natural phenomena. It, in turn, affects soils, relief, and animal life, to mention the most obvious relations. As vegetation varies, so do its associations. No single factor stands alone, be it an eroding stream or a burrowing animal. One responds to another and in return makes its contribution. A few inches difference in marsh elevation introduces a new plant. That plant in turn dies and decomposes and makes a place for yet another species. The river directs its silt to the west, the coast builds out, the sea takes control and builds a barrier beach of fragmented shell, and the ridge supports a woodland of live oaks.

It is one of the most important tasks of the geographer to know for any given place how the different aspects of nature are represented. He goes over his unvarying checklist: climate, relief, vegetation, soils, animal life, and drainage, and he notes the character of each. Then he asks, "How is each related to the others?" Finally, he distinguishes combinations of kinds of climate, relief, vegetation, soils, animal life, and drainage that persist over extensive areas. These areas of natural uniformity are his regions.

The picture of Louisiana's vegetation cover presented here applies to a period in the nineteenth century prior to industrial lumbering, prior to extensive ploughing of the prairies, and prior to disturbance of the marsh. A modern map of existing forest types made after industrial lumbering, after the conversion of the prairies to rice fields, and after the invasion of the marsh by trappers and oilmen shows considerable modifications.

The eastern third of the Florida Parishes is now designated as longleaf-slash, the middle Florida Parishes as loblolly-hardwoods, and West Feliciana Parish as mixed upland hardwoods. The bottomlands and certain adjacent uplands show about the same extent and same range of forest species as before. West of the Mississippi River, especially in the triangle between the Red and Ouachita rivers, there is a considerable decline in the area assigned to longleaf pine. The old shortleaf hills area in the northwestern part of the state is changed because of a much higher percentage of loblolly pines in the forest association. It may be repeated that the loblolly pine has the special ability to establish itself on abandoned fields and on areas denuded by lumbering. Of course, these conditions rarely existed a hundred years ago. Gone almost entirely are the canebrakes once so widespread in Louisiana. Their disappearance may be blamed on free-ranging cattle that found cane the very best winter feed, but also on the restrictions placed on woods burning, a practice that encouraged cane growth by burning out competing vegetation.

Human use of Louisiana, then, has clearly resulted in a reapportionment of the original vegetative species. This has come about through burning, lumbering, ploughing, and even planting. Additionally, new plants have been introduced, plants once foreign to the species belonging in the state. Some of these plants were brought intentionally, like rice, sugarcane, tobacco, and potatoes. Others came in quite by accident, such as the mesquite tree along the old trail leading from Natchitoches, Louisiana, to Nacogdoches, Texas. Some introduced plants, like citrus trees, live only when tended by man and eventually die out if left alone. Others, intentionally or acci-

Close-up of water hyacinth, an important species that is now a pest

Sam Hilliard

dentally introduced, have joined the original native plants and are regarded by most people as native to Louisiana. In this group are such familiar species as the Cherokee rose, crape myrtle, honeysuckle, pyracantha, trifoliata orange, tung-nut tree, Johnson grass, carpet grass, water hyacinth, alligator weed, Spanish bayonet, and the chinaball, or chinaberry, tree.

15
Resources

Wildlife and Fisheries

It must now be evident to you that nature has endowed Louisiana generously with those things useful to man. Commonly, a natural resource is regarded as becoming so only when man is able and ready to use it. For example, petroleum was not a natural resource for the Indians because they could not use it: neither was the state's vast stand of timber. Bottomland soils, on the other hand, were appreciated as a resource by both historic Indian and early European.

On the credit side of Louisiana's list of natural resources are: a climate combining abundant precipitation with a long growing season; a great area of first-class bottomland and terrace soils; petroleum, natural gas, sulphur, and salt, for all of which the state is a foremost producer; and a great reserve of fast-growing timber, even though there is little virgin growth left. In recent years, field surveys have discovered large amounts of commercial iron ore in central North Louisiana. It could be quite easily mined and may well become the basis of an iron and steel industry to serve regional needs.

There are other economic assets in the

Waterfowl flying over marsh

Elemore Morgan

Muskrat houses in marsh

form of water supply, wildlife, fisheries, and lesser items, some of which will now be discussed. The cutting of the state's forests and the exploitation of its petroleum and related resources have so tremendously altered the face of Louisiana that discussion of them will be reserved for special chapters in the section on human geography.

On the debit side there is a deficiency of metallic ores, such as copper, lead, aluminum, silver, and the like. There is some coal in North Louisiana, but it is not sufficient in amount or quality to be rated a first-class asset. If we now balance the ledger in the framework of the demands of the modern technological world, Louisiana's natural assets far outbalance its deficiencies. In a competitive world it is among the leading states in the wealth of its natural resources.

Wildlife

Louisiana's forests and grasslands have always supported an abundant and varied wildlife. Bear, panther, wolf, deer, and bison were among the larger mammals known to both Indian and European. Beaver, turkey, opossum, raccoon, rabbit, and squirrel are smaller forms still common to the state. Louisiana's extensive marshes and water bodies attract vast numbers of migratory waterfowl. Louisiana lies in the great Mississippi flyway, and it is the jumping-off spot for waterfowl that cross the Gulf. In the past the marshes seasonally yielded abundant returns to market hunters. Now they provide nationally known sport hunting.

But, interesting and worthy of discussion as these animals are, our interest here is in the fur producers that have given Louisiana first ranking in this industry during most of the present century. Mink, otter, beaver, raccoon, and a number of other small animals have yielded furs for a long time. But within the twentieth century it was the muskrat that gave Louisiana preeminence as a fur producer.

If the muskrat has been the backbone of fur production, the marsh has been the prime area for furbearers. Muskrat bones

87

are found in ancient Indian middens on Pecan Island, but in modern periods muskrats have not been abundant in the marsh. Historic Indians say nothing of them, and John James Audubon, writing in 1851, did not list the muskrat among Louisiana mammals. Speculation has it that a small group of these rodents always was in the marsh, and that in the late nineteenth and early twentieth centuries they multiplied greatly because of two occurrences. First, the burning of the marsh for cattle grazing greatly increased the stand of three-corner grass, the muskrat's favorite food. Second, the reduction in numbers of predators in the marsh, notably the alligator, permitted an increase of muskrats. In any event, persons now living can remember when muskrats first appeared in sections of the marsh.

The muskrat found the most favorable conditions in the brackish marsh, where three-corner grass is green in winter. Although it faced hazards of flood, drought, fire, and trap, the muskrat continued to thrive. Millions of pelts were taken each year; some 20,000 trappers were engaged

Marsh buggy, the modern way of traversing the marsh

Sam Hilliard

and their total annual earnings sometimes amounted to fifteen or more million dollars. This was true despite a winter trapping season limited to seventy to eighty days. The trappers burned over the marsh in late summer or fall to improve the feed and to make travel easier. They occupied their shacks with the drying frames set up around them, and paddled their pirogues along narrow *trenasses,* or canals, to visit their traps. It was not uncommon in a day when money was worth more than it is now for a trapper to clear $5,000 in the brief trapping season.

Trappers' camp

Louisiana Department of Wildlife and Fisheries

TABLE 2
Fur Harvest in Louisiana and the Nation
1976–77 season

Species	State harvest	U.S. harvest	State's percentage of total
Beaver	280	232,710	.1
Bobcat	2,997	72,220	4.2
Coyote	1,086	320,323	.3
Gray Fox	3,127	225,277	1.4
Red Fox	3,128	356,249	.9
Mink	54,858	320,823	17.1
Muskrat	965,889	7,148,370	13.5
Nutria	1,890,853	2,018,815	93.7
Opossum	44,851	1,064,725	4.2
Otter	11,900	32,846	36.2
Raccoon	254,435	3,832,802	6.6
Skunk	513	216,580	.8

SOURCE: Louisiana Department of Wildlife and Fisheries

The number of muskrats caught began to decline before midcentury, with the peak coming around 1946. However, even as late as 1957 Louisiana's take of 1½ million muskrat pelts was a fourth of the nation's total and kept the state in first place. Incidentally, in the same year Louisiana led in nutria (a newcomer), mink, and otter, and was sixth in raccoon pelts. Reduction in the number of muskrats has been brought about by several factors: a series of dry years, intrusion of salt water, storms, bad winters, eat-outs (where muskrat foraging was too heavy), and doubtless others. Basically, it seems the muskrat cannot share the marsh with increased human activity, particularly that connected with the petroleum industry. The muskrat thrives only in a limited section of the marsh; when that section fails him, he has nowhere else to go.

Despite marked resurgence in the number of muskrats taken in 1965–66, the big hope for the future of the Louisiana fur industry is the coypu, commonly called the nutria, a native of South America accidentally introduced into the marsh in 1937. The nutria is much heavier than the muskrat, weighing as much as twenty-five pounds. It is also much more adaptable to a variety of conditions, and is now found over most of southern Louisiana, even outside the marsh. It has also invaded extreme northern Louisiana. The nutria has not been very popular with trappers, nor as yet has it caught the

A coypu, commonly called nutria
Louisiana Department of Commerce and Industry

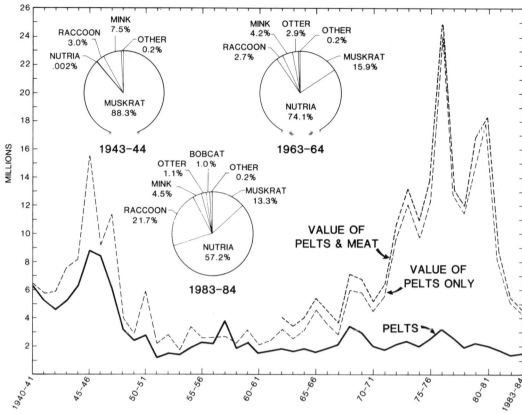

FIG. 21

Trapping in Louisiana, 1940–1984. Note changing importance of muskrat and nutria through time.

MLE, Carto. Sect., LSU
SOURCE: LA. WILDLIFE AND FISHERIES COMMISSION

fickle fancy of fur wearers. But certainly the fur has excellent qualities and the demand is increasing. Furthermore, there is a good market for nutria meat, chiefly as food for other furbearers raised in captivity. Another temporary market for the meat was the federal government's experimental program of screw worm eradication in which the fly larvae were fed nutria flesh.

A recent addition to the list of animals taken for their skins is the alligator. Long hunted for the prized leather that could be made from its hide, the reptile became scarce enough to be placed on the list of animals "threatened" to become extinct, but a ban on the trade in skins coupled with a well-enforced ban on hunting have led to a dramatic recovery in numbers. From its low point in the late 1950s, the reptile rebounded to become a nuisance in some areas by the early 1970s. Today, alligators are found in all parishes and are estimated to number half a million state-wide. Legal alligator hunting was rein-stated in 1972, and under stringent regulations it is now an annual event. The value of gator skins taken annually amounts to about 1½ million dollars (Table 3).

Fisheries

SALTWATER FINFISH

Until 1917, when the shrimp trawl was introduced into the state, Louisiana's combined catch of saltwater finfish and shellfish was exceeded by the harvest of its freshwater fisheries. The saltwater fish

TABLE 3
Alligator Harvest in Louisiana, 1972–83

Year	Number of hunters	Animals taken	Average length (feet)	$ Value of skins	$ Value per foot
1972	59	1,350	6.9	75,505	8.10
1973	107	2,921	7.0	268,994	13.13
1975	191	4,420	7.4	258,791	7.88
1976	198	4,389	7.1	512,240	16.55
1977	236	5,474	7.3	488,499	12.23
1979	708	16,300	7.0	1,711,500	15.00
1980	796	17,692	6.7	1,609,972	13.00
1981	913	14,870	6.9	1,821,575	17.50
1982	1,184	17,142	6.8	1,621,633	13.50
1983	945	16,154	6.9	1,452,568	13.00
Total	5,337	100,712	7.0	$9,821,277	$12.99

SOURCE: Louisiana Department of Wildlife and Fisheries

resource is still somewhat of an unknown quality and quantity. For a long time it was not large because of the difficulties in getting fish to distant markets before they spoiled. Furthermore, most of the methods of commercial fishing employed in this country originated in New England, and they have been slow to migrate down the Atlantic coast into the Gulf.

There are certainly variety and quality in our saltwater finfisheries. Snapper, redfish, flounder, trout, pompano, drum, sheephead, and others are of unexcelled eating quality. However, a great fishery is not built upon variety but rather on the large mass of a single species of uniform size demanded by modern commercial techniques of catching and handling. If true, it is not clear just why the Gulf should lack great concentrations of fish. Some students have observed that there is little vertical movement of the water to bring nutrients up from the ocean floor. Therefore, they say, there is a deficiency of nutrients in the upper layers of water. The plankton that feed on the nutrients are less abundant in the upper Gulf layers, and so are the fish that feed on the plankton. Other students do not accept this explanation.

Investigation in recent decades has revealed that there are tuna off the Louisiana coast in numbers sufficient for a commercial fishery. But the most successful bulk fishery has been for the menhaden, or pogy, the so-called American sardine. This abundant fish is seined in great numbers in summer and early fall. Vessels move into Louisiana seasonally from the Atlantic coast, where crews were trained and boats and methods were developed. The fish is processed for oil, animal food, and fertilizer in plants located at Cameron, Empire, Morgan City, Abbeville, and near Houma.

FRESHWATER FINFISH

The importance of Louisiana's freshwater finfisheries is steadily declining because of deteriorating conditions in the Mississippi River and other inland waters. Pollution, reduction in backwaters and flooding, and improved fishing equipment all have contributed to a decline in numbers. In recent years there have been

Pogy boat sucking menhaden out of net   Louisiana Department of Wildlife and Fisheries

extensive fish kills on the Mississippi. Some come with the first cold; agricultural pesticides, scarcity of oxygen in the water, and industrial waste have all been blamed for the damage.

Prior to 1917, when Louisiana's freshwater fisheries led in value, the catfish, spoonbill, buffalo, and gaspergou were important, in that order. Spoonbill, catfish, and even garfish roe have been collected and sold as caviar. With today's decline, what were once considered inferior species—garfish and choupique—are being caught and marketed. Fish kills affect garfish less than other species.

SHELLFISHERIES

Since about 1919 Louisiana's shellfisheries, including mollusk (oyster) and crustaceans (shrimp and crab), have risen to dominate the state's fisheries. The state's shrimp have long supplied the country's

markets, and its oysters, crabs, and crawfish are of growing importance. Leadership in this resource can be attributed primarily to the Mississippi River, which provides nutrients, needed mineral salts, and a balance of fresh and salt water. For years our shrimp have led the nation's production. They exist in some variety, even excluding the distantly related small river shrimp. They vary in size with age. There are the medium-sized lake shrimp and the jumbo shrimp, or prawns, from the continental shelf. It has been established that shrimp spawn at depths far out on the shelf. The young then move in to shallow embayments where they feed and grow. As they become larger they move out toward the spawning grounds.

Prior to 1917 most commercial shrimp were caught with long seines operating from beaches. In 1917 the trawl was introduced from Atlantic waters. Within two

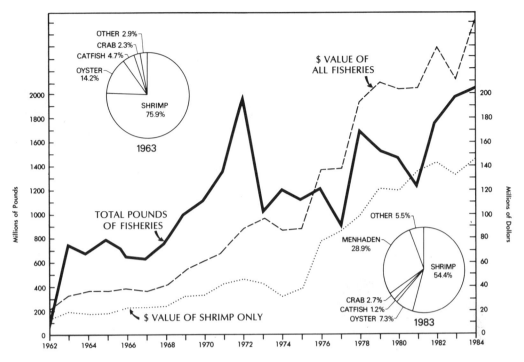

FIG. 22

Finfish and shellfish harvest in Louisiana, 1963–1983

years the catch had doubled. Fishing was carried on from small vessels operating in bays and nearshore Gulf waters. In 1937 jumbo shrimp were discovered out in deep shelf waters. Offshore operations called for larger vessels and mechanized equipment. Shrimping became big business, for the demand was insatiable, and

Large shrimp trawlers at festival
Louisiana Department of Commerce and Industry

prices rose from $3 to $140 per barrel. At present there is a great deal of "night skimming"; boats are hauled in on trailers to skim off the shrimp in shallow waters and then moved to another promising spot.

At first, shrimp were marketed fresh, which limited the distance over which they could be transported. Shrimp were canned as early as 1867 but the method was not entirely successful until the invention of a can liner in 1875. In 1873 drying of shrimp on open wooden platforms was introduced by Chinese fishermen. By 1924 as much as 28 percent of the catch was dried; at present the amount is less than 5 percent. This process, however, cannot command the choice, large shrimp. In 1934 the quick-freeze process was introduced, and since 1946 it has been the prevailing method of preservation.

No new shrimping grounds have been discovered in Louisiana since 1937–38. For causes only partially understood, shrimp fluctuate in numbers from year to year. It is hoped that measures can be taken to preserve the well being of this most important Louisiana fishery. Attempts are now being made to produce shrimp in enclosed ponds, a kind of shrimp farming. If the experiments are successful, a future supply of shrimp is assured.

In some spot or other in the Mississippi's deltaic system there have always existed ideal conditions for the production of oysters. The river provides nutrients and needed mineral traces, such as copper. At flood stage, fresh water favors early growth. As the river falls, salt water invades the beds to sharpen the oysters' flavor. Unfortunately, oysters cannot migrate like shrimp, and favorable conditions shift locality with shifts of the river's discharge. If the water is continuously fresh, the oysters die; if too salty, they are attacked by borers. In order to guarantee ideal conditions, oyster "farming" was introduced in the last century by experienced Dalmatian fishermen. Old shell, or cultch, is planted in areas favorable for early growth. On this cultch the minute oyster, or spat, attaches itself. When of proper size the oysters are moved to saltier water for "topping off," that is, to improve their flavor.

Both human and natural forces seem to combine against oysters. The petroleum industry competes for ground and labor. Perhaps the greatest natural enemy of the oyster is the conch, and now saltwater intrusion has carried the "conch line" shoreward, thus reducing the area free of saltwater predators. In 1965 Hurricane Betsy destroyed many beds while at the same time reviving some old ones. In recent years oyster production has remained constant. Some 112,000 acres are

Oyster lugger   Fred Kniffen

under lease for oyster cultivation or fishing, and there are applications to the state for as many more. Annual return is around $6,000,000, about equally divided between the catch of raw and processed oysters.

Crabs, among Louisiana's shellfish, rank third in commercial value. With modern fishing methods and an abundant supply rated of excellent quality, crabs are increasing in importance. The freshwater crawfish has recently attained notable commercial value. Long prized locally, the crawfish is now being processed and marketed widely. The natural supply is too uncertain to meet the increased demand, so that crawfish "farming" in ponds, introduced many years ago, is now a profitable business.

Natural conditions in coastal Louisiana are unparalleled in their excellence for the production of shellfish of the finest quality. But increasing competition for the waters has introduced new hazards such as saltwater intrusion and pollution. Experimentation now under way may enable us to cope with or offset these dangers and assure a future supply of shellfish.

16
Miscellaneous Resources and Conservation

In the humid eastern United States, water considered as a natural resource is a recent concept. Somehow, water, like the air, was taken for granted and no value was attached to it. But, quite suddenly, water has emerged as a resource of primary concern. Not only amount but also condition of water are matters for national discussion and legislation. Plans for treatment and distribution are of tremendous scope. In this new evaluation Louisiana finds itself in a fortunate position with respect to total available water. But in another aspect, waterpower, Louisiana has the lowest potential of any of the fifty states.

In the age when waterpower was used for all kinds of milling, Louisiana made wide use of what it had. Gristmills, sawmills, and small manufacturing plants were situated wherever it was possible to pond water and have sufficient fall to turn the mill wheel. At high-water stage, Mississippi River water was carried over the New Orleans levees to power mills set at lower elevations than the river level. When the river dropped, the mills ceased to operate. On the river itself were anchored raft mills, rising and falling with the water level, their wheels turned by the current.

There may be a few watermills operating in Louisiana today, but after the adoption of steam power in the nineteenth century, the use of waterpower declined greatly. With the rise of hydroelectric power in the twentieth century, Louisiana's deficiency in streams with sufficient gradient inhibited this development. Fortunately, Louisiana has abundant mineral fuels with which to develop electrical power. Water as a useful resource, however, is quite a different matter. Louisiana is perhaps as adequately supplied as is any other state. Abundant water supply is as important as deepwater navigation in drawing industry to the Mississippi below Baton Rouge.

Water supply is divided into two general categories, groundwater and surface water. Groundwater is derived from wells. The source may be many miles away, where surface waters move through porous rock layers beneath the surface. Surface water comes mainly from streams, although some is obtained from lakes. As with groundwater, much of the surface water is brought by streams from other states. In Louisiana, the Mississippi River system is the main source of surface water. Disregarding quality of surface water, it is quite abundant in Louisiana except in an area between the Atchafalaya and the Mississippi in South Louisiana, and in southwestern Louisiana generally.

Pure and soft groundwater is even more unequally distributed over the state. Moderate to large quantities of soft water occur in the Florida Parishes, in Rapides Parish and west to the Sabine River, and in the northern triangle between the Red and Ouachita rivers. Little or no drinkable

Overshot water mill. Such mills were operable only in favored locations, places with a stream gradient high enough to impound water to a level above the wheel.

William G. Haag

Turbine or tub mill. Much more common in Louisiana than the overshot mill, this type could be installed in creeks with gentle gradients. This particular mill was located in Sabine Parish about one mile from Hodges Gardens. The photo above shows a small pond upstream from the mill, and the photo on the left is a view from downstream showing the vertical shaft connecting the power source to mill stones above. Fred Kniffen

97

groundwater is obtainable in the area east of a line connecting Donaldsonville with Morgan City, in an east-west belt through Natchitoches, and in western Caddo Parish. Consideration of the total groundwater and surface water for various areas reveals the inequities in their distribution (Map 28). Especially blessed are the Florida Parishes and the northern triangle. Most deficient in both is the Lafourche area, where cisterns are commonly used to collect rainwater and surface water must be piped from a distance to supply both cities and rural sections.

Water is used for domestic purposes, for irrigation, and by industry. The heaviest use for irrigation is in the rice section of southwestern Louisiana, and much is used in East Carroll Parish, also for growing rice. The relatively large amounts of water used in Tangipahoa and St. James parishes are for irrigating berries and vegetables. In industrial use of water by cities New Orleans is well in the lead, followed, in order, by Baton Rouge, Lake Charles, and Monroe. No other industrial area in the state uses it in comparable amount. The bulk of water used for industrial purposes comes from surface rather than groundwater sources.

Despite an abundant water supply, we are not immune to problems of shortages,

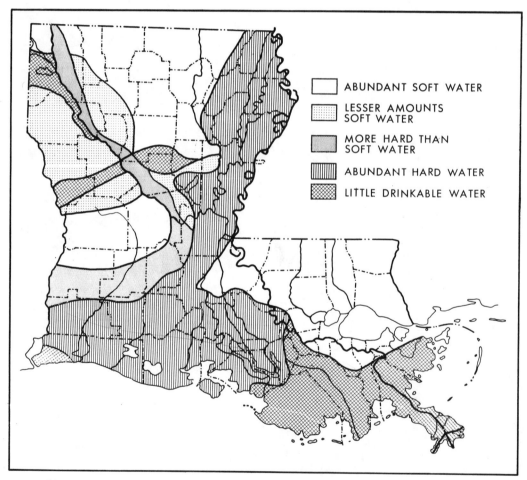

ABUNDANT SOFT WATER

LESSER AMOUNTS SOFT WATER

MORE HARD THAN SOFT WATER

ABUNDANT HARD WATER

LITTLE DRINKABLE WATER

MAP 28
Water from wells

pollution, and saltwater intrusion. Louisiana is in a better position than most other states; we count our water supply as a prime asset. Nevertheless, as our economy becomes more industrial and less agricultural, the problem of maintaining, not to mention upgrading, water quality becomes increasingly complex. Most wastewater discharges cannot be or are not being completely treated. Furthermore, particularly since World War II, many new types of chemical waste are being produced, for which methods of treatment have not been developed. Knowledge is sorely lacking about the effects of these wastes on the quality of the receiving streams.

Minor Natural Resources

Among the minor natural resources of Louisiana are clam and oyster shells, used for road surfacing and as a source of lime; sand and gravel from the terrace streams; clays for bricks from a variety of sources; and peat moss, abundant but little used. It is important that Louisiana possesses these resources, but the modes of securing and using them are not distinctive to the state. They would be the same in Texas or Mississippi. However, another and a lesser resource and its exploitation are confined largely to Louisiana. This natural resource is Spanish moss.

By no stretch of the imagination, then, can Spanish moss be considered a major natural resource of Louisiana. Yet it *is* a natural resource, and its exploitation is one of the most interesting and picturesque of the folk economies remaining in the state. Its uses become fewer as it faces the competition of synthetic products. Perhaps it will finally lose all importance as a commercial resource.

Botanically, Spanish moss is not a moss but is a member of the pineapple family. It is epiphytic, that is, air nourished, rather than parasitic upon host trees. Further, it does not smother trees, though it does grow luxuriantly on dead trees. It feeds on dust from the air and propagates by seeds and also by strands that are carried to new hosts. It grows at the rate of about an inch per month, rapidly enough to guarantee a renewed supply if properly gathered. It grows best in low, damp areas. Cypresses and live oaks are the favorite host trees, and the Atchafalaya Basin is the region of its greatest abundance.

Indians used Spanish moss as swaddling for infants and as tempering in wattledaub construction. European settlers used it for tempering in clay for chimneys, ovens, and houses. They found that it made good feed for horses and cattle, and they discovered that, like the horsehair that cured moss resembled, it was good stuffing for mattresses, pillows, and upholstering. It served as a textile, being spun and woven into bridles, cinches, and saddle blankets.

Only partially preserved today are the old, highly developed techniques employed when the gathering and curing of moss was a lively industry. The moss was gathered from downed trees in the wake of logging or by actually climbing the trees. It was gathered most easily from a tower on a floating scow, the moss being secured by a blunt hook on the end of a long pole. The rate of growth provided a new picking about every three years. The green crop had to be retted, or cured, in order to remove the outer cortex from the core. Piles of wet moss developed a bacterial action that loosened the cortex and if continued long enough made the core black like horsehair. Drying was a short process. Then the cured moss was carried to the gin, where cortex and trash were removed. The dark core was then baled for shipment. Most of it was used for automobile upholstery and furniture. Now, such synthetics as foam rubber have about destroyed this folk industry. Only one moss gin remains in operation today.

Conservation

It is the function of conservation to assure the wise use of our natural resources. It is not the purpose of conservation to save everything, but rather to distinguish the relative importance of resources for the present and for the future. In order to carry out the assignment properly we must distinguish between renewable resources, like water, timber, and even soils, and nonrenewable resources, such as petroleum, gas, sulphur, and salt.

We may recover from mistakes made with respect to renewable resources, but we cannot bring back wasted minerals. If we can foresee atomic energy as a replacement for petroleum in the future, we need be less concerned over heavy use of petroleum in the present. But we may look further and see that petroleum is a source of many chemicals and synthetic materials important in our economy.

As conservators our concern, then, is primarily with Louisiana's nonrenewable resources—its minerals. It should be our object to see that they are never wasted directly, that they are not diverted to uses where a renewable resource would do, and that income derived from them by the state is set up at least in part as a sinking fund against a future when they will be gone. And we should consider, for example, whether our natural gas can best be used in Louisiana, or whether it should be exported for fuel to areas where coal occurs in abundance.

There are cases where so-called renewable resources are threatened with destruction. We are then faced with decisions as to which of the contending activities takes precedence. Suppose we are told that in coastal Louisiana we cannot have oysters and muskrats at the same time the area is being exploited for petroleum. What shall our decision be? What are the values to be used in arriving at an opinion? Upon the wisdom of our decision rests the future economic health of our state. Citizens must be concerned with these matters. Because geographers deal professionally with human use of the earth, they should point the way to wisdom in utilizing natural resources. In subsequent chapters the human use of some of our major natural resources will be examined in the light of what has happened in the last hundreds of years.

17
Man in Louisiana

Up to this point we have emphasized natural rather than human Louisiana, and quite properly so because the earth had to be suitable before man could occupy it. We have dealt with the millions of years during which Louisiana was formed by the forces of nature, rather than with the few thousands of years since man has appeared. We have learned what these natural forces have created and continue to create in Louisiana. That part of our study covered physical geography. Some geographers are interested principally in this province of geography, and they are called physical geographers. Human, or cultural, geographers are those whose primary interest is man. Physical geographers study the processes whereby nature constructs and modifies the face of the earth. Human geographers attempt to understand man's activities in modifying the earth to suit his needs and wishes.

Despite the relatively short time that man has occupied Louisiana, we have described and weighed natural features and conditions by human values rather than by nature's terms. In nature there are no Latin names for trees, oil is no more valuable than water, a snake is as noble as an eagle, a hurricane is nothing to be dreaded. Thus, even in our study of something much larger and older than we are, we cannot escape applying our values—our ideas of inferiority or superiority—to the animate and inanimate parts of nature.

In less than three hundred years European man has made changes so great that explorers of 1700 would likely not find very much familiar in the Louisiana of today. Some of the changes have been unintentional. Certain kinds of plants were destroyed by fire; others took their places. Erosion dissected fields planted on too-steep slopes. Weed plants drifted in and established themselves. But most of the changes are the result of man's planned activities, such as the clearing of forests, the introduction of new plants and animals, the creation of stock ponds or lakes, the building of roads, cities, factories, and tank farms. You might refer again to the pictures of primitive and industrial landscapes in the first chapter of this book. Your imagination can supply almost innumerable examples of human changes.

Human geographers are not the only students interested in man in Louisiana. So are historians, sociologists, economists, and anthropologists. What aspects of man's occupance of the land are distinctly geographical? First, the human geographer is concerned with man's imprint on the land, how man changes the earth's surface, how there are likenesses and differences from place to place. Most of the things in which the geographer is interested are material and substantial and can be measured and pictured, though he realizes that thoughts and ideas underlie material things.

Second, the human geographer is interested in the relationship between man's works and the natural qualities of that section of the earth in which they lie. He is concerned with location, which he shows on maps. He matches man's works with climate, resources, relief, drainage, and other natural conditions. Eventually he is in a position to say that man's use of the earth has been wise or unwise, that man should give up certain activities or take advantage of some unused opportunities. The geographer may ultimately be able to say that, given certain natural conditions, man tends to choose to do certain things.

It is clear that man behaves differently now, or at least in a more complex manner, than he did centuries or even years ago. It is equally clear that people in one place often do not live in the same manner as those living far from them. It is a fundamental part of the human geographer's task to compare peoples of different times and different places in order to better understand them all. He must seek an outline or plan by which to make comparisons. He finds the basic elements of the outline in man's primary economies, how man gains a living. There is a simple pattern of living, representative of man's animal needs, that is common to all mankind, regardless of time or place. It consists of shelter, sources of water and food, and means of communication. Among primitive man these needs might be satisfied by a brush shelter, a river, a reef of edible shellfish, and trails connecting them.

The satisfaction of men's needs is just as necessary today as it was at the dawn of history. People still must have shelter, water, and food. And it is essential that they move about to supply their wants. More people occupy more of the earth and use more of its resources. New needs have been added to those of primitive man, but today's occupation of the earth differs by degree rather than by kind from that of thousands of years ago. It is thus in man's occupance patterns, the imprint of his living on the land, that we can compare peoples of all times and places.

And why is it that man's mode of living today is so much more complex than it was a thousand years ago? It is not that man is more intelligent today. It is because his accumulated store of knowledge makes his technical know-how more and more capable of satisfying his necessities, real or fancied. By contrast, animals of today behave exactly as they did thousands of years ago. They cannot accumulate and transmit knowledge. Man's ability to do so distinguishes him from animals. This ability permits the growth of human culture.

There are instances of two groups of people, say, Americans and Chinese, whose lands are not greatly different in their resources and whose knowledge of technology is about the same. Yet, they do things quite differently. American and Chinese houses do not look the same, nor do their villages or fields. *Value system* is the term used to describe a group's notions as to what are the right and wrong ways to do things. Often such ideas cannot be explained rationally. Each member of a group builds a particular kind of house, or raises cattle in a certain manner simply because his people have always done it so. That is the way people are.

In summarizing human geography, we may say that it deals with man's imprint on the earth and the relation of that imprint to the nature of the land where it is found. Occupance patterns are everywhere basically alike. They may not look alike, but they function alike in that they all must provide for man's basic animal needs as well as his acquired human needs. Increases in technical complexity have come with the passage of time because man can learn, retain, and add to his knowledge from one generation to the next, things no animal can do. Occupance patterns based on the same technology vary from place to place having similar natural qualities because the people have different values. The accumulated learning of a group and its values constitute that group's culture.

Now it should be clear that the basic economies with which we are so concerned became increasingly complex through time. The simplest economy of all was gathering or collecting, in which food was obtained by the simplest methods. Digging roots, collecting clams or birds' eggs, and gathering nuts and berries are examples. Another stage was reached when the development of weapons and tackle made hunting and fishing important sources of food. Advancement to this stage does not mean that collecting or gathering was abandoned.

A third stage came when plants and animals were domesticated and men could be farmers and herdsmen. Then, as living became more and more complex, some devoted their time to making tools and weapons, while others traded the surplus produced by their group for desired articles from another group. Today we would call these activities manufacturing and commerce. All these stages and even more have been represented in Louisiana. Remember that all stages are still represented in some manner to this day.

As we should now realize, there are sections of the earth where man has so altered the surface as to obscure nearly all that is natural. Residents in such areas may well get the idea that man's wisdom and technological knowledge are such that he has nature under control. However, every now and then nature asserts itself. Man has not yet learned how to prevent destructive hurricanes and tornadoes or even disastrous floods. Yet, he commonly disregards these threats and occupies almost any part of the earth he chooses. The complexity of his occupation of the land has made him far more vulnerable to natural disaster than were his primitive predecessors.

18
Prehistoric Indians

We group together as prehistoric Indians all the peoples who lived in what is now Louisiana before the first Europeans arrived. Perhaps they were not Indians like the ones we know. Our information about them must be gained entirely from the things they left behind them, things that somehow were preserved until the present, generally in mounds, middens, village sites, or workshops. We find stone and bone tools and weapons; animal and human bones; pottery, whole or in fragments; seeds; post molds where house posts were once fixed in the ground; imprints of basketry; and the like. This kind of evidence may give us a pretty good notion of how these people lived, but we have no idea of what language they spoke or what the tribes were called. There is no written record for prehistoric times. That is the big difference between the prehistoric period

Excavated midden. The plain layers are river deposits lying between midden deposits.

William G. Haag

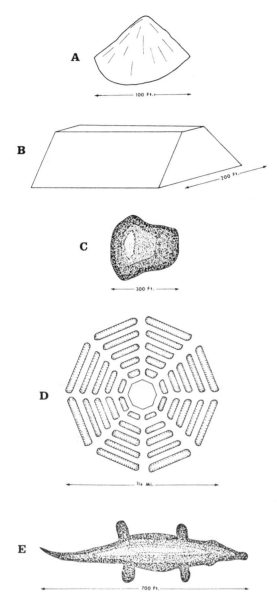

FIG. 23
Prehistoric mound types. (A) burial mound;
(B) temple mound; (C) bird effigy; (D) earth-
works; (E) alligator effigy

mounds, flat-topped pyramidal temple mounds, animal-shaped effigy mounds, and fortificationlike earthworks are the common shapes. The purposes of the first two are clear. In Louisiana, effigy mounds shaped like alligators and birds likely had to do with religious or social practices. Some of the earthworks might have been fortifications; others we can only guess at.

Middens are dump heaps. They are composed of the refuse of a group that lived nearby: shells, bones, broken pottery, tools of stone, horn, and bone, and the black earth that results from the decomposition of organic matter. Village sites were commonly situated on middens; otherwise they were on flat ground adjacent to mound groups, or stood alone, unassociated with mound or midden. Sometimes the shapes of houses can be determined, or evidence of a stockade around the village may be found. Workshops were places lived in temporarily, say, near a source of gravel from which tools and weapons were made. Workshop sites are common along gravel-bearing streams such as the Upper Amite River.

Man probably first appeared in what is now Louisiana about twelve thousand years ago. This first Louisiana man we say was in the Lithic stage or culture. His economy was not the most primitive, for he was capable of hunting the large animals abundant in those days, some of them now long extinct. Just what did the various parts of the Louisiana of those days have to offer a primitive people? Which was better, pine hills or swamp? Perhaps some other natural region was better than either.

The coastal marsh had much to offer primitive people. There was abundant animal life. It had clams that could be gathered in almost endless supply. Turtles, for example, could be easily caught. There were many useful and edible plants. On the negative side, there were noxious insects and destructive storms. But, all in all, the marsh was good for primitive man.

and the historic period, when Europeans introduced writing.

The plainest evidence that people lived in Louisiana in prehistoric times comes from the mounds and middens. Mounds are structures built of earth or shell according to some plan. Cone-shaped burial

105

Oyster (left) and clam shells   Fred Kniffen

To the north of the marsh were the prairies, stretches of grassland between strips of woods bordering the rivers. The prairies seem not to have had much that was useful to primitive Indians. The best areas were along the streams, where trees and swamp provided fair hunting and gathering.

The floodplains of the major streams, with their broad swamps and ridges of higher ground, were nearly as good as the marshes. Animal life, fish, roots, and berries were there in abundance. And when agriculture was introduced, the floodplains were the very best areas for this purpose.

In prehistoric times and long afterward, streams remained the most-used highways. The Indians had no wheeled vehicles, no beasts of burden and no roads. They built excellent dugout boats to utilize a readymade, maintenance-free system of waterways. The combination of productive bottomlands and water transportation meant that population was strongly concentrated along the streams.

Finally, there were pine flatwoods and hills, probably the least attractive places for primitive people to live in Louisiana. Game was not plentiful and neither were the plants that could be gathered. The soils were not good for primitive agriculture. The best places to live were, as

might be expected, along the larger streams.

If the pine flatwoods and hills were not the best places for people with a simple economy to live, they did have resources that brought the Indians back to them again and again, at least for short visits. The most important of the resources were gravel and stones, which could be found along at least some portion of nearly every stream. From these gravels and stones were made most of the Indians' arrowpoints, knives, drills, and other weapons and tools. Gravel was a valuable commodity, to be traded to the tribes of southern Louisiana where it did not naturally occur.

The other highly important resource of the pine hills was salt, necessary to people living to a considerable extent on vegetable food. From the salty water of the salines or interior salt domes a crude salt was extracted by evaporation. Salt was another highly valued trade article for which the manufacturers might get skins, feathers, wood for bows, sharks' teeth, and other much-desired items.

The sites that can be identified as Lithic in age, the oldest in Louisiana, have been found associated with streams draining the terraces and on Avery Island. Very likely they once existed in the floodplains and possibly along the shore of the Gulf. The floodplain has been deeply covered by silt, and the shore has been invaded by the sea during the past ten thousand or so years. The earliest known inhabitants, then, were primarily hunters of large game and secondarily fishermen and gatherers.

As time went on, there was less dependence on the hunting of big game, perhaps because many of the larger animals became extinct. Just why is not clear. Gathering became relatively more important, and perhaps nearly two thousand years ago agriculture appeared. Agriculture brought domesticated plants such as maize (corn), squash, beans, and the sunflower. It meant a more settled life and a source of food more dependable than anything else except the gathering of clams along the coast. Agriculture also gave a greater importance to the floodplains of the streams, both large and moderately sized; the regular flooding that gives rise to the word *floodplain* brought a renewal of soil productivity and continuous good harvests.

The chart showing the sequence of Indian cultures in Louisiana reveals that as time went on agriculture became increasingly important (Table 4). Even so, the harvesting of clams in coastal waters remained important for considerable numbers of peoples almost to historic times. The matching of certain economies with certain natural regions of Louisiana,

an association that has survived into the present, became set in prehistoric times. If the map of Indian economies is compared with the map of natural regions in Chapter 2, it is evident that the pine flatwoods and hills and the prairies were largely, though not entirely, areas to be visited occasionally, chiefly as sources of gravel and salt, and less importantly for hunting and the gathering of such items as edible acorns. The great attraction of the coastal areas was clams. From their shells, enormous middens were built. In addition, there were many edible roots and seeds and much animal life. Quite likely coastal agriculture was limited by the very small amount of arable land. The major economic activity in the great

MAP 29
Indian economies

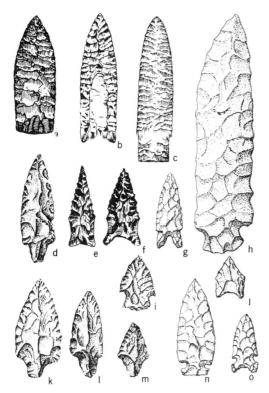

FIG. 24

Prehistoric projectile points. Types a, b, c, d, and e are the oldest.

floodplains of the Red and Mississippi rivers was agriculture. Fields were located wherever natural or man-made openings in the forest occurred. Some were upland sites, but the bottomlands were favored because of their higher fertility and because they were less affected by drought. Stream banks, especially point bars, were used for quick crops after the spring floods had abated, but only if the soils were not too sandy. Remember that these latter areas were also excellent for hunting, fishing, and the gathering of edible plants.

Each culture in the succession had to provide for the needs of its members. Beyond that there were many things that distinguished each culture from all others: the forms of tools and weapons, the rise and decline of mound building, and the like, as described in the chart. Then there were great groupings of mounds and

earthworks, which marked certain sites and cultures. One of the earliest was the Poverty Point culture site on Bayou Macon in West Carroll Parish. Here there are two huge effigy mounds and the remnants of a third shaped like birds, and the remains of a concentric series of eight-sided ridges. These ridges are about eight to ten feet high and a hundred feet apart. The outside ridge is some three quarters of a mile in diameter. The purpose of the ridges is not clear, but the whole site shows that for a long time a large group of people had in mind a plan of construction that they saw through to completion. Further, these great structures were not built for any practical purpose, such as subsistence or protection. Clearly, the execution of such an ambitious and complex undertaking indicates a high level of organization and thought, hardly the work of primitive savages.

During the Tchefuncte period two large effigy mounds were constructed of clam shells, one at Weeks Island and the other on Grand Lake south of Lake Arthur. About half of the former still remains, but the Grand Lake mound was completely destroyed for its shells. Marksville culture

Poverty Point, an ancient site in West Carroll Parish that dates from more than three thousand years ago

TABLE 4
Prehistoric Cultures and Their Characteristics

Louisiana Chronology	Basic Subsistence	Other Characteristics	Distribution
Historic (A.D. 1700)	Agriculture-Gathering Hunting-Fishing	Large centers of population. European influences.	Distribution widely scattered along streams. Along modern Mississippi River south to Buras.
Caddoan Mississippian Plaquemine (A.D. 1300–1700)	Agriculture-Gathering Hunting-Fishing	Some temple and burial mounds. Palisaded villages. Shell middens in coastal areas. Influence from east.	Caddoan on upper Red River. Mississippian down valley to mid-Louisiana and along eastern coast. Lafourche-Mississippi. Plaquemine throughout state.
Coles Creek (A.D. 950–1300)	Agriculture-Gathering Hunting-Fishing	Elaboration of Troyville culture. Shell middens, earth mounds.	Distribution similar to Troyville but more widespread. Middle interior to coast. Grand Cheniere–Pecan Island.
Troyville (A.D. 500–950)	Agriculture-Gathering Hunting-Fishing	Temple mounds. Ceremonial centers, specialized hunting and fishing sites. Shell middens in coastal Louisiana.	Named for Jonesville site. Older Lafourche-Mississippi course. Bayou Barataria region. Cheniere Perdue.
Marksville (A.D. 100–550)	Agriculture-Gathering Fishing-Hunting	First conical burial mounds. Shell middens in coastal Louisiana.	Type site at Marksville. Greatest development in interior Louisiana. Same areas as Tchefuncte in southwest Louisiana. Red River–Teche. Early St. Bernard deltaic distributaries.
Tchefuncte (200 B.C.–A.D.400)	Gathering-Fishing Agriculture	Earliest pottery. Basically coastal culture with large shell middens.	On coastal stream courses and oldest cheniers. Beach ridges around Lake Pontchartrain. Salé-Cypremort, early St. Bernard deltas.
Poverty Point (1700 B.C.)	Intensive Gathering Hunting-Fishing Agriculture likely	Poverty Point objects and microflints. Large earthworks at Poverty Point. Eastern coastal shell middens.	On interior terraces, buried streams in the delta, and old beach ridges.
Lithic (back to 10,000 B.C. or older)	Hunting Fishing-Gathering	Possible association with extinct fauna. Camp sites. Isolated artifacts in terrace deposits.	In association with stream valleys draining terraces. Avery Island.

is named for the site near the city of Marksville, which consists of a large number of earthen mounds surrounded by an earthen wall and a ditch or moat. Fortunately, this site is preserved as a state park. There once existed a walled group of mounds at Jonesville, one of which was said to have been ninety feet high. The Jonesville site, generally attributed to the Troyville culture, was once as impressive as the Marksville site. It is now almost entirely gone.

19
Historic Indians

A few years after Columbus' voyages to the New World, the first Europeans appeared in Louisiana, and about 1700 they came here to live. The beginning of the historic period for Louisiana, then, is commonly placed at 1700, because those first white settlers left written accounts of both the country and its people. These descriptive accounts are valuable sources of information about the Indians, for they often recorded what the Indians thought and said about many things. Thus today's students of Indian cultures have much more evidence to study than those tools, weapons, and pottery that have been preserved largely by accident. We regret that the early explorers quite often recorded only the things about the Indians that interested them and left out information we would very much like to have. Before we blame them too much, we might think that future students will wonder how we could have been so stupid as not to record many things that they will be interested in.

This written information has helped scholars reconstruct the culture of the Indians as it was just before the Europeans began to bring great changes. As geographers we are interested chiefly in where and how these historic Indians lived. We see immediately that they continued to prefer the desirable floodplains to the less attractive upland areas. Judging from both the archaeological and his-

torical records, the coast and its resources seem less used than before. Perhaps agriculture had become more reliable and thus relatively more important as a source of food. In any case, the coastal population was surely less at the time of European contact than it had been five hundred or a thousand years earlier.

As shown on the map of historic Indians, Louisiana Indians belonged to several linguistic groups, with differences among them as great as those separating English from Chinese. Tunican, Atakapan, and Chitimachan belong to the Tunican language family. The differences among them were about the same as those between French and English. Caddoan was a second family, and Muskhogean, a third. Muskhogean proper, spoken by the tribes living in eastern Louisiana, was much like the Choctaw speech of Mississippi. A second variety of Muskhogean, Natchezan, was spoken by the Tensas and Avoyel tribes in Louisiana. And almost every village in Louisiana had a resident or two who knew Mobilian, a Muskhogean tongue spoken by a tribe living near what is now Mobile, Alabama. Mobilian was, like the sign language of the Plains tribes, a means of communication among peoples whose languages were mutually unintelligible.

Each of the linguistic divisions was divided into several tribes. A tribe was an independent political group that had a sense of belonging together and that oc-

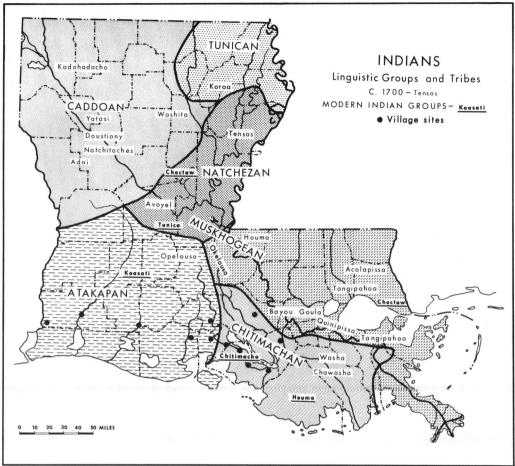

MAP 30

Linguistic groups are shown by different patterns. Tribal names of modern groups are underlined; those not underlined are shown as of approximately A.D. 1700.

cupied a recognized territory. Several tribes sometimes joined into a confederation without losing their independence. As the map so clearly shows, the tribes were almost all located along major streams or on high ground at the edge of marsh or swamp. This supports the idea we have stressed that marshes, swamp, and bottomlands were best for hunting, gathering, fishing, and agriculture, and that waterways were the major routes of travel.

Over and above these important differences in the value of the terrain, there were differences in resources that led to varying ways of living in North and South Louisiana. For example, in South Louisiana, Indian houses were commonly made of palmetto. In Central Louisiana, they were solid cabins consisting of a heavy framework, a filling of earth, and a protective covering of cane mats. Northwest Louisiana houses were beehive-shaped frames thatched with bundles of grass. Even more directly related to the resources, coastal Louisiana produced highly valued sharks' teeth and an excess of feathers and meat. These products were traded northward for large animal skins, stone, and the best wood for bows—*bois d'arc,* or Osage orange.

We may now look at the various tribes and tribal groups a little more closely. A number of the important Atakapa villages were situated on high ground just to the north of the marsh. The Atakapa concentrated on the produce of the marsh and shore and did not emphasize argiculture to the same extent that their neighbors to the north did. The Chitimacha villages clustered about the waterways of the Lower Atchafalaya Basin. Their inhabitants raised swamp living to a high art. They built the very best pirogues in Louisiana and made fine baskets out of cane. Despite such heavy dependence on the swamp, they grew tall corn and other crops on the well-drained levee land back of their villages. The Muskhogean tribes and the Koroa gave maximum attention to agriculture, although some had access to extensive swamp and marsh and made use of them accordingly. The Caddoan tribes of the Red River were agricultural, but after the coming of the Europeans they were easily persuaded to take up horses; consequently, hunting became relatively more important.

Looking at the Indians of about 1700, we can say in general that they were sedentary farmers who lived in villages and supplemented their crops with generous participation in hunting and fishing. Spring was a time for fishing, when the fish ascended the streams in great numbers to spawn. Summer was crop-growing time. With the fall and winter coolness after the harvest, hunting became a major pursuit. This is an annual schedule not totally unfamiliar today.

Those Indians of 1700 were perhaps some fifteen thousand in number, fewer people than live in many modern Louisiana towns. What could so few people do to change the face of the land? The mounds and middens we have mentioned, but certainly many Louisianians live and die without ever seeing a mound. The unintentional changes that these Indians made were much more important but are much more difficult to identify and measure. Probably the principal instrument of change used by the Indians

Indian house type: cabin

Indian house type: grass house

Indian house type: palmetto house

was fire. They used fires for a number of purposes, but certainly in many cases the fires got out of control and had effects that the Indians never intended. Some practiced what is known as slash-and-burn agriculture. They girdled trees to make them die, lose their leaves, and let

Modern deadening of older trees to encourage growth of cotton

Roland Harper Collection, University of Alabama

the sun get to the ground. Small brush was cut, piled, and burned, thus creating a clearing for planting and incidentally adding potash fertilizer from the ashes to the soil. Fires were set to produce better grazing and so encourage the presence of game. Fires were also set to clear the ground under nut trees so that the crop could be more easily gathered.

Clearing the forest for agriculture and repeated burning created grassy openings, some of them now referred to as Indian old fields. The openings encouraged the greater growth of sunloving plants, or heliophytes. In heavily forested areas burning tended to destroy hardwood trees. This encouraged the growth of pines, especially the longleaf, a tree particularly resistant to fire. There can be little doubt that the pure longleaf forests that once covered much of Louisiana were the result of burning.

But, as we view the Louisiana of today, with its great cities, networks of highways, tall buildings of steel and glass, and great manufacturing plants, and then think back to the scene as it was in 1700, there certainly seems to be very little connection. What if the Indians of that time made no significant use of the resources of the state? We live in another age, and things have different values in our culture. For example, petroleum and natural gas meant nothing to the Indians. Gravel, used by the Indians for tools and weapons, serves a far different purpose today. Just the same, the Indian and European cultures as they met in 1700 were not so far apart that the Europeans could scorn all Indian ways. European settlers quickly took over many Indian plants such as maize and tobacco. They used the same water highways and selected the same places as did the Indians for establishing settlements. So, there was considerable continuity from Indians to Europeans.

Today, the Indians in Louisiana number fewer than those living here in 1700. Even if we accept the census figure for 1980, 11,951, that many Indians out of the total population of the state cannot be

TABLE 5
Indian Population in Louisiana

Indian Population, 1700–1980

Date:	1700	1890	1900	1910	1920	1930	1940	1950	1960	1970	1980
Population:	15,000	628	593	780	1,066	1,536	1,801	409	3,587	5,294	11,951

Indian Population by Parish, 1980

Acadia	23	Iberia	97	St. Charles	68
Allen	233	Iberville	24	St. Helena	4
Ascension	76	Jackson	16	St. James	2
Assumption	21	Jefferson	1,371	St. John the Baptist	36
Avoyelles	46	Jefferson Davis	34	St. Landry	32
Beauregard	27	Lafayette	209	St. Martin	26
Bienville	21	Lafourche	829	St. Mary	385
Bossier	186	La Salle	142	St. Tammany	303
Caddo	382	Lincoln	35	Tangipahoa	84
Calcasieu	257	Livingston	71	Tensas	—
Caldwell	—	Madison	5	Terrebonne	3,272
Cameron	7	Morehouse	15	Union	18
Catahoula	17	Natchitoches	122	Vermilion	34
Claiborne	2	Orleans	501	Vernon	232
Concordia	23	Ouachita	104	Washington	29
De Soto	24	Plaquemines	283	Webster	53
East Baton Rouge	505	Pointe Coupee	10	West Baton Rouge	18
East Carroll	1	Rapides	428	West Carroll	16
East Feliciana	20	Red River	13	West Feliciana	17
Evangeline	18	Richland	10	Winn	20
Franklin	6	Sabine	774		
Grant	24	St. Bernard	290		

a very influential group. Furthermore, the Koasati and the Choctaw are descended from tribes that migrated into the state after the coming of Europeans. Despite their relative unimportance today, the Indians left us one obvious heritage: place names. If you look at names of streams in Louisiana, you will find a great number with *bayou* and *bog* or *bogue* as part of them. To these we may add *hacha* and *okhata*, and we have Indian names for different kinds of water bodies: hacha for river; bog or bogue for creek; bayou; and okhata for lake. Then there are Indian names for colors: *lusa* or *loosa* for black; *houma* or *humma*, red; and *hata*, white. There are some familiar adjectives: *falaia* or *falaya*, long; *chitto*, big. Now let us combine some of the Indian terms into familiar names: hacha-falaia or Atchafalaya; boglusa or Bogalusa; bog-falaia or Bogue Falaya. Other familiar Indian names are Calcasieu, Istrouma, Natchitoches, Bistineau, Catahoula, Coushatta, Manchac, and Ponchatoula. We *do* owe a debt to the Louisiana Indians.

20
Explorers

We have said that in about 1700 the Europeans came to Louisiana to stay. But for some two hundred years before that they had been prodding and probing, trying to see what kind of country the new land was. It was most difficult for the explorers to make accurate maps of what they had found. It was almost impossible for them to get an accurate longitudinal, or east-west, location; therefore we are still not sure when Louisiana and the Mississippi River were first seen by a European and shown on a map.

In 1502, only ten years after Columbus arrived in the New World, there appeared in Europe the Cantino map, which shows what is clearly Florida and the Gulf Coast. One of the many streams shown is named *Rio de las Palmas* (River of Palms). Some scholars have thought this to be the Mississippi, but there are many reasons to believe that it is not. In 1519 a Spanish explorer named Pineda sailed westward along the coast and reported that he had seen the mouth of a large stream. Maps based on his information show this mouth as a large bay separated from the Gulf by a long point. This form resembles Mobile Bay and bays on the Texas coast, but not the bird's-foot delta of the Mississippi.

In 1528 a party under the direction of another Spaniard, Nárvaez, sailing westward along the Louisiana coast, detected the presence of a large stream nearby by finding fresh water far out at sea. Among Nárvaez' men who survived the wrecking of their small boats west of the Mississippi was Cabeza de Vaca. De Vaca wandered westward for several years before he reached Spanish settlements in Mexico. As the result of his reports, two great expeditions were organized to explore what is now the southern United States. These explorers hoped to find riches of silver and gold to match those discovered in Mexico and Peru. Hernando de Soto led the expedition to the section that included Louisiana.

De Soto landed in what is now Tampa Bay, Florida, in 1539. It was 1543 when the remnants of his party found their way out of the mouth of the Mississippi on their way to Mexico. The party had spent some time in Louisiana and had crisscrossed the northern part of the state. They were favorably impressed with the luxuriant growth and the mild climate, but they complained of the severity of the winter they spent at the mouth of the Arkansas River. They found the extensive swamps of the southern part of Louisiana somewhat forbidding. They saw no bison, or buffalo, in the whole of what is now the southeastern United States, a point to remember for future reference. Most disappointing to them was the failure to find gold or silver.

In northeast Louisiana, along the Mississippi, the Spaniards found a dense population of Indian farmers living in villages and towns. De Soto's men gave them some of the pigs they were driving along for food. For a while the pigs thrived on the forest mast, but likely disappeared after a few years. It is probable that the Indians retained none of the domesticated plants or animals they borrowed from these early European contacts. But what these Indians had certainly gotten from Europeans by de Soto's time were infectious diseases, some of which were harmless to Europeans but killed the Indians by the thousands.

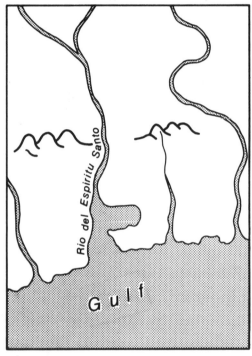

MAP 31
The De Soto map of 1544, showing a large river flowing into the Gulf

As a result of de Soto's trip and the information it provided, maps showed a *Rio del Espiritu Santo* (River of the Holy Spirit) to represent the Mississippi. But still the mouth of the river does not look like it should, extending out into the Gulf. On these maps it still resembles Mobile Bay. Perhaps the poor representation of the Mississippi indicates a lack of further interest on the part of the Spaniards in

the area when it failed to yield the riches they sought. It supports the idea that de Soto's men left Louisiana by way of the Atchafalaya River rather than the Mississippi. In any event, no other large expedition visited Louisiana for nearly 150 years, and then it was a French group coming from the north, down the river.

Leader of the French advance down the Mississippi into Louisiana was René Robert Cavelier, Sieur de La Salle. La Salle was a native of France and a resident of Canada. He was interested in exploration as well as in gaining wealth from the fur trade. Hearing from the Indians of a "great water" to the west, he thought it to be the Pacific. After Joliet and Father Marquette had descended the Mississippi to the vicinity of present-day Memphis and proved that it was not the Pacific, La Salle led a move to explore and develop the great valley. Early in 1682 he started downriver from the Illinois country with a large, rather slow-moving party. As they neared Louisiana they saw European articles among the Indians, especially fowl and pigs, which the natives did not have when de Soto first saw them. In Louisiana the explorers saw the Tensas tribe, the Quinipissa, and the Tangipahoa. Northeastern Louisiana, so abundantly peopled in de Soto's time, had already lost a large part of its population.

La Salle reached the mouth of the Mississippi in April, 1682. He claimed, and this is very important, all that great basin drained by the Mississippi River. This meant that southwestern and southeastern Louisiana, where the rivers run directly into the Gulf and not into the Mississippi, were, strictly speaking, not included in what La Salle named *Louisiane* (Louisiana) after King Louis XIV of France. On the way back upstream, La Salle saw Indians hunting bison in the marshes south of the site of future New Orleans on the east bank of the river. Recall that there were no bison in Louisiana in de Soto's time. Here is a remarkable instance of a large, wild grazing animal's actually extending its range after the arrival of Europeans.

La Salle saw that if France were to hold her vast new territory, the basin of the Mississippi, she must establish a settlement near the river's mouth. Therefore, in 1684 La Salle came from France with several hundred colonists aboard ship, only to miss the mouth of the Mississippi, perhaps intentionally, and land in Texas. The colony was a failure and La Salle was assassinated by his own men. Nevertheless, the establishment of a settlement was clearly necessary. So a new expedition was organized under the direction of the Canadian-born Frenchman Pierre le Moyne, Sieur de Iberville, whom we know simply as Iberville. Two ships carrying several hundred men set out from France in 1698. Late in the same year the ships reached the vicinity of modern-day Biloxi, Mississippi, and anchored off Ship Island while Iberville explored the country, looking for the mouth of the Mississippi.

Iberville's trip up the Mississippi was very important because it led to the discovery of many geographical facts that were important later (Map 32). Leaving Ship Island, so named because it provided good anchorage for the ships, the party discovered another small island to the west. They named it Cat Island because of the many opossums or raccoons

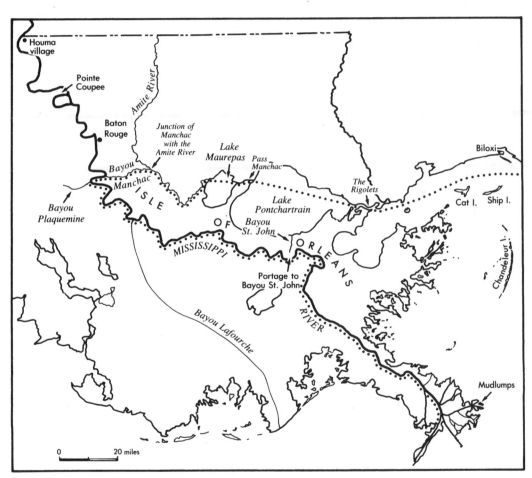

MAP 32
Significant landmarks associated with Iberville's ascent of the Mississippi River

on it. The Chandeleur Island arc was discovered on February 2, 1699, Candlemas Day, and was given the French equivalent of that name. When Iberville approached the mouths of the Mississippi, he found them in flood and somewhat shrouded in fog. He noted "rocks" resting in fairly deep water; doubtless these were mudlumps such as we have described. Iberville's party had moved many miles upstream against a stiff current when the men encountered some of the same Indians they had seen and left behind in Biloxi. Seeking an explanation of their unexpected appearance, Iberville followed the Indians to the future site of New Orleans. There they pointed out the portage that led to Bayou St. John and so to Lake Pontchartrain and on by water to Biloxi.

The party ascended the river to a point on the west bank where a large distributary carried floodwaters out of the Mississippi to the Gulf. We now know that stream as Bayou Lafourche. Above Lafourche they saw Bayous Plaquemine and Manchac, also active distributaries of the flooded Mississippi. Above the Manchac, and also on the east bank, Iberville encountered the first high ground he had observed since leaving Biloxi. This was the last place downstream where the river flowed against the bluff formed by the Prairie Terrace. This high ground was called *Iti-houma* (Istrouma) by the Indians, presumably because of a red pole standing there. We know this site better by its French name *Baton Rouge*. Above Baton Rouge the party saw Pointe Coupee, the nearly severed neck of what is now False River, and still farther above that they came upon the Houma Indian village near the present Angola prison farm.

On the return trip Iberville descended Bayou Manchac (the "back way" to the Amite River), then followed a route that took him through Lake Maurepas, Pass Manchac, Lake Pontchartrain, and the Rigolets to the Mississippi Sound. He had

thus encircled the Isle of Orleans, and had additionally traversed the sites of New Orleans, Baton Rouge, and Pointe Coupee. He had found the important distributaries of the Lower Mississippi— Bayous Manchac, Plaquemine, and Lafourche. He also had gained a poor notion of the navigability of the Lower Mississippi for oceangoing vessels. The swift current and shallow bars of a flooding Mississippi seemed to mean that it could not be navigated by ships.

After the explorations of La Salle and Iberville, maps finally began to present a reasonably accurate picture of conditions as they were. The Gentil map of 1700, based on La Salle's and Iberville's information, shows a clearly recognizable Lower Mississippi. And the name *Mississippi,* an Algonkian term brought down from the north, replaced *Rio del Espiritu Santo.*

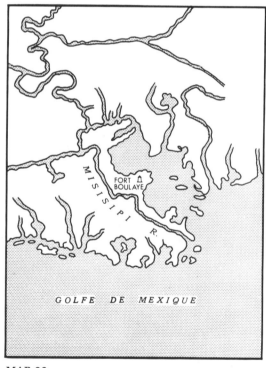

MAP 33
The Gentil map of 1700 portrays the river much more accurately than the De Soto map.

Long after Iberville's time, extensive sections of Louisiana remained little known to Europeans. Even so, primary exploration was over. The succeeding stage—permanent settlement—was initiated by Iberville. It became the dominant European activity in Louisiana. It will be our concern in the succeeding chapters.

21

European Settlers and Settlements

In 1699, when Iberville decided to establish a permanent settlement, it was not in Louisiana, but instead at Biloxi, in Mississippi. He recognized that the Mississippi River was the great central artery on which colonization must focus. However, he was of the opinion that it was too difficult to get ships upriver and thought that the settlement should be on the Mississippi coast, where the ships could anchor in security. From Biloxi it was possible to get to the Mississippi by either Bayou St. John or the Manchac route.

But in the same year, Iberville's young brother Bienville, returning from an exploring trip down Bayou Lafourche, encountered an English ship in the Mississippi at what is now called English Turn. He convinced the English captain that he was trespassing on French territory, and the ship turned downstream and sailed away. This incident frightened the French into establishing a small fort, Boulaye, at a point on the east bank about fifty miles above the mouth of the Mississippi. Although this was the first French settlement in what is now Louisiana, it disappeared after a few years and so cannot be counted as the first permanent one in the state.

Biloxi may not have been a bad spot for a ship anchorage or for access to the Mississippi, but it was a poor site for farmers. In 1701, the colony was moved from Biloxi to a site on Mobile Bay, where, it was hoped, natural conditions would be more favorable for agriculture. However, improvement was slow. In 1713, when the French financier Antoine Crozat was granted a commercial monopoly of Louisiana, the economic condition of the colonies was not good. In 1713, of several hundred persons in five small communities stretching from the Mississippi to Mobile Bay, only thirty-five were farmers. On the poor coastal soils they produced some vegetables and fowl. Food items such as wheat flour, sugar, molasses, rum, and salt meat had to be imported. A major obstacle to agriculture was the lack of familiarity with local conditions. Europeans knew nothing of Gulf Coast soils or climate, and most imported crops did poorly at first. It was deemed unwise to move farther inland to better soils because Indians friendly to British traders were believed ready to attack.

The main trouble with the colony was that its members were little interested in settling down to farm. Many of them were soldiers who hoped to find quick riches in gold; others were French-Canadian trappers and fur traders. The principal exports of the new settlements were furs, hides, bear oil, and game for food.

In 1714 the first permanent settlement in Louisiana was founded—Natchitoches. It was established for two purposes: to assert the French claim to lower Louisiana and to develop trade with the Spaniards in Texas and to the south. The site was

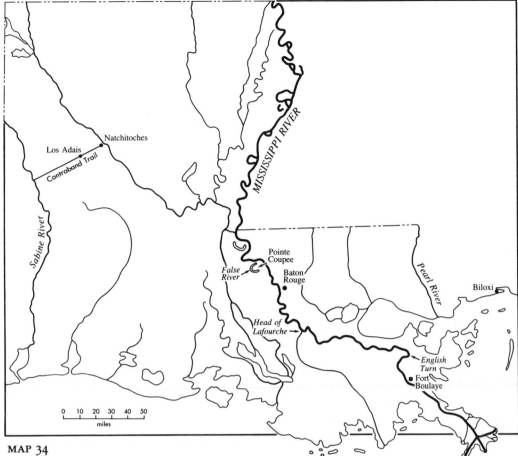

MAP 34
Index map of important early sites

wisely selected. It lay on high ground on the navigable Red River, below the Great Raft. To the west the land was high and well drained, and thus land transportation was comparatively easy.

To counter the French settlement, the Spaniards established a post at Los Adais, a few miles southwest of Natchitoches. Between Natchitoches and Los Adais was the accepted boundary separating French and Spanish territories. Natchitoches was on what was then the Red River, a tributary of the Mississippi. Los Adais may have been thought to be on drainage entering the Gulf west of the Mississippi. This boundary line is geographically important because it indicates a recognition of La Salle's territorial claim, that

Louisiana coincided with the Mississippi drainage basin.

The hoped-for trade with the Spaniards did develop, but hardly to the extent expected. There was illegitimate trade along what was frequently called the Contraband Trail (the Natchitoches-Nacogdoches Road). This trade was in the form of horses that the Indians stole from the Spaniards and brought to sell or trade to the French.

An unplanned economic development of the Natchitoches settlement was the growing of corn, cotton, and tobacco, which thrived on the rich soils of the Red River bottoms. What happened at Natchitoches was part of a general development along the great floodplains of the state. It became evident that the rich bottom soils could produce profitable

crops, especially indigo and tobacco. It
also became evident that few Europeans
or Indians were willing to undertake the
hard work necessary to clear the fields
and raise crops. The solution was found
in African slaves. Five hundred arrived in
1716, and many more came after 1718,
when the Company of the West, Crozat's
successor, assumed control of the colony
under Bienville's direction.

After 1718 other important developments began to take place. By 1721 the
vagrants and convicts who had constituted most of the forced French immigrants were being succeeded by capable
and serious settlers from Europe. Bienville saw clearly that the economic future
of the colony lay in the development of
commercial agriculture on the productive
floodplains. Indigo, tobacco, cotton, and
rice were seen as possibilities, not to
mention older subsistence crops like
maize. But difficulties arose. For example,
there was the problem of distributing the
rich lands to the new settlers. Speculators
were eager to get large sections and then
let them lie idle until they could be sold
for a high price. A law preventing the
holding of large sections of undeveloped
land for long periods of time was put into
effect.

Division of the lands along the river
followed a system used in northwestern
France along streams and in reclaimed
marshlands. It consisted of measuring off
a width along the high ground of the
natural levees paralleling the stream, then
extending it into the backland swamps.
The details as worked out in Louisiana
meant that the width of a grant was
commonly eight arpents. Since an arpent
is about 192 feet, the width was roughly
1,500 feet. The depth of a grant became
standardized at forty arpents, or nearly
8,000 feet, about 1-1/2 miles. No one
apparently anticipated what the effect of
the French system of inheritance would
be. To this day it is not uncommon for
land to be divided equally among all the
heirs. In this case, the holding is sliced

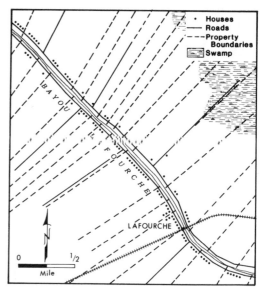

MAP 35
*Linear settlement patterns were the hallmark of
the French.*

lengthwise, thus producing an ever-nar-
rower front, or width, but retaining the
forty-arpent depth.

In 1718 Bienville urged the founding of
a community on the Mississippi. Certainly he supported the development of
agriculture, and he knew it would succeed only on the rich bottomlands. The
company officials and traders were opposed to such development, favoring the
old settlements to the east—Biloxi and
Mobile—where commerce was already established. Nevertheless, Bienville got his
way and New Orleans came into being.
The specific site was determined by the
location of the portage to Bayou St. John
with its access to the Gulf Coast and to
the east, and the existence of a relatively
high natural levee. Remember, much of
present-day New Orleans is at or below
sea level.

Among those directing the planning of
the new settlement was a French engineer
named Adrien de Pauger. This remarkable man understood well the problems
involved. Since there were initially no
levees to protect New Orleans, the site

had to be laid out on the narrow natural levee slope between the river and the backswamp. That meant the area to be occupied had to be elongated parallel to the Mississippi and had to be shallow in depth. It was de Pauger who selected the sites for public buildings around what we know today as Jackson Square. But most outstanding was his diagnosis and prescription concerning the difficulties of navigating the river below New Orleans. He explained how the river extended its channels by depositing natural levees and then scouring to considerable depths between them. He understood how the river created shallow bars at its mouths where it reached the sea. These hazards to navigation, he said, could be flushed out by the current if the ends of the passes were confined between artificial jetties. This idea was put into practice by an American engineer, James B. Eads, in 1878, more than 150 years after de Pauger's time.

In 1722 Bienville wore down his opposition and had New Orleans made the capital of Louisiana. He proved that ships could cross the bars and ascend the river. Levees were made to surround the settlement. A stockade, moat, and blockhouses protected it from attack. By this time there were other settlements on the Mississippi: the German Coast (to be described in the next chapter); at the head of Bayou Lafourche; on the Manchac; at Baton Rouge; at Pointe Coupee; and at Natchitoches on Red River. Note that all were on streams. The back country remained nearly as wild as it had ever been.

22

New Settlers, New Trade, New Crops

By the 1720s enough people had moved into the colony to establish a small but productive agricultural community. By no means were all the Europeans who farmed along the river wealthy plantation owners with slaves to do the work. Some were small farmers who did their own work. Among these were the Germans of the *Côte des Allemands* (German Coast). These people began arriving about 1720 and established themselves on the Mississippi River "coast" of what are now St. Charles and St. John the Baptist parishes. At that time *côte* (coast) referred to the natural levees and not to the backswamp. Some of these Germans came from an abandoned colony in Arkansas. Others came directly from Europe. Most were very poor. They fought Indians and floods, cleared the ground, raised vegetables and fowl, and made butter. This produce they carried in small boats to the New Orleans market. They were thrifty and industrious people, who showed that small farmers could thrive on the productive river-bottom soils.

It is difficult to appreciate the difficulties faced by the Germans in moving from one kind of country to a very different one. Most of them came from the Rhine River Valley. The climate to which they were accustomed was one of cool summers and mild winters. In the old homeland they grew crops such as wheat, grapes, and flax; not one of these could grow well in Louisiana. They found the summers oppressively hot. The forest they had to clear from the natural levees was dense. They had to learn to eat corn (maize) and rice. Dairying, the making of butter and cheese, was far more difficult than it had been in the Rhine country. The Germans were good pioneers because they realized that Louisiana, however difficult, offered opportunities beyond anything available to them in Germany. They were so successful that by 1803 the area was called *Côte d' or* (gold coast).

Before too long the Germans lost their language and their identity through absorption by the larger French population. About the only reminder of them today is many of the family names found in French Louisiana. Some of these names still sound quite German: Wiltz, Weiss, Keller, Schexsnaider, Rixner, Montz. There are others we probably think of as being French: d'Arensbourg, Chance, Leche, Vicknair, Folse, Trosclair, Oubre, Tregre, Webre, Toups, Himel, and Rome. Aside from the names, there is very little that is German to be observed along the German Coast today.

The early large-plantation crops raised for export were indigo, rice, and tobacco. Indigo found a ready market in Europe. Rice was important as a local food. Among poor people it was a substitute for wheat bread, to be used especially in soups.

An old account suggests that Louisiana's distinctive method of producing river rice was discovered quite by accident during New Orleans' early years. It is said that during a hurricane a storehouse containing rice was destroyed and the grain stored there for use as food was thoroughly scattered. But there appeared at the edge of the backswamp a good stand of rice which was harvested and consumed. So, Louisianians learned to plant at the lower edge of the natural levee's backslope in time to take advantage of the spring flood and then to harvest the grain during the dry period of late summer and fall. Modifications of this method remained in effect as long as river rice was important in Louisiana's economy.

Tobacco, particularly that grown in what is now St. James Parish, in the late 1700s came to be cured in an unusual manner that gave rise to a highly regarded black tobacco known the world over as perique.

Maize was another important crop, used especially as feed for animals, and by poor people and slaves. Cotton was a common crop, much of it used locally for making cloth. Cotton was expensive because of the great amount of hand labor needed to separate the lint from the seed. Figs were introduced early from southern France and did well. Citrus fruits were brought in from the Old World through the West Indies. They grew well and their quality was the best, but periodically the

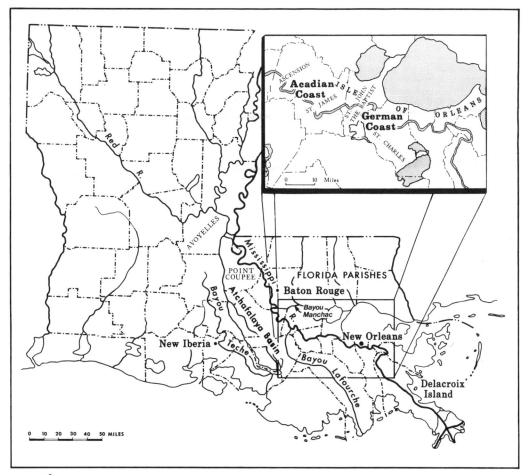

MAP 36
Index map showing details of early spread of settlers

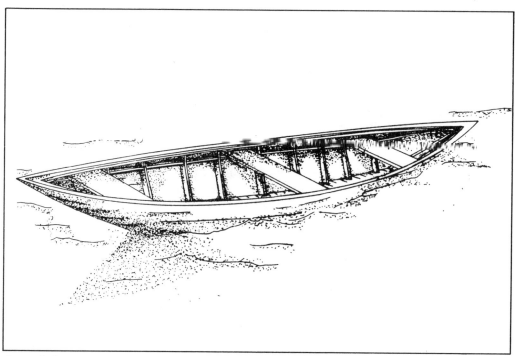

An early bateau

trees were killed by unusual cold and had to be replanted. Sugarcane was introduced early in the 1700s but was not granulated into sugar until the 1790s.

Early in the settlement of Louisiana considerable trade developed with another area of French settlement that was called the Illinois country. Part of the goods brought down to New Orleans were for local consumption; others were exported. Only goods of high value for their weight could be carried back upriver, for transportation both ways was in what were called *bateaux*. The bateaux of those days were made of planks and had sharply projecting bows and sterns; they were flat bottomed, and were up to forty feet long and nine feet wide. A bateau was propelled with oars, poles, and, occasionally, sails. Sometimes in going upstream it was necessary to send the crew ashore with a rope to tow the vessel, a practice known as lining or cordelling.

The bateaux came down from the Illinois country to New Orleans in De-

cember. Among the articles they brought for sale or trade were wheat flour, to make bread for the wealthier Louisianians; corn; bacon; hams from hogs and bear; corned pork; dried bison meat, commonly called jerky; beeswax; tallow, leather, and furs; bear grease, good for many uses, including hair pomade; lead and copper for bullets and cooking pots; and wool. Back upstream in February went tobacco, sugar, cotton, and such luxuries as spices and silks; part of these were imports to Louisiana by sea.

The French were not the only Europeans dealing with the Indians. British traders moved west from Charleston and were trading with tribes along the Mississippi at the time the French arrived.

Louisiana and the Illinois country were united by more than language and nationality. Today there are still countrysides and towns in Missouri and Illinois that immediately suggest Louisiana. Houses look like those of French Louisiana, and there are the same arpent-strip land divisions fronting on the streams.

Occasionally some of the crew of the descending bateaux were Indians from the Illinois country. Other Indians came in their canoes to winter in southern Louisiana. Some camped on the property of the German farmers and spent the winter months hunting waterfowl. In spring they returned to their homes in the North.

All this description of boats tends to emphasize the importance of water transportation. Even so, an edict issued early in the French period stated that property owners along the Mississippi had to construct and maintain roads (which were little more than paths) parallel to the artificial levees for which they were also responsible. With the building of river roads it was possible to go upstream as far as the roads extended with pack animals or wagons, which was sometimes much easier than working a loaded boat up against the current.

In 1763 there ended a war in which the British had opposed France and Spain. As a result of their victory, the British got a part of Louisiana, the portion of the drainage basin of the Mississippi east of the river, with the exception of the Isle of Orleans. The British also got the territory west of Mobile to the Mississippi. This meant that what we now call the Florida Parishes became British. All the rest of Louisiana, the Isle of Orleans, and that portion west of the river was ceded by France to Spain. British control of the Florida Parishes still did not provide free access to the sea for British Americans living upriver, for Spain still held the mouth of the Mississippi. Not until the Louisiana Purchase in 1803 and subsequent negotiations with Spain was free navigation of the river achieved.

The difficulties of war times and especially the changes in territorial ownership after the war caused dissatisfaction and unrest for some and offered new opportunities to others. For example, many Indians, particularly Choctaws, who had been friendly to the French, found themselves suddenly in British territory. They moved west of the river to live under more friendly officials, and at the same time they found better hunting grounds, where the game was not depleted as it was east of the river. British colonials from the Carolinas and Virginia found their way to the productive blufflands of the Felicianas, brought with them tobacco, their major crop, and instituted practices quite alien to the French ways of doing things.

But the largest and most influential new group to enter Louisiana at this time was the Acadians. These people were French refugees from eastern Canada, from which they had been expelled by the suspicious British. Many wandered far and wide, finally to find refuge with other French people living in Louisiana. The first Acadians had arrived by the 1760s, and they came by the hundreds and thousands during the next thirty years.

Little actual change in language or custom occurred when Spanish rule succeeded French in what was then legally Spanish Louisiana, but the Acadians avoided the Florida Parishes, then under British rule. The Acadian Coast, consisting of the two parishes next above the German Coast, St. James and Ascension, was one of the first extensive areas of their settlement. They went down the broad levees of Bayou Lafourche. They went to the Pointe Coupee settlement, which lay across the river from British Feliciana. They went westward up the Red River to the productive Avoyelles section. They pushed by water across the Atchafalaya Basin to the broad Teche levees and the eastern borders of the prairies.

The Acadians were quite different from the French who had come from Europe and the St. Lawrence Valley. They were poor and they were small farmers (*petits habitants*). They were very strong in the Catholic faith, had large families, and held tenaciously to their ways. They quickly absorbed nearly every alien group that came in contact with them—Germans and Spanish, for example. At the beginning they were poor and inexperienced, but, like the Germans, they worked hard and emerged as very good peasant farmers. Unlike the Germans, however, they were less likely to own slaves. In 1803 the Acadian settlements were predominantly white.

1803 Populations	German Coast	Acadian Coast
whites	1,571	2,059
slaves	2,666	1,282
totals	4,237	3,341

In their shift to Louisiana, the Acadians experienced changes as great as did the Germans. In Acadia, they produced apples, wheat, and flax, and utilized a variety of berries and other wild products, none of which grows in Louisiana. They had to learn to like rice, corn bread, and sweet potatoes and to replace flax and wool with cotton for weaving textiles.

Today the distinction between Acadians and others of French descent is not always clear. But we do know at least that among the French family names most frequent in Louisiana, Broussard, Landry, LeBlanc, Hebert, Boudreaux, Mouton, and Martin are Acadian, while Bernard, Gremillion, and Fontenot are not. The term *Acadian* or *Cajun*, though often loosely applied, is recognized as belonging properly to those descended from the French inhabitants of Acadia, now Nova Scotia. *Creole* is a term much more difficult to define. It was originally applied to the Louisiana-born of European descent. There were in Louisiana, therefore, French, Spanish, and even German Creoles. The term has been loosely extended to include people of mixed blood, a dialect of French, a breed of ponies, a distinctive way of cooking, a type of house, and many other things. It is therefore not a precise term and cannot really be defined.

23
European Settlement Patterns

When the Spaniards took over the administration of Louisiana they generally confirmed the established French practices in granting land to new settlers. The grants along the Mississippi and other streams were commonly six to eight arpents wide and forty arpents deep. The grantee, under threat of losing his land, was given three years to clear the property back for a distance of two arpents, build and maintain levees, and construct a road forty feet wide next to the levee. He then had to dig parallel drainage ditches the length of his property from levee to backswamp, and he had to build culverts over the ditches where they crossed the road.

This system of running property lines at right angles to the river, from front lands to backswamp, worked out very well for those grants located on the outside, or convex side, of a meander, for here the lines kept getting farther and farther apart away from the river. The owner had an increasing width of land, with more to cultivate and more backswamp for timber. But what of the grantee who got his land on the inside, or concave side, of the meander? His property lines quickly converged so that his cultivated acreage was much reduced, and he might have too little or too much backswamp. Few people wished to have property on the inside of meanders. The Spanish authorities wanted the land continuously occupied so that someone

would be responsible for building and maintaining levees and roads. To bring this about they granted twice as much frontage, or twelve arpents, on the points that occupied the inside of meanders. If this was not attractive enough, the land was sometimes granted outright to neighboring owners.

Across the great Atchafalaya swamp, in the grassy prairies of the Attakapas and Opelousas districts, the grazing of cattle was frequently more important than field agriculture. A long, narrow strip of land

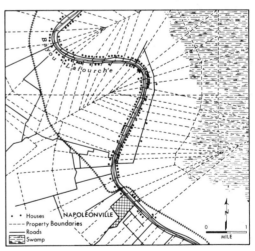

MAP 37
Landholding boundaries (dashed lines) and houses (black dots) indicate the manner in which settlers arranged their holdings. Note how landholdings taper from front to back on the inside and outside of bends in the bayou.

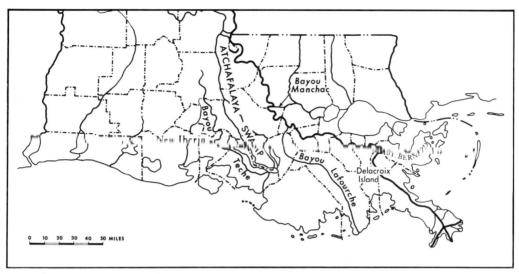

MAP 38
Index map of important landmarks

might be all right for growing crops, but it was a poor shape for a pasture. The Spaniards were experienced cattle raisers, and they changed the system in some instances and granted square or rectangular leagues. A Spanish league of those times was nearly 4,500 of our acres, so this made a fair-sized ranch, or *vacherie,* as it was called by the French.

It has been pointed out that in Louisiana two systems of beef cattle raising met—the Spanish system coming from the west, and the Anglo-Saxon system coming from the east. A whole series of items—saddles, bridles, ropes, clothing, and the like—was different for the two. But more important, with the Spaniards, cattle raising was a special activity. The Spanish vaquero did nothing but look after the herd. Among the Anglo-Saxons, raising beef cattle was one part of general farming. The cattle ran loose in the woods most of the year. Seasonally the farmer became a cowboy, rounded up the animals, branded and marked them, then forgot about them for the rest of the year. It is not surprising that Spanish cattle were better bred and generally in better condition.

The Spaniards also imposed strict regulations on the handling of cattle. They had to be marked with the owner's brand by the time they were eighteen months old; otherwise, they were shot. The Spaniards knew that rules were necessary if the quality of the cattle was to be maintained. They did not want the open range infested with wild, unclaimed animals.

The Spaniards got the notion that if they planted colonies of Spanish-speaking immigrants among the Louisiana French they might, in time, build a colony sympathetic to Spain rather than to France. Consequently, late in the eighteenth century, they brought to the New World groups of Isleños. These people were called Isleños because many of them, although not all, came from the Canary Islands. One group was settled at Delacroix Island in what is now St. Bernard Parish. Here alone the Spanish language lives to this day in Louisiana.

Other colonies were set up in the Valenzuela district on Bayou Lafourche, on Bayou Manchac, and at New Iberia on Bayou Teche. The New Iberia colony was settled by people from mainland Spain. They were primarily interested in raising cattle, and they helped to install in French Louisiana the Spanish methods of handling range cattle. Southwestern prairie

130

and marsh Louisiana became the easternmost extensions of the Spanish-American cattle complex that dominated the western United States and extended southward through Latin America.

Spanish attitudes and methods regarding cattle stood in marked contrast to those of the upland, piney-woods Anglo-Saxons, as pointed out above. The latter combined western European traditions with traits acquired on the Atlantic seaboard and carried them westward. Annual burning of the woodland pastures and drives to market were other features of the Anglo-Saxon system.

Like other minority groups settling in French Louisiana, the Spanish-speaking settlers were largely absorbed by the French. There remain today many family names of Spanish origin borne by people who are otherwise French Louisianians. Among these Spanish family names are Cortinas, Rodrigue, Gomez, Perez, Chavez, Gonzales, Martinez, Suarez,

Romero, Sanchez, and Dies. Aside from some square and rectangular land grants, the Spanish left little else that has permanently marked the land and is distinctly Spanish.

There were, therefore, in the latter part of the eighteenth century two quite distinct major rural settlement patterns, one French and one British colonial. The

Half-timbering with brick nogging   Fred Kniffen

A Creole house   Fred Kniffen

131

French pattern was based in the arpent-strip holdings we have described. Remember that there was a road on the front lands next to the levee. The houses of the inhabitants were set along this road, at right angles to it, so that the dwellings at the front of narrow strips constituted a continuous curving line of houses, just as they would on a street if it were not straight. Such a linear form is called a line settlement and, because the houses are close together, it is referred to as an agglomerated pattern (Maps 35 and 37). Villages were little knots along the line. In the villages were overshadowing churches and graveyards with vaults above the ground.

French houses, like the French settlements, were quite unlike those of the British areas. In the first place, the French never built log houses like those of the British. If they used logs for buildings, they were set upright in a trench (*poteaux en terre*), like the timbers in a stockade or palisade. The upright logs were plastered over and topped with a palmetto thatch roof. The floor was simply the tamped earth. Such houses survived in South Louisiana until a few years ago.

The French Creole houses, many of which survive to this day, were much more elaborate. They were constructed over a very heavy framework of timbers, jointed and pegged together. The spaces between the timbers were filled with brick (*briquette entre poteaux*), or clay rolls clinging to sticks (*bousillage*). Over the outside and hiding the construction was a board siding. The siding might be omitted where the front porch overhang protected the wall. The wall was plastered and whitewashed, strongly contrasting with the unpainted cypress siding covering the rest of the house.

These houses were more or less square in plan, had gabled or hip roofs and deep front porches built into the structure of the houses rather than being stuck on. Chimneys were centrally located in the smaller houses and never built on the

Paling fence   Fred Kniffen

outside of the structures, as they were on the houses of British settlers.

Around the yard of the French dwelling was a paling fence made of cypress slabs driven into the ground close to each other. The fences kept chickens, hogs, and other marauders out of the yard and vegetable garden. Field fences were of a type we know today as post and rail. Heavy posts were set into the ground, and then holes or slots were cut through them, into which cypress rails were inserted. The French were more careful than the British were about confining their stock. For example, pigs were kept penned until fields were harvested and then turned loose to glean what was left of the crop.

The Anglo-Saxons of the Florida Parishes divided their land into irregular holdings by a system known as metes and bounds, which means that boundaries run independently of a regular survey system. On their large farms they often built their houses and barns in a spot remote from those of their neighbors. This meant that the roads connecting them with some village center were highly irregular. Such an irregular system with widely separated houses we call an isolated, or dispersed, pattern (Map 39). Each individual farmstead might occupy a clearing, with miles of forest between it

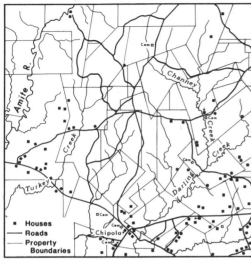

MAP 39
Irregular survey and settlement in St. Helena Parish. Compare to the patterns shown on Map 35.

Saddlebag house   Fred Kniffen

"I" house   Fred Kniffen

Dogtrot house   Fred Kniffen

and the next one. Graveyards were commonly family affairs. They were kept free of grass by annual "scrapings."

British buildings of the early days in Louisiana were largely made of logs. The logs were placed horizontally, one over the other, and joined at the corners by methods introduced into America by Germans. Chimneys were nearly always on the outside at the gable ends of the houses. Some of the houses had two separate parts with a passageway between them. These we call dogtrot houses. When the settler became well-to-do and wished to build a finer home, he constructed an "I" house. This might be a framed house with siding over the outside. The main part of the "I" house was one room deep, two or more rooms long, two full stories high, and had outside, gable-end chimneys. Rooms, porches, and even columns might be added in almost endless variety, but the basic part of the house was always the same.

The Anglo-Saxons also used rived paling fences for yards and gardens; but to surround cultivated fields they built snake, or worm, fences of split rails. These fences could be readily moved, for they were not fastened into the ground. It was a tradition brought from Europe, particularly by the Scotch-Irish, that cattle and hogs had the run of the woods. So it

133

was the British practice to fence stock *out* of their fields rather than to pen stock, turning them loose only after the harvest, as the French did.

There was a fundamental difference in land use between the small French farmer of the bayous and the small Anglo-Saxon hill farmer. The former occupied the deep, fertile soils of the floodplains. He cultivated the same ground indefinitely. The hill farmer had to shift his fields every few years because of soil impoverishment. He followed the Indian practice—slash and burn—in clearing new fields. The larger trees were girdled so that they would die, lose their foliage, and so permit the sun to get to the ground. Within the deadenings thus cre-

Snake rail fence   Sam Hilliard

ated, the brush was cut and it and other trash were piled and burned. Likewise in Indian fashion, the old fields could be reclaimed after a few years and cultivated

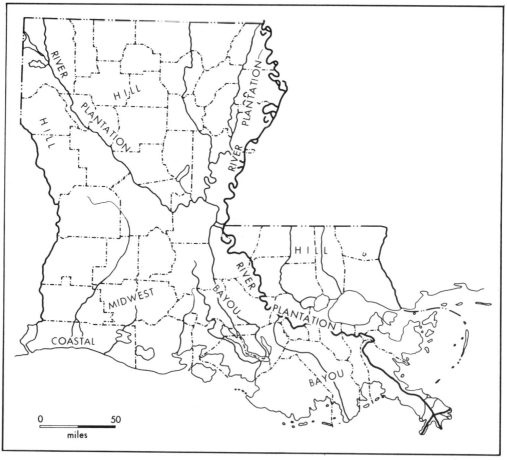

MAP 40
Distribution of rural settlement types

134

again. Eventually the dead trees fell to the ground and stumps rotted out, resulting in a truly cleared field.

The great differences between the French and British as illustrated in their settlement types extended into many other practices. For example, whenever possible the French ate wheat bread baked in their outdoor family ovens and they felt that corn was fit only for animals and slaves. The British relished corn bread baked in iron pots called Dutch ovens. The French used terms like *bayou*, *prairie*, and *coulee* to name natural features, while in British-settled areas there appear terms like *creek* and *branch*. To this day these differences between French and British Louisiana are very much in evidence.

Map 40 illustrates the distribution of rural settlement types in Louisiana. It designates hill, bayou, coastal, river plantation, and Midwest. The hill type applies to the Anglo-Saxon, dispersed settlement described above. The bayou type is the linear French settlement. The coastal type refers to the distinctive linear settlements of the cheniers. River plantation includes the large landholdings devoted to commercial crops, to be described shortly. The Midwest pattern came into being only with the settlement of the prairies and the rise of prairie rice as a commercial crop. This pattern is described in Chapter 28.

24

New Boundaries and New Commercial Crops

With the conclusion of the American Revolution in 1783, a change in international boundaries took place. The new United States claimed the 31st parallel as its southern boundary. However, the Spaniards claimed everything northward to and including Natchez. Finally, Spain and the United States agreed on the 31st parallel as a boundary. This meant that no part of present-day Louisiana belonged to the United States. Nevertheless, the Florida Parishes remained chiefly Anglo-Saxon in people and customs. This cultural structure was reinforced because American settlers, welcomed by the Spanish, continued to pour in.

It was in the years after the Revolution that indigo developed a disease so deadly that it became necessary to find a substitute for Louisiana's main export crop. Sugarcane was the answer. Cane had been grown in Louisiana for about fifty years but not in great quantities, and it had been used chiefly as a source of syrup for local use. Now the planters tried it in earnest. Experts from the West Indies were brought in, and sugar-making became a reality in the last years of the century.

The growers realized that climate has a great deal to do with successful production of sugarcane. For a while, Bayou Manchac was regarded as the northern limit of cane growing. North of there the planters were to substitute cotton for indigo, despite the expense involved in pro-

cessing it. South of the Manchac the boom in sugar went on at a great pace. Plantations grew larger and more numerous. Small landowners were displaced and they moved back from the river to the east or west across the Atchafalaya to the Teche and the prairies. It became increasingly difficult for the small holders to compete, especially since, as property owners on the river, they had to maintain levees and roads.

The sugar plantation came to have a very distinctive settlement pattern, in part derived from the older indigo plantations and in part copied from the sugar plantations of the West Indies. The plantation was agglomerated, in that the buildings were close together. The layout of streets and buildings was planned so that it formed a square or rectangle, in contrast to the homes of small farmers that were oriented to the curving river road. There was the "big house" of the owner, set up to and facing the river road and the boat landing. Back of it or to one side was the overseer's house. Back of that were the quarters, rows of houses all exactly alike and set square to the street. Then there were the commissary, the mule barns, and other outbuildings. Dominating the whole settlement was the sugarhouse with its tall chimney, visible for miles and not to be confused with any other work of man.

The sugar plantation of the early days was pretty much a closed community. It had its own people who lived there permanently. There was work to be done throughout the year, aside from planting, tending, harvesting, and processing the cane. There were roads and levees to build and maintain. There was wood to cut, to be used as fuel for cooking, for heating, and in part for operating the sugarhouse. There were important food crops—rice and corn—to grow for people and animals. There really was no season without important work to be done.

You will see from the description that a sugar plantation settlement pattern of the early years was very much like one of today. This should not be taken to mean that sugar planters are too old-fashioned to make changes. They were quick to take advantage of new technical developments that would aid in the processing of cane into sugar. For example, as early as 1822

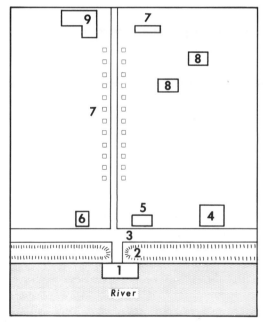

MAP 41
Type of plantation settlement pattern. Distance from the river to the sugarhouse is approximately half a mile. (1) landing; (2) levee; (3) road; (4) "big house" (usually occupied by the owner); (5) manager's house; (6) store; (7) quarters; (8) barns; (9) sugarhouse

cane was being ground with steam engines instead of with horse or mule power, as can still be seen in some parts of the state. In 1830 a vacuum pan for boiling the juice was invented, which was a great advance over the open kettle.

Sugar was such a profitable crop that its growing was extended farther and farther north, at one time up Red River to Natchitoches. In some years this was successful, but in others an early frost might reduce yields or even destroy the crop altogether. Gradually the area came to be limited by a 250-day growing season, which is defined as about the 31st parallel. Rainfall, too, is important, for sugarcane needs lots of water. Commercial production of sugarcane is restricted almost entirely to the bottomland soils of the Mississippi and Red rivers. Even here, cane does much better on the front-land soils than on the heavier and wetter soils toward the backswamp.

Sugarcane farming in Louisiana reached a peak of prosperity in the 1850s, when there were some 1,500 plantations in operation. A great number of the fine plantation homes were built at this time, reflecting the favorable economic situation.

The Louisiana Purchase, in 1803, followed a brief return of Louisiana from Spain to Napoleonic France. When the young United States took over the vast territory, there was naturally a shift in boundaries. But the Florida Parishes were not involved, only the Isle of Orleans and the area west of the river. Spain, in whose possession the Florida Parishes remained, stated correctly that they had not been involved in the original transfer from France to Spain and hence were not part of Louisiana. This claim could hardly be disputed, but the people of these parishes wanted to be part of the United States. There was a revolt, a short period of independence, and then late in 1810 the Florida Parishes became part of the United States.

In the southwestern section of Loui-

MAP 42
Area of Louisiana Purchase, 1803

siana the settlement of boundary disputes
did not come so quickly. Remember that
Louisiana originally was defined as the
drainage basin of the Mississippi, and
southwestern Louisiana is not drained by
the Mississippi system. French Louisiana
and Spanish Texas had generally recognized this fact, and the boundary between
them had roughly followed the drainage
division. After the Louisiana Purchase the
United States claimed lands west to the
Sabine River, and Spain claimed everything east to Rio Hondo, a small stream
near Natchitoches. No agreement was
reached until 1819, when the Sabine was
accepted as the western boundary of
Louisiana. Before the final settlement,
southwestern Louisiana was a "neutral
ground," or even, perhaps, a no-man's
land that offered refuge to those living
outside the law.

About 1810 there began another great
agricultural boom—in cotton. The time
was ripe for a cheap textile material,
because power looms were at hand for
cheap weaving, and the growth of cities
meant new markets. But, most important,
the cotton gin had been perfected, and
the time-consuming hand separation of
lint from seed was a thing of the past.
Louisiana was ready to participate in the
boom, for it had great areas of rich land,
some of which had been under cultivation
for a hundred years, and much more that
had never been broken.

The cultivation of cotton was not confined to the bottomlands; it spread into
the blufflands and even into the hills. The
large plantation developed mainly in the
bottomlands and blufflands. Because the
roads were so poor, most of the transportation of baled cotton was by water. The
great expansion of cotton growing in
Louisiana came with the development of
the steamboat, which also appeared in the
early nineteenth century. By midcentury
every stream, if navigable only at high-
water stage, had steamboats pushing into
it to bring in supplies and carry out
cotton.

The early cotton plantation pattern of settlement was much like that of the sugar plantation, except for the obvious substitution of a gin for a sugarhouse. In fact, during unfavorable times, when the tariff on sugar imports was low, sugar plantations turned temporarily to cotton growing. But there was a distinction other than crops. That was the difference between upland and lowland plantations. Lowland plantations showed strong French West Indies influences in methods of operation and in the architecture of the buildings. The upland plantations in the British-American areas showed a strong tradition of log construction and favored the "I" big house previously described.

If the upland plantation was not derived from the West Indies plantation, neither did it come directly from the plantations of tidewater Virginia or South Carolina. It seems to have been developed wherever the settlers encountered extensive sections of highly productive land. In Louisiana that meant the blufflands and the northern portions of the Red and Mississippi river valleys. The cultural background of the people who developed these plantations was that of the upland, rather than the tidewater, South.

The early cotton plantation, then, was much like the sugar plantation in its compactness and orderly arrangement of buildings and in its self-sufficiency. When the Civil War ended, cotton plantations, unlike sugar plantations, commonly adopted a system of tenant farming. The quarters of the tenants were moved out onto the land they farmed. Each tenant cared for his own stock, so that there were no large central mule barns to house the animals. Today, with the abandonment of tenancy, the pattern of the cotton plantation again has become compact, with quarters and tractor sheds concentrated around the big house.

With the spread of plantations in the bottomlands and blufflands, what was happening in the large areas of hill lands?

The virgin hill soils possessed a considerable degree of fertility. Where they lay within reach of water transportation, there was large-scale production of cotton, with slaves and other plantation features. However, within a few years the topsoil fertility declined, and erosion became a problem, especially on steep slopes. Large-scale cotton production then left the hills and became more and more confined to the fertile and erosion-free bottomlands. The abandoned lands became part of the system of subsistence farms so characteristic not only of the Louisiana hills but of the whole upland South.

Cotton as a cash crop found its way into the remotest hills. It could not be extensively grown because the soils were not good enough and, more important, because of poor transportation facilities for getting it to market. Its presence on the hill farms in no way interfered with the established pattern of subsistence farming. The chief food crops were sweet potatoes, corn, turnips, and black-eyed peas. There were also green vegetables, sugarcane for syrup, free-ranging hogs for meat, and some cattle. Hunting regularly added to the meat supply. There was a permanent garden plot near the house and fenced outfields surrounded by woods. These fields were shifted every few years to permit renewal of soil fertility. Plowing was usually straight up and down slope, in the manner brought from northern Ireland. Late in the eighteenth century William Dunbar, a scientific agriculturist and friend of Thomas Jefferson, is said to have introduced contour plowing into the Natchez district. Whether he did or not, contour plowing became universal on hill lands by 1900 and is still practiced wherever row crops are planted on hillsides. Contour plowing was adopted because it reduces erosion, adds no expense, and can be practiced on small, isolated fields. In short, it fits the subsistence system of agriculture. Related to contour plowing is the practice of terracing. Terraces are small ridges of earth, similar to levees, that are built across fields to prevent erosional gullying by controlling excess water runoff. Terraces are especially useful in minimizing erosion on very steep slopes, but are expensive to build and maintain. Not until the twentieth century, when government subsidies and technical aid became available, did terracing become common among small farmers. Both contour plowing and terracing leave distinctive imprints on the landscape.

The subsistence farm survived in some hill sections of Louisiana well into the present century. Even today many small farmers produce much of their own food, lumber, and firewood, but the subsistence farm is a thing of the past. In the modern world few are satisfied with such an existence.

25
The Last Hundred Years

The state enjoyed considerable prosperity throughout the first half of the nineteenth century, but between 1861 and 1865 the Civil War interrupted Louisiana's peaceful growth. Geographically, the war was a conflict over control of the Mississippi River. The North wished to hold the river in order to separate the South into two parts, and to maintain the traffic to and from the Gulf so important to its midwestern states. The North took New Orleans early in the war, occupied Baton Rouge, and eventually subdued Vicksburg and Port Hudson. The South successfully defended the Red River and stepped up the exploitation of the interior salt domes as a source of salt for the Confederacy.

After the war most Louisianians returned to their former occupations. Slavery had been abolished, but both planter and slave, as well as farmer, merchant, cattleman, and hunter, lived pretty much as they had before the war. Not until near the end of the 1800s did the state experience significant change.

A hundred years ago Louisiana had about a million inhabitants. There was only one real city, New Orleans. Most Louisianians lived in the country or in small towns, and agriculture was their main source of livelihood. Trapping, lumbering, and fishing were not nearly as important as they became later. Some salt was produced, but petroleum, gas, and sulphur were unheard of as Louisiana products.

The distribution of population over the state was not the same as it is now. There were few permanent inhabitants in the coastal marshes. Those who lived there practiced a little agriculture and cattle grazing on the cheniers to the west and on barrier islands such as Grand Isle, on old natural levees, and on the Five Islands to the east. The prairies, too, were not heavily populated. On the prairie streams, especially to the east, were the line settlements of the Acadians and others of French descent. On the open prairies were grazing cattle and little else. Along the streams of the Atchafalaya Basin, from the Teche to the Mississippi, were the line settlements of the small farmers and the great plantations. Sugarcane was the principal crop. In the blufflands east of the Mississippi, along the Mississippi itself, and along the Upper Red River were more plantations where cotton was the chief crop. In the pine flatwoods and hills were dispersed farm clearings where cotton was the cash crop and stock ran loose in the woods, which were cleared of their underbrush by annual burning.

During the past hundred years the face of Louisiana has been transformed by technical and economic developments and by growth and shifts of population. Of chief geographical importance are the emergence of means of transportation, control of the Mississippi, settlement of the prairies, mineral production, shifts in agricultural emphasis, industrialization, and the growth of cities.

We will begin our discussion of important geographical developments in Louisiana during the past hundred years with transportation. Of course, transportation is actually a series of techniques that make geographical developments possible.

We have already described the importance of bateaux in the early commerce of European Louisiana. Even before them, the local dugout pirogue and the northern canoe were used by settlers who carried on a limited trade. What happened in the evolution of transportation was a combination of growing demand for the carriage of goods and people and an increasing technological efficiency in meeting those demands.

As we have seen, waterways were the first highways because they were ready to use. No settlement could be far from a usable stream in the early days. Even so, there were many difficulties in traveling by water, many problems to solve. Going downstream was quite easy, but what about going upstream against the current? And suppose, with all the streams running north and south as they do, that one needed to go east and west?

Large, heavy-timbered flatboats carried the produce of the Mississippi Basin to New Orleans. They were constructed in wide variety, but they all had great capacity and all were cumbersome. Sometimes they were loaded with various live animals, such as cattle or hogs. Then they were called arks. They also were called broadhorns, because the long sweeps used to guide them might rise from either side like the horns of a steer. They served well on a downstream course, and they could be broken up and sold for their timber in New Orleans. Only rarely were they dragged back upstream.

The early bateau was a much easier boat than a flatboat to work upstream. A better solution was the keelboat, so called

A keelboat

Harper's Weekly

because its frame consisted of ribs set in a central foundation timber, or keel. The keelboat was a long vessel with a considerable cargo capacity. It rested lightly on the water, so that it projected below the surface only a foot or so. This meant that the portion of the craft against which the current pushed was reduced to a minimum. Some keelboats were open in the center; others were decked over and had a cabin for passengers. All had a cleated walkway on either side. Along these the crew walked rapidly forward, set their poles on the river bottom, and then pushed the boat upstream as they slowly walked aft. When the water was too deep for poling, the crew went ashore and scrambled along the water's edge, cordelling or lining the vessel with a long rope. At times, when the shore was bad for walking and the water swift and deep, the crew leaned over the side, grasped the willows on the bank and pulled the boat upstream. This was known as brushing or bushwhacking. In calm water the keelboat was rowed, or it sailed before a favorable wind.

We have seen that not all needs for transportation could be supplied by streams, for the streams did not always go where people wanted to go. Sometimes they were too difficult to navigate, particularly upstream. As a result, roads were built at a very early date. Some of the earliest were those built along streams parallel to the levees. These roads connected residents along the stream, and they provided an easier route up swift streams. One of these roads that survives is the River Road along the Mississippi, situated about where it was originally laid out over two hundred years ago.

Two famous early Louisiana roads were laid out east and west across the direction of the major streams. One was the Natchitoches—Nacogdoches Road that we have talked about. The other was the Old Spanish Trail, which ran west from Baton Rouge, got with difficulty through the Atchafalaya Basin, then made its way across the prairies over somewhat easier terrain. Its crossings of prairie streams are still recognizable.

Other roads might be called simply feeders, in that they connected occupied back country with points on navigable streams. Such was the case with the Felicianas. There the good bluffland soil early led to the establishment of upland plantations, first for the growing of tobacco and, later, for cotton. You will recall we mentioned that the roads worked themselves down through the distinctive soil (loess) of the area in steep-sided trenches called guts. Many of them, most unused, can be observed even today, paralleling modern highways. The roads reached the Mississippi at landings such as Bayou Sara (St. Francisville) and Port Hudson.

Other early roads were built for military purposes, to permit the quick movement of troops through country otherwise unprovided with more than paths or trails and with no usable waterways. One such was the Jackson Military Road, built to connect Nashville, Tennessee, with New Orleans. This road, parts of which can still be seen, came through the eastern part of the Florida Parishes to Madisonville on the north shore of Lake Pontchartrain. From there, connection with New Orleans was by boat across the lake. These are a few of the early roads. Others are shown on the map accompanying this section.

Building roads, until very recent times, was a difficult matter. They had to be built on naturally high ground, on ridges or along natural levees, wherever possible. Bridges were too expensive and difficult to build. If streams were shallow enough they were forded. If they were too deep to ford, traffic had to be ferried across. Roads built on sandy soils were not made impassable by rain, but if built on clay, rain made them almost useless for wheeled vehicles.

Special methods had to be used where there was no possibility of avoiding difficult terrain. Short, boggy spots could be

143

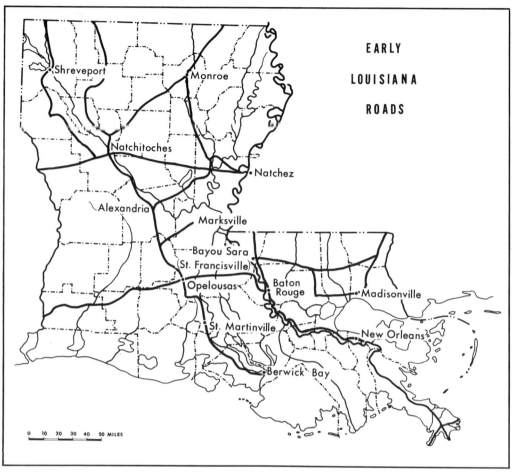

EARLY

LOUISIANA

ROADS

0 10 20 30 40 50 MILES

MAP 43

Early roads were the only means of getting about in places where boats couldn't go. Early roads were crude, often little more than trails, but as population and traffic increased they were improved.

made passable by placing logs side by side to make a firm but rough surface, a practice called corduroying. Much smoother were plank roads, which were made of heavy boards nailed to stringers to produce an all-weather surface. The most remarkable solution of all was the construction, in 1874, of a covered road for a distance of nine miles east of Shreveport. The earth was graded up into a ridge. A roof on posts shed the rain and kept the road firm and dry. The comple-

tion of the railway between Vicksburg and Shreveport in 1887 put the covered road out of business.

It is interesting to note how a new technique can make old practices obsolete. It is difficult for most people at any given time to believe that there can ever be any advance over their ways of doing things. Persons yet living remember the time when there were no automobiles and no airplanes; the steam locomotive was thought to be the ultimate advancement in transportation. So it was with the early roads we have discussed. They were built and maintained where waterways did not serve better. They were certainly regarded as the last word in transportation. With the coming of railroads, to be considered in the next chapter, the roads fell into disuse and were no longer kept in repair. The modern system of highways came into being only well into the twentieth century when the automobile became a practical mode of transportation. For a hundred years the through road connecting major cities was insignificant as a means of communication.

26

Steamboats, Railroads, and Modern Transportation

With the introduction of the steamboat early in the nineteenth century there was a great revolution in transportation, which more than ever emphasized the importance of waterways. The steamboat was a significant technical advance over the keelboat, because its power was provided by an engine and not by men.

Steamships were first developed in arms of the sea where there was little or no current. They sat fairly low in the water and their engines were below deck. Such a vessel was the *Orleans*, which came downriver to New Orleans in 1812. The trip downstream from the Ohio River, where the ship had been built, was quick and easy. But it was a very different story when the steamship started back upstream, because its engines lacked the power to push the vessel against the

A side-wheeler steamboat

Baton Rouge *State-Times*

current. The *Orleans* thereafter spent its years on the lower river; it clearly was not the type for the Mississippi.

Then there entered the contest to design a proper vessel the same Henry Shreve who, many years later, was to clear the raft out of Red River. His first solution was to build a vessel with engines powerful enough to buck the current of the Mississippi. His steamship, the *Enterprise*, did make its way up the river, but it had to work so hard that it was all but torn to pieces. Power alone was not the answer.

Shreve was an experienced riverman, and he called on his years of observation to help him put into practical form a revolutionary idea. It was that the steam*boat* should rest *on* rather than *in* the water, like a steam*ship*. This is the essential difference between a river steamboat and an ocean or lake steamship. As part of the change, Shreve put the engines on the deck and laid them down instead of standing them up, as on steamships. There was an engine on either side, each connected independently to the paddlewheel on its side. This enabled one wheel to go ahead while the other reversed, giving the vessel great maneuverability. The name of the first new kind of vessel was the *George Washington;* the year was 1816. With this new kind of design, the steamboat came to dominate the rivers in a very few years.

Steamboats invaded every Louisiana stream that was navigable, even if only at flood stage. They reached a peak of importance about 1860. Old maps show the extent to which they penetrated nearly every nook and cranny of the state. Evidence is in the form of symbols showing head of navigation (the farthest point navigable upstream) on rivers no longer used. The maps also give names of steamboat landings long since forgotten. There are old pilots' guides showing distances to landings on streams now hardly known. Within the last fifty years there was regular steamboat service across Lake

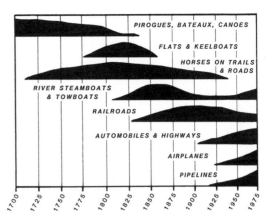

FIG. 25
Changing transportation modes through time

Pontchartrain between New Orleans and Madisonville. A line of packets ran regularly between Plaquemine on the Mississippi and points on Bayou Teche. French Settlement, on the Lower Amite River, was connected by steamboat with New Orleans; there was no direct communication of any kind between French Settlement and the northern part of Livingston Parish, the parish in which it lies. After 1860, the rise of railroads reduced the steamboats to less and less importance; they reached a low point about 1900.

Modern towboats that push great clusters of barges carry an increasing amount

Modern river barge passing under Sunshine Bridge
Don Nugent

147

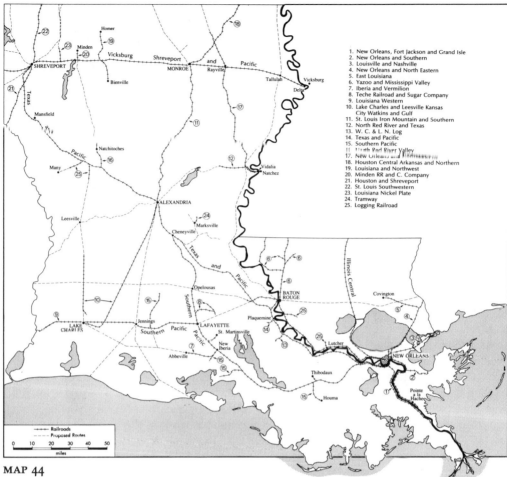

1. New Orleans, Fort Jackson and Grand Isle
2. New Orleans and Southern
3. Louisville and Nashville
4. New Orleans and North Eastern
5. East Louisiana
6. Yazoo and Mississippi Valley
7. Iberia and Vermilion
8. Teche Railroad and Sugar Company
9. Louisiana Western
10. Lake Charles and Leesville Kansas
    City Watkins and Gulf
11. St. Louis Iron Mountain and Southern
12. North Red River and Texas
13. W. C. & L. N. Log
14. Texas and Pacific
15. Southern Pacific
16. North Red River Valley
17. New Orleans and Pikhninniiiiiiii
18. Houston Central Arkansas and Northern
19. Louisiana and Northwest
20. Minden RR and C. Company
21. Houston and Shreveport
22. St. Louis Southwestern
23. Louisiana Nickel Plate
24. Tramway
25. Logging Railroad

MAP 44

Railroads in Louisiana in 1895. A number of additional routes are shown as "proposed," but not all were eventually built.

of cargo, but this is a very different matter. Traffic is largely restricted to the Mississippi and the western portion of the Intracoastal Canal; cargoes are primarily the products of the oil fields. The old steamboats carried people and the products of the countryside—cotton, livestock, and the like—and brought the goods needed by every individual. Steamboats were a part of everyday life; towboats and barges are remote from our ordinary experiences.

Railroads came to Louisiana at a comparatively early date—in the 1830s. Their first function was to provide an all-weather roadway for areas that could

afford them. Like the roads they replaced, they were essentially feeders of the steamboats on the rivers. One of the earliest ran between Clinton and Port Hudson, to connect a rich cotton-producing hinterland with the Mississippi. Serving the same purpose was an early railroad between Woodville, Mississippi, and Bayou Sara on the river. Another in New Orleans ran between the Mississippi and Lake Pontchartrain, thus connecting the two navigable waterways. Still another ran between New Orleans and Proctorville (modern Shell Beach) on Lake Borgne, in hopes of providing a route to the sea as an alternative to the difficult mouths of the Mississippi River.

By the 1850s the railroads were moving into direct competition with water trans-

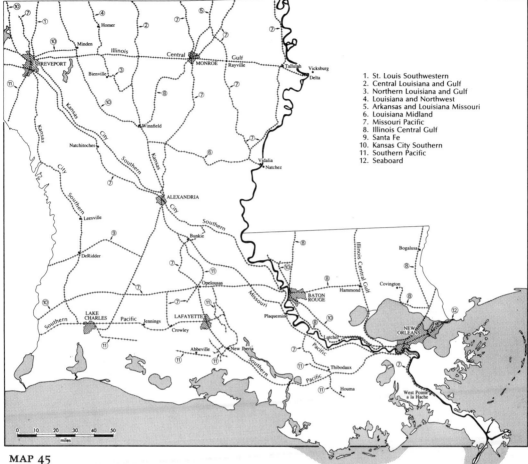

MAP 45
Present-day railroads in Louisiana

1. St. Louis Southwestern
2. Central Louisiana and Gulf
3. Northern Louisiana and Gulf
4. Louisiana and Northwest
5. Arkansas and Louisiana Missouri
6. Louisiana Midland
7. Missouri Pacific
8. Illinois Central Gulf
9. Santa Fe
10. Kansas City Southern
11. Southern Pacific
12. Seaboard

port. The forerunner of the Illinois Central line was pushing its way between New Orleans and Chicago. Everywhere the railroads won out. They took over passenger traffic quickly and cut heavily into freight. Railroads reached a peak of mileage in Louisiana during the early twentieth century, especially when the period of industrial lumbering produced hundreds of miles of logging track.

Today the railroads must meet the competition from other means of transportation: automobiles, buses, trucks, planes, pipelines, and river barges. Passenger traffic has largely been lost. In freight traffic the railroads have shown that they can hold their own by devising new and faster means of carrying goods.

Modern highways are part of the automobile era that came of age only in the second quarter of the present century. They are possible because of new construction skills and almost unlimited public financial support. Now all-weather

The Luling-Destrehan Bridge across the Mississippi

Louisiana Highway Department

149

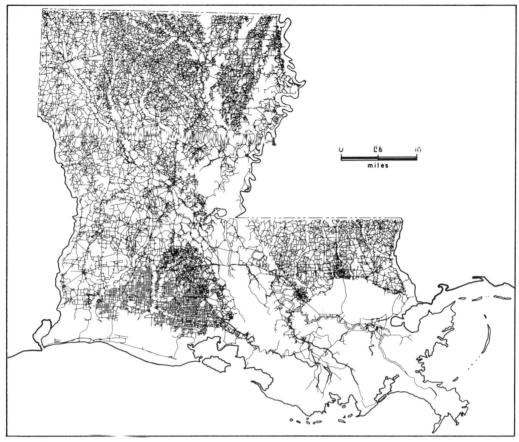

miles

MAP 46

Roadways of all types in Louisiana as of 1960.
Note how few penetrate the great alluvial
valley of the Mississippi and the coastal
marshes. Note too the rectangularity of the
road pattern in the southwestern prairies and
the irregularity of roads in the Florida Parishes
and in northern Louisiana. Such patterns in
the Florida Parishes reflect irregular survey,
whereas in northern Louisiana the survey was
rectangular but topographically is such that
the roads cannot follow survey lines.

roads can be built over any terrain and
thus can follow straight lines across even
swamp and bog (Map 46). Great bridges
span the Mississippi, and ferries have
become things of the past. It is notable in
many rural communities that the trunk
roads of today have almost no reference
to the local inhabitants but instead are
designed for through traffic across the

area (Map 47). This necessitates a new
series of feeder roads from farms to the
new highway. Thus, the patterns of settlement and communication are altered by
changed values and technical abilities.

Even if it is now possible to build
highways almost anywhere, it will be a
long time before a new road pattern dominates the state. The map of present Louisiana roadways still reflects terrain
difficult for road building, systems of land
survey, density of population, and other
factors (see Map 46). Note how few the
roads are in the marshes and in the
swampy areas of the Mississippi alluvial
valley. The flatness of surface, the recency
of agricultural settlement, and the application of the township survey system
outline the prairie section almost exactly
with a dense system of north-south and
east-west roads. In the alluvial valley the

roads are largely confined to the levees. In hilly North Louisiana the terrain has led to an irregular system of roads on the divides between the streams.

Pipelines for carrying petroleum and natural gas first appeared early in the century. Now they constitute a tremendous network over the state. Even though they are mostly buried, they leave unmistakable surface evidence in the form of straight swaths through forests, special bridges across rivers, compressor stations, and clusters of neat "company" houses for the families of pipeline employees (Map 48). To be mentioned in the same context are the cross-country paths of electric power lines, a fairly recent addition to the scene brought by a new ability to convey electricity for long distances and by a greatly increased demand for electric power.

Airplanes have become major means of transportation only since World War II. Airports and navigational aids are obvious markers on the land. Transportation by air is clearly still in its infancy as

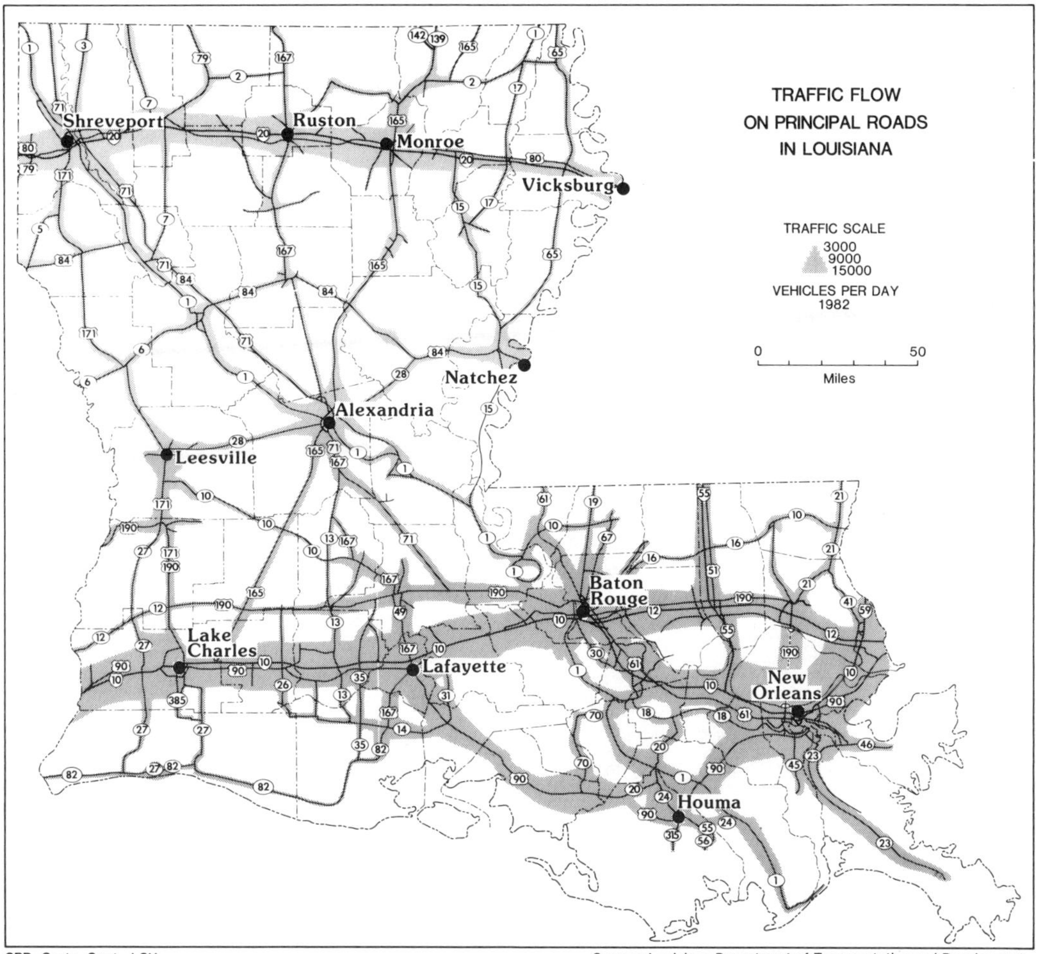

MAP 47

Only major highways are shown on this map. Traffic volume is shown in gray. The widths of the gray lines are proportionate to the number of vehicles passing per day.

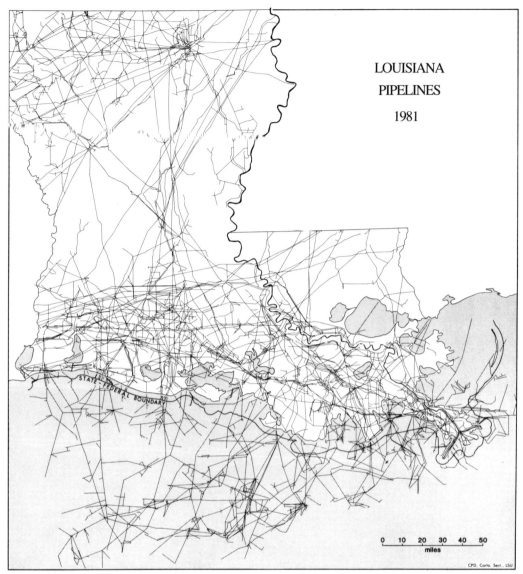

LOUISIANA
PIPELINES
1981

STATE-FEDERAL BOUNDARY

0   10   20   30   40   50
              miles

CPD, Carto. Sect., LSU

MAP 48

*Pipelines serve as important transportation
arteries, carrying a variety of liquids, mostly
oil and gas.*

indicated by rapid change, ever larger
planes, increased capacity for freight, and
the search for larger facilities. The question of to what extent planes will be able
to directly serve the smaller communities
remains unanswered.

As geographers our main concern with
transportation is the matter of its effects
on the earth's surface. Some of the direct

ones are implied by what we have discussed. We have mentioned one of the
indirect ones in referring to the effects of
new, through trunk roads on rural service
roads. There are many others. One may
think of the decline of businesses in small
communities after automobiles made it
possible to shop in larger towns. There is
the obliteration of buildings that accompanies the construction of a superhigh-
way through cities. There is the
orientation of prairie towns to the railroad, with streets at an angle with the

cardinal directions, showing that the railroad was there first. Along the Mississippi there are ghost towns that were once thriving ports that died with the decline of steamboat traffic. There are other former river towns that show an attempt to adapt to changing dominance of types of transportation: along the levee is crooked Front Street with century-old buildings, now largely abandoned. Perhaps a mile away is a newer business section along the railroad. Then a bit farther away is the newest, most thriving section along the highway.

Modern transportation has certainly caused the decline of many towns, and it has definitely strengthened others. Nevertheless, the major centers of the modern transportation system were major centers during steamboat and railroad supremacy. There is no great city that owes its existence entirely to highways or air facilities. New Orleans remains the focus of the transportation system, just as it has always been. Baton Rouge, Shreveport, Monroe, Alexandria, and Lake Charles date back to the older days of transportation. Is this because these places are so superbly located for all forms of transportation, or is this continued dominance simply a matter of inertia on the part of other communities?

27
Controlling the Mississippi

We learned early in our study that the Mississippi River is the most important single part of Louisiana's natural endowment. The greater part of the state was built by the Mississippi. The river has provided our best soils, created conditions favorable for aquatic life, and provided a highway for water transportation. It has even been a subject for song and story. But we are interested primarily in control of the Mississippi by man, the prevention of floods, and its improvement for navigation.

Great and uncontrolled floods have occurred ever since man has lived on the river. When Iberville's party ascended the stream in 1699 it was in flood to such an extent that Iberville was for a while uncertain that it was actually the Mississippi. Historical accounts state that in 1782 and again in 1840 the river flooded the whole countryside between the blufflands. So, flooding is not a new thing; what is new is human vulnerability to damage. The Indians did not suffer from flooding. They lived on the higher sections of land and awaited the retreat of high water to plant their crops. Europeans occupied more and more of the floodplain, extended their farms to the limits of the natural levees, and built their towns there. Nothing they could do could guarantee freedom from damage by high water.

The building of artificial levees on top of the natural ones was the first effort at protection. This came early; we have mentioned levees for New Orleans in 1722 and also the Spanish law that obliged land grantees along the river to build and maintain levees. As late as 1829 a public act required the building of levees throughout the state. Once started, levees were necessary everywhere, because each individual holding or town could not be completely surrounded by dikes, an island in the floodwaters.

Although levees solve some old problems, they introduce new problems as well. One is the matter of backwater. Obviously all streams and their tributaries cannot have levees. How would rainwater run off? Levees keep water out of streams as well as in them. When major trunk streams are carrying floodwaters, their levels rise between retaining embankments instead of flowing over their banks as they would without dikes. The high waters of the larger streams push back up the smaller tributaries. Eventually this backwater reaches a place where there are no levees and inundates the surrounding bottomlands.

During the late nineteenth century large areas of Avoyelles, Catahoula, and La Salle parishes became so subject to backwater flooding that farmers were forced to give up agriculture. At the same time there was a greatly increased northern market for fish, and rail transportation providing ice and carriage to market was present. The combination drew the

Artificial levee

Louisiana Department of Commerce and Industry

deposed farmers into fishing, which they were taught by experienced fishermen from as far away as the upper Mississippi and Ohio rivers. Prosperity was the lot of the fishermen until the 1950s when flood control and pollution began reduction of the catch. No longer prosperous, the fishermen have returned to the almost unfamiliar occupation of farming. Soybean fields have replaced swamps, and old fishing boats are now watering troughs for livestock.

Another problem introduced by levees was of a quite different nature. This was the temptation of those living on one side of the river to break down the levees on the other side, so relieving the pressure of the high water. Naturally, each side wished to protect its own levees from destruction. Horseback patrols and dynamited levees were not uncommon only some fifty years ago. Quite unintentional

was the flooding caused by rice farmers who opened the levee so their crops could be irrigated. Too often the operation got out of control and a crevasse and flooding resulted. In 1850 an act imposed a fine and imprisonment on anyone making an unauthorized cut in the levee. A pipe over the levee through which water could be siphoned was an acceptable solution to the problem.

Prior to the Civil War the building and maintenance of levees were controlled locally, which meant the absence of broad supervision and the prevalence of rivalries. During the war the levees quite naturally were badly neglected and fell into disrepair. In 1872, the federal government took on a large measure of supervision of the levees. Although there remained a great deal of local control, there was now an overall view of the problem of flood control. Special problem areas could be sought out and the re-

Repairing break in artificial levee   Elemore Morgan

sources of the national government brought to bear on them.

Despite better supervision, flood-control measures were not sufficient to prevent the highly destructive flood of 1927. After that year the U.S. Army Corps of Engineers took over direction of planning and construction. An experiment station established at Vicksburg, Mississippi, had for its function the understanding of the river's activities, at both flood and normal stages. Plans called for a revision of the levees, a changed alignment of the river, and the construction of spillways, or emergency outlets.

Levees were made higher, broader, and stronger. New techniques made the work much faster, with substitution of power draglines for mule-drawn slips. Attention was given to the nature of the ground on which the embankments rested, to see that it would not disintegrate with high water. Where the river indicated a tendency to open a channel across a neck and so create a cutoff, new levees were laid out, and efforts were made to assist the river in performing the operation by digging a new channel. It was assumed that decreasing the length of the river's channel would increase its velocity and so hurry the floodwaters into the Gulf.

Flooded church, Concordia Parish, 1973
Sam Hilliard

156

In Louisiana, the Mississippi itself is completely bordered by artificial levees, except for that portion of its course which impinges against the high terrace bluff on the east bank north of Baton Rouge. Where the river moves west away from the bluff sufficiently to expose good agricultural floodplain, it is necessary to build a levee from the bluff around it on three sides. Such a situation exists at the 35,000-acre Angola prison farm in West Feliciana Parish. The average height of the Mississippi levees above their base on the natural ground level is about twenty-five feet. One would expect that this should increase in height toward the mouth of the river, but instead it becomes lower. Particularly toward its mouths the Mississippi loses rather than gains volume,

Concrete revetments   David Prior

since it lacks tributaries and can rapidly distribute its flow into the broad Gulf through many outlets. Louisiana rivers

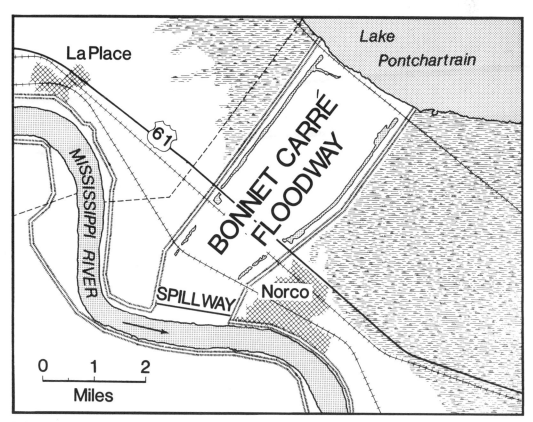

MAP 49
Designed to protect New Orleans from floods, the spillway gates may be opened to divert water into Lake Pontchartrain.

157

Ship passing along the Mississippi during high water appears to tower over cemetery.

David Prior

other than the Mississippi lack such well-developed artificial levee systems.

Two major spillways, the Bonnet Carré and the Atchafalaya, are fairly recent innovations designed to help dispose of flood waters harmlessly. Each is capable of carrying large volumes of water out of the Mississippi to the Gulf, thus relieving the pressure on the levees of the lower river. Such relief is necessary, for the leveed Mississippi channel at New Orleans can handle only 1,250,000 cubic feet of water per second (cfs), far less than the

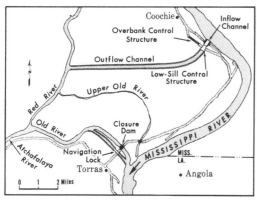

MAP 50
Solution to the Atchafalaya problem? Stability was achieved by controlling discharge from the Mississippi into the Red-Atchafalaya System.

maximum flow of the river. Bonnet Carré Spillway, built in the 1930s, is a two-mile-wide, five-to-six-mile-long channel that can divert 250,000 cfs from the Mississippi to Lake Pontchartrain. It has been used several times, successfully keeping the height of water on the New Orleans levees at a harmless level (Map 49).

The Atchafalaya Spillway is a much larger structure, 15 miles wide and capable of diverting over 600,000 cfs from the Mississippi to join the Red River's flow. During extreme high water the Morganza Floodway is opened, pouring an additional 500,000 cfs or more into the eastern portion of the Atchafalaya Basin. First opened during the severe flood of 1973, the Atchafalaya system managed to keep Ole Man River from topping his levees, but at many places river water was within a few feet of the levee crest.

Although the modern levee and diversion system dates from the 1920s and 1930s, the Atchafalaya system had its origins much earlier. Beginning in 1840 the raft choking the head of the Atchafalaya was removed to permit navigation between it and the Red and the Mississippi. From a common point it is 155 miles to the Gulf by the Atchafalaya; by the Mississippi, 325 miles. Slowly the Atchafalaya began to take more and more

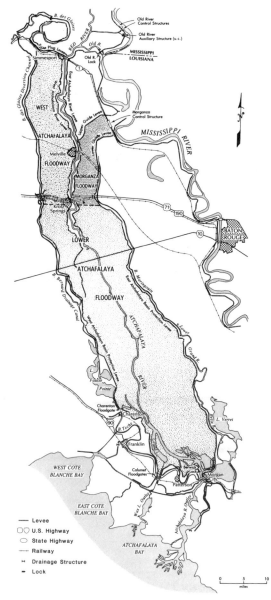

the sea, with no current and with salt-to-brackish water. Certainly this would improve navigation by eliminating silt-depositing water. But one change would be irreparable—the loss of abundant fresh water in the lower river for industrial and domestic use. The solution to the problem has been to sever the Atchafalaya from the Mississippi except for controlled discharges of water and navigation locks (Map 51). The Atchafalaya is now the lower course of Red River. The reduction of the amount of water discharging into it should prevent the Atchafalaya from further deepening and broadening its channel.

The chief difficulty in improving the Mississippi for navigation centers on the bars at the river's mouths. Not only do the bars reduce the depth of channels, but the different temperatures of river and Gulf waters induce another hazard to navigation in the form of fogs. From an earlier chapter you will remember that in 1718 Pauger, the French engineer, suggested that channels could be scoured naturally across the bars if confined by artificial levees. This was put into effect by James Eads in 1878 at South Pass. To this day South Pass maintains a depth across the bar of about 30 feet and requires little dredging. The same solution was tried at Southwest Pass, the other principal navigation channel, but those jetties did not work so well. The bar would silt up to a depth of 18 feet if left

MAP 51

The entire Atchafalaya floodway from Old River to the Gulf

water from the Upper Mississippi by enlarging its channel. A few years ago it was taking one third of all water coming down the Mississippi, and no Red River water got into the Mississippi. The threat was real and imminent that the Atchafalaya would take over the water from the Upper Mississippi completely, leaving the Lower Mississippi simply a long arm of

Morganza control structure　　　　　David Prior

alone. Dredging during the flood season is required to maintain a depth of 40 feet.

An alternative to the natural routes across the bars lies in a newly constructed channel, the Mississippi River-Gulf outlet, running southeast from New Orleans some 76 miles to the open sea, as compared to 116 miles through the lower river. This new channel was opened for use in 1960, but its complete success is by no means assured. Connection by lock with the Mississippi is slow, and it is difficult to maintain a channel through unstable marsh deposits.

Above the bars the river naturally maintains a channel depth of 35 to 40 feet, with very little assistance, 240 miles upstream to Baton Rouge. Above Baton Rouge the river shallows in a number of spots to depths prohibitive to deepwater vessels. There, maintenance for inland navigation consists primarily of removal of snags and the installation of lights and other aids.

28
Settlement of the Prairies

The prairies of southwestern Louisiana were the last of the great regions of the state to become truly settled and to make a distinctive contribution to the state's agricultural economy—the growing of prairie rice. A major reason for the lateness of the area's development was the absence of adequate transportation. The streams ran the wrong way and were hardly sufficient in size to permit navigation. The situation was changed in 1882 when the Southern Pacific railroad was completed, thus establishing through transportation between the prairies and the outside world.

Prior to the period of major settlement the prairies were subject to three cultural influences. From the east came the Acadian French to establish along the prairie streams a true South Louisiana settlement pattern. The land was divided in arpent strips; the farmstead buildings stood on the frontlands and formed a linear pattern; the houses were commonly of the Creole type; the fences were a yard paling fence and field post-and-rail type. In every front yard there was a chinaball, or chinaberry, tree, its branches clipped back to provide firewood and to thicken the crown for better shade.

Cotton, corn, potatoes, and other crops were raised in the lighter soils of the levee, largely for home consumption. The *platin* or *marais* ponds were crudely fenced to keep the animals out, and on their shallow floors were raised crops of

"providence" rice. This term meant that if Providence provided rain and other necessary conditions there would be a crop. The rice served primarily to feed the people at home. Around the farmstead were hogs and chickens, also for local consumption.

In the open areas was the cash crop, cattle. Cattle were handled according to the methods of the Spaniards to the west, but with French terms substituting for Spanish ones. For example, *vacherie* was used instead of *rancho*. This was the second important cultural influence, the Spanish cattle complex. Cattle were driven to market, or at least to landings where boats would carry them on to New Orleans. The prairie dwellers thus were not dependent on other means of transportation. The third cultural influence

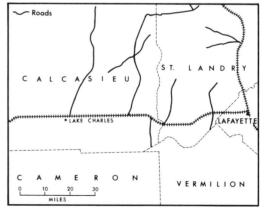

MAP 52
Southwest Louisiana in 1884

was that of Anglo-Americans, generally coming from the north. This influence was relatively light. It seems to have contributed such items as certain barn types, outside chimneys, Dutch ovens, and corn bread.

The completion of the railroad in 1882 brought a flood of settlers and boom times to the prairies. Here was land to be had for fifty cents an acre, or it could be homesteaded. Additional land could be had free as a timber claim, on which the claimant planted trees in the treeless prairies. Two favorite trees were pine and catalpa, the latter used principally for fence posts. To this day one can see square plots of trees that were timber claims.

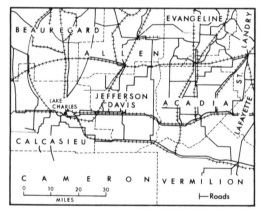

MAP 53
Southwest Louisiana in 1917

New parishes were created, the better to serve the administrative needs of a greatly increased population. Among them were Allen, Jefferson Davis, Evangeline, and Acadia. New towns were planned and laid out where there had been open land. Because these towns were laid out in advance, they tended to have very regular streets, parallel to and at right angles to each other, and straight with the cardinal directions, unless they were adjusted to a deviating railroad. Some of those towns that have survived to the present are Crowley, Jennings, Kaplan, Welsh, Rayne, and Iowa.

Comparison of the two maps, one for 1884 and one for 1917, illustrates some of the changes accompanying the settlement of the prairies. The 1884 map appeared two years after the completion of the railroad. It was already the main artery of transportation. From it post, or mail, roads ran across the country in all directions, following the easiest routes, regardless of property or survey lines. At this time the prairies were unfenced, open cattle range. The inhabited areas were chiefly along streams. There were only four prairie parishes: Calcasieu, Cameron, St. Landry, and Vermilion.

The 1917 map shows the fundamental changes completed. Post roads largely ran north-south and east-west with square turnings. This pattern of roads reflects the township survey system applied to flat country. It means too that people are living on farms in the open prairies and are no longer restricted to streams. Principal towns are situated on rail lines. Beauregard, Jefferson Davis, Allen, Evangeline, and Acadia parishes were added to the four original parishes through subdivision.

Among the new settlers were large numbers of Midwesterners, farmers who knew prairie land and were attracted by its cheap price in Louisiana. They thought to bring with them the corn-hog economy that had worked so well in the Midwestern prairies, but this system did not succeed in the Louisiana prairies. And in seeking a substitute these farmers happened upon rice, which the Acadians of the prairies had been raising in a rather haphazard manner. The Midwesterners were accustomed to growing grain crops like wheat, oats, barley, and rye. They saw rice as simply another grain that could be grown by methods with which they were familiar.

The one thing they had to learn was to irrigate. Rice is irrigated not because it demands so much more water than other crops, but because water controls weeds and helps to keep the harvest clean. Rice

Turn-of-the-century housing in southwestern Louisiana Fred Kniffen

grows well in standing water; most weeds will not.

At first, water was drawn out of a stream by buckets fastened to a chain operating on a sprocket turned by a steam engine. This first pumping operation took place in 1888. Growing a crop of rice takes about 40 inches of water. Some 18 inches come from rain that falls at the right time; the balance of 22 inches must be provided by irrigation. To supply irrigation needs, water was drawn so heavily from streams that their level fell and salt water began to flow in from the Gulf. In the Mermentau River system it was necessary to build a dam to keep out the salt water. Another source of water was found in wells. Inevitably the problem of too little or too poor water arose, and it remains unsolved today.

Prairie soils are ideal for irrigation in that they have an impervious claypan about a foot deep that keeps the irrigation water from seeping away. The level surface of the land aids the distribution of water over the fields. The large levees of old ice-age streams run down the gentle Gulfward slope of the prairie area from north to south. Along them may be built the main irrigation canals. From them, field ditches run down the levee slopes to the fields. The field dikes are built suffi-

ciently high to ensure that the ground gets about an eight-inch cover of water. Since individual field levees must always lie at the same elevation, they are curved around the field like contours on a map. At the present time, levelers are reducing wetted fields to one constant slope so that levees may lie in parallel straight lines and be reduced in number by as much as 40 percent. Another departure from the past is a trend toward the replacement of open canals by buried pipes, thus reducing the loss of precious water between source and field.

The Midwesterners used the same machinery and methods they had previously employed in grain growing: seeders, binders, shocks in the field, and steam threshing machines. As in grain-growing areas, they advanced to the use of combines, great machines that cut and thresh in one operation. Planting has been modernized by the use of planes to scatter seed and fertilizer over the fields. All this represents an enormous change from the simple hand methods employed with "providence" rice. And it is vastly different in concept and execution from the production of river rice, which is of Louisiana origin and applied to the levee backlands of the Mississippi system.

Crop and cultural antecedents have

House type built by midwesterners moving into southwestern Louisiana Fred Kniffen

Seeding rice by plane Louisiana Department of Agriculture

combined to give the prairies a highly distinctive settlement pattern, vastly different from the pre-railroad pattern. These flat lands, like those of the Midwest, permitted the full development of the General Land Office system of square townships and sections applied to unsurveyed portions of Louisiana after the Purchase in 1803. Roads followed section lines and made square turnings; fields were rectangular in shape. Farmsteads were dispersed, their buildings clustered behind a windbreak of planted trees and set square to the road and the cardinal directions. The houses of the Midwesterners were like those of their former home: great, square, two-story white houses with pyramidal roofs, or modified "I" houses, one room deep and two stories high. Barns were big and often painted red. One still feels in this section of Louisiana that he is in a remote land, quite unlike the river-bank settlements, or equally unlike the settlements of the flatwoods and hills.

Rice elevators in prairie town Sam Hilliard

Prairie towns too are distinctive, with their clustered rice elevators like the railroad towns of the grain-producing Great Plains. Recently, with the use of combines and the harvesting of rice in a moist condition, driers—great tall structures—now flank the elevators.

The Midwestern settlement pattern, so distinct a few years ago, is beginning to fade before modern development and a new cultural invasion. No Midwestern houses have been built in a long time, and the old ones are becoming scarcer. Further, there has been a continued invasion by Acadian settlers from the bayous and prairie margins to the east. Their fields are smaller, their headlands larger, their crops more varied, and their Acadian houses of a very different character. Ears of maturing corn are "broken" downward to ward off water and birds. And thus does a new settlement pattern begin to emerge.

Rice is no longer a continuous crop. There is rotation with grass pasturage and soybeans. At the same time, newly developed varieties of rice promise to raise production of this profitable grain and bring it into even greater importance among Louisiana's major commercial crops.

29
Industrial Lumbering

Lumber was mentioned as one of Louisiana's earliest exports, but it may be said that until the late nineteenth century, the state's forests were almost untouched. Then, in a matter of thirty-five years, Louisiana's virgin forests were depleted. This was the period of industrial lumbering with which we are concerned.

The main American market for lumber was the heavily populated Northeast. The forests of that area had been cut first, and then the lumbering industry moved west toward the Great Lakes and south through the coastal states. With the threatened exhaustion of the Lake States' timber, lumber interests moved southward into Arkansas, Mississippi, and Louisiana. Louisiana was the target of two movements, one from the North and one from the eastern South. When they met, the frenzied activity was like that of a swarm of locusts that drops down without warning, remains for a while, and then departs, leaving a barren waste.

Of course, there had long been some lumbering in Louisiana and some exploitation of the pine forests for naval stores—tar and turpentine. Pine logs were floated downstream to sawmills, especially in the Florida Parishes and southwest Louisiana. The pine forests were used for grazing cattle and hogs and were kept free of underbrush by annual winter burning to bring a fresh growth of grass. Cypress had a variety of local uses, for example, as lumber, for sugar boxes, for cistern staves. Sawmills were widespread from the earliest times. They were powered successively by human labor, by horses, by water, and by steam. We have described an ingenious application of water power in New Orleans, where water from the flooding Mississippi was piped over the levee to turn a sawmill below. As early as 1811 a steam-powered mill in New Orleans was destroyed by workmen who felt that it led to unemployment. Despite the abundance of timber, even as late as the 1880s it was

Turpentining pine trees   Elemore Morgan

cheaper to buy imported pine lumber from the large-scale mills of Alabama than it was to purchase it from the small Louisiana mills. At that time, industrial lumbering had reached Alabama but not Louisiana.

The introduction of industrial lumbering, in about 1890, completely revolutionized operations. There was some hasty extraction of turpentine before trees were cut. Sawmills of huge capacity were set up and operated twenty-four hours a day the year around. A network of railroads in the pine woods replaced slow movement by streams. Largely because natural conditions were so different, two contrasting modes of operation in the lumber woods developed: the cypress and hardwoods of the swamp, and the pine of the flatwoods and hills. Methods differed, and to a large extent so did participants. The two had their separate sawmill towns and separate markets.

Merchantable cypress is said to have grown naturally in every parish of the state, but the area of great concentration was in the Atchafalaya Basin. Other stream bottoms and the swamps around Lake Pontchartrain made relatively minor contributions of cypress timber. As late as 1818 a government survey found the stands of cypress virtually untouched. Another survey made in 1833 showed that some of the cypress had been stolen, but not much. In 1849 the swamplands were transferred from the federal government to the state of Louisiana, and the Timber Act of 1876 opened the cypress lands for sale. By 1880 outside investors and lumbermen were buying the cypress lands for from twenty-five to fifty cents an acre.

In the old, leisurely days of cypress lumbering the "swampers," who were mostly Acadians and northern lumberjacks, went into the woods in the fall, lived in crude camps, suffered attacks of malaria, and felled the enormous trees. On the "spring rise," when the woods were deep in water, the logs were poled

out individually to points where they could be made into rafts and towed to the sawmills. The swampers spent their summers in the sawmill towns, usually situated on the higher land bordering the great swamp. Among the old cypress towns were Harvey, Patterson, Morgan City, Lutcher, Plaquemine, and Ponchatoula. Most of these places were not exclusively lumber towns, for they have survived the death of the industry. But there were some exclusively cypress sawmill towns that have disappeared, leaving little trace.

Primitive hand methods did not last long into the period of industrial lumbering. First, there had to be faster and more certain methods of getting the cypress logs to the mills. Two ingenious systems were developed. One employed a pullboat, which basically was a big barge on which was mounted a powerful steam engine turning a drum that held a half mile or so of heavy cable. A straight canal was dug to a preselected site, through which the pullboat was towed; with it went the quarter boat, an office boat, and a kitchen-dining boat. From the pullboat, narrow openings were cut in all directions to a distance of a half mile. Along these openings the logs were dragged with the cable to the pullboat, where they were made into a raft and towed to the mill. Areas recently logged by pullboats can easily be detected from the air by the patterns of intersecting lines that look like the spokes of a rimless wheel.

The other mode of cypress logging was with narrow-gauge railroads. The roadbed was made of tree trunks cut and arranged for the purpose. The main line ran into the forest, sending branches off on either side at intervals of a quarter mile. The skidder, which pulled the logs to the railroad, was a powerful steam rig mounted on a flatcar. Sometimes a "high line" from a tall, trimmed tree serving as a mast near the track was used so that the logs could be lifted through the air rather than dragged on the ground. A steam

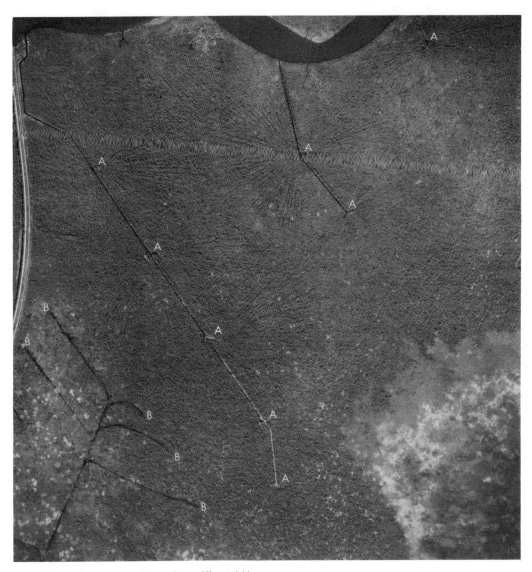

Logging in the swamp. Note the pullboat (A) and railroad (B) traces.

"jammer," or derrick, mounted on a flatcar loaded the logs onto cars for the trip to the mill. Railroad logging, too, leaves its distinctive pattern, readily recognizable from the air.

If woods methods were improved, so were the sawmills. In the old days waterpowered saws moved leisurely up and down like a handsaw to make lumber out of logs. Then came the circular saw, which operated with steam and cut much faster. In 1889 the bandsaw was introduced. It is a continuous band, or saw, which stands upright and runs always in one direction. It too so greatly increased the capacity of mills that by the 1890s lumbering in Louisiana was big business. The great period was from 1910 to 1914. In 1914 Louisiana led the nation in lumber production. By 1925 the big period was over, with most of the mills gone and millions of denuded acres left behind.

Pine lumbering followed its own distinctive course. It involved several large areas—the Florida Parishes, the Ouachita-Red river triangle, and southwest Louisiana (the area between the Red and the Sabine rivers). In the beginning, oxen pulled the logs from the woods to the stream banks. There the logs were dumped in and "driven" downstream to the mills. Railroads also invaded the pineries, much after the manner of logging in the cypress woods.

The idea prevailed among lumbermen that taxes on timberlands and the high investment in equipment made it mandatory to get the timber out as fast as possible. To do this they never halted operations. Company towns, with log ponds, mills, houses, churches, and schools, were built central to the timber holdings. The life of such a town probably averaged less than twenty years, for by that time logging operations were too far from the mill. It was cheaper to move the mill and town and abandon the site than to bring the logs in from a distance. This has been referred to as a "cut out and get out" policy. As a result, many of the old pine towns were completely abandoned. In some cases, about the only evidence left of their former presence is the old log pond, its artificial nature indicated by the presence of a straight shore where the dam is located. Some of the towns once important for pine lumbering survive as modern communities, such as Lake Charles, Winnfield, and Bogalusa.

Pine achieved commercial importance a little later than cypress. As late as 1891 pine land was still available at $1.25 an acre. The big start came in 1900, although in 1909 much cheap pine timber was still to be had. In 1914 Louisiana's production led the nation. By 1918 there were twelve

Modern sawmill

Louisiana Office of Forestry

Modern tree farm

Louisiana Office of Forestry

million cutover acres and they were increasing by 250,000 to 300,000 annually. By 1920 operators saw the end and were looking westward to the virgin forests of the mountain and Pacific states.

The aftermath of industrial lumbering in the sense of its geographical effects represented on the land can hardly be appreciated by one who had not known the country before. We have referred to the imprint of logging operations that are visible from the air and to the evidence of abandoned pine towns. We might mention old railroad grades in the same areas, some of which have been converted to modern roads. More important, even if we are largely unaware of them, are the changes in vegetation. In some areas, pine was completely eliminated where

destructive steam skidders were used. Scrub oak, formerly controlled by regular burning, took its place. Other denuded areas were used as sheep pastures.

The forest is still very important as a Louisiana resource, mainly because of our climatic advantages that induce a rapid growth of trees. Vestiges of the old methods of cutting and milling are to be found in many small operations, most of them in pine stands, but some in bottom hardwoods and cypress. More important for our future is the "sustained yield" notion, which involves using the same land again and again to grow a crop of trees. But this does not belong to the period and stage of industrial lumbering. Instead, it is a special kind of agriculture and will best be discussed under that heading.

30
Mineral Resources

Probably no human activity has been more important in altering the face of Louisiana than has the discovery and use of petroleum and its associated resources. The direct results are seen in the derricks of drilling wells, offshore platforms, refineries, tankers, and the like. Indirect results are the great industrial complexes that exist because of petroleum resources. There are new concentrations of population around activities based on petroleum.

The prehistoric Indians surely saw oil seeps and may have skimmed petroleum off water to use for medicinal purposes. In the 1820s waterwell diggers were extremely disgusted when they encountered gas instead of water. About the same time, teamsters used oil from seeps to lubricate the axles of their wagons. The Indians and early European inhabitants of Louisiana did not seek out and use oil because they did not have the mechanical knowledge necessary to do so. Further, they had no way of using it.

Prior to its production in Louisiana, petroleum had been brought out of the ground for fifty years in other parts of the United States, chiefly as a source of kerosene for lamps. Drilling for oil was first carried on in Pennsylvania. The surface of Louisiana is quite different from that of Pennsylvania, so that for a long time no one suspected that Louisiana would become the greater producer of petroleum. What really intensified the search was the invention of the automobile and the demand for gasoline and lubricating oil. The first notable discovery in this part of the country came not in Louisiana but in Texas.

Petroleum in the Gulf Coast area occurs to a great extent in salt domes, some of them showing at the surface and others deeply buried. Prospectors for petroleum in the early 1900s knew nothing about salt

Early oil field with derricks. Now such structures are removed after the well is drilled.

Louisiana Department of Commerce and Industry

domes, and looking for petroleum was almost a blind search. Sulphur water and gas seeps that burned with a red flame were regarded as favorable signs. However, it was largely an accident when in 1901 the great Spindletop dome near Beaumont, Texas, was discovered. As soon as it was operating and producing gusher wells, men looking elsewhere for petroleum judged that they should seek out places where there was a natural elevation of the ground above the surrounding level. All the necessary conditions seemed to be met—gas seeps, sulphur water, and a slight elevation of the ground—on a farm near Jennings, Louisiana. Sure enough, in 1901 a gusher was struck at a depth of 1,800 feet. This well sanded up and had to be abandoned but oil had been found in Louisiana, and soon there were other discoveries.

Jennings was an established field by 1902. New discoveries to the east came in rapid succession. Anse la Butte, east of Lafayette, was brought in in 1902. The Mississippi River seemed to be a barrier to farther extension to the east. Not until 1935 was the Baton Rouge field, east of the river, discovered. Even today, production east of the Mississippi in the Florida Parishes is limited. This may mean different geologic conditions, not clearly understood, rather than an absence of petroleum in the ground. In 1906

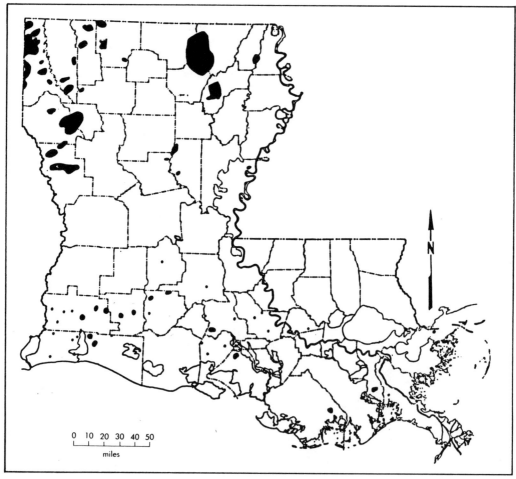

MAP 54
Map of oil and gas fields in 1935

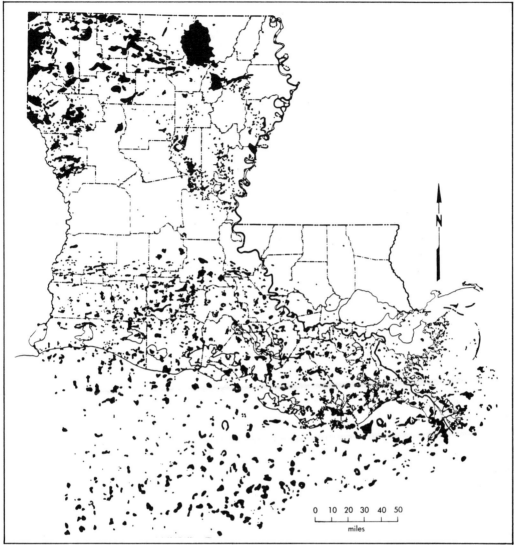

0 10 20 30 40 50
miles

MAP 55

Map of oil and gas fields in 1981. Note the increase over that of 1935. Note also the barren area across the "waist" of the state and the presence of offshore fields in the Gulf.

a discovery in Caddo Parish marked the first production in North Louisiana. There, most of the sources are anticlinal or domed geologic structures (some quite large), rather than salt domes, as is the case in South Louisiana. From Caddo Parish, discoveries and production moved east, reaching Delhi in 1947. In recent years the main activity and the greatest

production have been in quite different areas, in the deep delta, offshore, and inland at depths of 15,000 to 20,000 feet. There remains a considerable belt of largely nonproductive ground between the producing areas of North and South Louisiana (Maps 54 and 55).

On a surface devoid of any evidence of a petroleum industry in 1901, developments in Louisiana followed at a rapid pace. The first pipeline, from the Jennings field to Beaumont, Texas, was built in 1901. The huge refinery complex in Baton Rouge got its start in 1903. By 1910 there

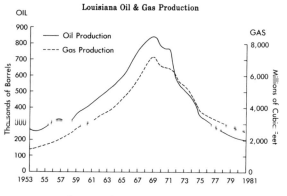

FIG. 26

Oil and gas in Louisiana. A look at this graph reveals why the state now suffers from declining revenues. Production of oil was lower in 1981 than in 1953.

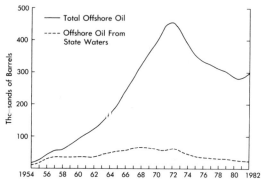

FIG. 27

Offshore oil production

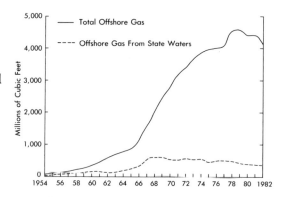

FIG. 28

Offshore gas production

were three major pipelines: the first ran from Jennings to Beaumont; the second from Caddo Parish south to the coast; and a third from southwestern Louisiana to Baton Rouge. By 1916 Louisiana ranked fifth among the forty-eight states in production, and by 1919 the state had fifteen refineries. During the depression years of the 1930s crude petroleum dropped to ten cents per barrel and glutted the market. In 1938 experts thought that with a billion barrels produced to that date, Louisiana's natural store was half exhausted. By 1947 two billion more barrels had been produced! Today Louisiana ranks third behind Texas and Alaska in annual production. In gas production it is second only to Texas and only by a small amount, 6.4 million cubic feet to 6.1 million cubic feet.

Despite such phenomenal growth, Louisiana's future in oil and gas production is not bright. The peak was reached around 1970; since that time production has declined sharply to levels approximating that of 1954. New discoveries are being made, but many of the older fields are now nearly depleted.

Exciting recent development has been along a geologic formation known as the Tuscaloosa Trend that stretches from

Avoyelles Parish southeastward through Baton Rouge to a point near Slidell. Long suspected of being rich in gas, the Trend was first tapped by Chevron in 1975 near False River. Since that time other fields were developed at depths around 20,000 feet, but the recent decline in demand coupled with the high cost of recovery has limited development.

The decline in production within the state has been partly offset by development offshore. Located outside the three-mile coastal waters claimed by the state, fields on the continental shelf now yield more than that of the entire state.

Methods for producing and processing petroleum and associated products are constantly being improved. For a long

174

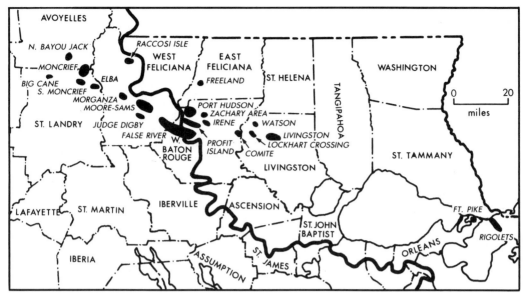

MAP 56

Map of producing fields along the Tuscaloosa Trend in 1984

time, natural gas was largely a wasted by-product of oil production. Then, in 1917, a process was perfected for the conversion of gas to carbon black, a substance necessary in making tires, ink, carbon paper, electric insulators, and other articles. The great Monroe gas field, discovered in 1909, came into full use. With the building and perfecting of pipelines, gas could be transported north to be used for home heating and cooking and for industrial purposes.

The search for oil and gas naturally led to the exploitation of associated minerals, sulphur and salt. Sulphur, with its many industrial uses, became an important product of South Louisiana with the invention of the Frasch process in 1941. Sulphur lies in the caprock overlying the salt in salt domes. The sulphur cannot be removed by direct mining, since it frequently is deep-seated and occurs in small stringers. By the Frasch process, hot water is pumped into the caprock and melts the sulphur to a liquid, which is then forced to the surface. An associated mineral, salt, likewise has been produced

in great abundance by actual mining of the solid rock. The Five Islands have been the almost exclusive sources of Louisiana's salt production. Additionally, brines derived from salt domes are used in chemical plants, as in the Solvay process for making sodium carbonate or soda ash, an ingredient of many manufactured products.

Offshore drilling platform. As many as twenty wells may be drilled from such a structure.
David Prior

The search for minerals deeper and deeper in the earth necessitated new technical developments. In 1901 the drilling rig used in Louisiana used the old cabletool method of Pennsylvania, in which the bit was simply lifted with a line, then dropped. The rotary rig was developed in the early 1900s. This method, which may be compared to a brace and bit, was a great improvement. In 1907 the limit of drilling depth was 3,000 feet. By 1937 rotary rigs were penetrating to 10,000 feet. This was regarded by some as an absolute limit beyond which steel drill pipe would not withstand the strain. By 1956, wells were drilled to 21,000 feet. Combined with ability to go deep is a new ability to control direction. Wells can be drilled straight down or at an angle. It is possible, and sometimes necessary, to drill several wells from one platform.

The most spectacular field development has been the advance of drilling through the marshes and out into the open Gulf. The marshes were difficult enough. Marsh buggies, large-wheeled vehicles capable of operating over land or water, were used for the preliminary work. Canals were dredged to drilling sites, where more and more rigs mounted on barges were used. Oil might be carried out in barges or, if it were produced in sufficient amount, a pipeline might be built.

Venturing into the open water of the Gulf introduced new difficulties: the problem of setting up a solid platform and the risk of destruction by a hurricane. Initially, the drilling platforms remained close to shore and were restricted to shallow water. The first well drilled in the Gulf was completed in 1933. It stood in twelve feet of water half a mile off Creole, Louisiana. Gradually they were moved seaward into deeper water. By 1955, forty offshore rigs were operating 50 miles or more from shore. By 1986 more than 7,000 wells were operating offshore from Loui-

Refinery complex

Don Nugent

176

siana. Rigs capable of operating in several hundred feet of water have been built; others are designed for even greater depths. Much of the offshore drilling technology was developed in Louisiana, and Louisiana workers helped develop offshore fields in the North Sea, South America, and Southeast Asia. Furthermore, the offshore rigs have withstood well the fury of recent hurricanes.

The platforms and rigs are but a minor part of the total imprint of petroleum operations in coastal Louisiana. On the shore are installations including residences, shops, anchorages for service vessels and crewboats, landings for helicopters serving the drillers, pipelines bringing petroleum ashore, and even the refuse from the platforms deposited on beaches by onshore winds. At night one sees the flares marking the distant offshore operations.

The refineries and other facilities that handle the raw petroleum products have kept pace with the other improvements in the industry by enlarging their capacities and promoting new efficiency. The Baton Rouge refinery has the largest capacity of any in the United States and is surpassed by only one in the world. It is a maze of tanks, towers, laboratories, office buildings, and transportation facilities. Gasoline, kerosene, lubricating oil, paraffin, tar, and road oil are among the products coming directly from petroleum. Use has been found for by-products that once were wasted. Then there is a whole family of rubber and chemical plants directly dependent on the refinery for raw materials. And there are power plants, cement plants, and alumina plants that have been attracted by abundant and cheap fuel.

Examination of the maps showing producing fields and pipelines (Maps 48 and 55) reveals how intricately and thoroughly Louisiana is marked by petroleum. Roughly south of an east-west line through Baton Rouge and south of the Florida Parishes lies the great producing area of Louisiana. The greatest oil yield comes from the modern Mississippi delta and the older deltas just to the west. Oil is found to the west, but there the percentage of gas production rises. There is something of a production gap north to the latitude of Alexandria. From there the number of fields increases northward, with great gas production to the east and more oil to the west.

Oil pipelines form an intricate network over most of the state, even fingering in from the Gulf and crossing areas where there is little or no production. Lines tend to converge on Baton Rouge and other processing and shipping centers. The gas pipelines clearly serve local needs, but just as frequently they move out of the state toward some distant market.

It is natural to take for granted the complex imprint of petroleum in the Louisiana of today. It is difficult to think of a Louisiana without it, as was the condition only seventy years ago. It is part of our task as students of geography to realize and visualize the importance of man's role in changing the face of the earth.

31
Agricultural Shifts

We have seen how Bienville in the early 1700s envisioned a Louisiana given over to the production of commercial plantation crops—indigo, tobacco, and rice. And we have seen how the Germans and Acadians became successful small farmers, growing most of the things they needed, and in addition producing a cash crop that provided money to purchase the necessities they could not grow. The British of the flatwoods and hills lived in a manner similar to that of the Acadians and Germans. Their chief crop was corn, for it provided food for man and beast. The same was true of sweet potatoes. Beans completed this trio of subsistence crops.

By the end of the 1700s some commercial crops disappeared, to be succeeded by others. When indigo cultivation diminished, sugarcane and cotton came to the fore. Neither of these was a new crop. Technology made them profitable, as cane growers learned how to crystallize sugar and the cotton gin created a cheap source of textiles. Rice grown along the river became less important. Late in the nineteenth century prairie rice emerged as a leading commercial crop. Tobacco became less and less important and finally became restricted to St. James Parish and the production of perique. Of course, the commercial crops were often subsistence crops as well. Sugarcane was widely grown for syrup, the only sweetening for many small farmers. Cotton was a source of home-woven textiles as well as a money crop. Both rice and tobacco were commonly grown for home consumption.

The production of livestock, particularly cattle and hogs, was both a commercial and a subsistence enterprise. The raising of cattle found in Louisiana the meeting ground of two contrasting systems, as we have seen. In the southwestern part of the state was the easternmost extension of the Spanish system; in the flatwoods and hills was the piney woods system. Hogs were produced in both areas and were subject to the same contrasting methods of husbandry.

Until well into the twentieth century, Louisiana was overwhelmingly a rural and agricultural state. Most commercial and industrial enterprises were related to agriculture; even timber-cutting was done by farmers and planters. Such great dependence on agriculture, and especially on a few cash crops, proved again and again to be economically hazardous. The failure of a single commercial crop or a drop in prices or change in tariff had widespread effects, because so many people were dependent upon it for their living. National and state leaders urged farmers to diversify, that is, to raise several cash crops. They pointed out the opportunities in new kinds of production, such as the annual expenditure by Louisianians of some thirty million dollars annually for out-of-state dairy products in an attempt to stimulate in-state production.

Changes certainly have come to Louisiana agriculture in the twentieth century. Some old crops are now of less importance, and new ones have been introduced. There have been changes in the size and operation of individual farms. And, of particular geographical importance, new distinctions in agricultural practices have arisen among the various areas of the state. Some of the changes have resulted from planning and research, such as that which commonly comes from the agricultural experiment stations. Better livestock, increased dairy production, new emphasis on broilers and eggs have all been fostered by scientific research. Other changes have not been anticipated, as when federal government acreage controls of sugarcane, rice, and cotton led to big increases in soybean and cattle production. Acres of cutover land unfit for field agriculture suggested tree farming. Technical developments changed crop emphases, reduced tenant farming, and increased farm size. For example, the replacement of horses and

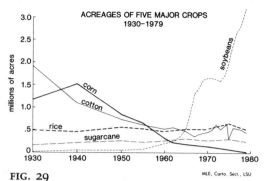

ACREAGES OF FIVE MAJOR CROPS
1930–1979

MLE, Carto. Sect., LSU

FIG. 29

Changes in acreage of the five major crops through time. Note the spectacular rise in soybean acreage after 1960.

mules by tractors reduced the acreage of animal feeds grown on one-crop farms. Expensive mechanical cotton, grain, and cane harvesters reduced the demand for labor and increased the acreage that can be cultivated by an individual operator. New crops such as tung nuts, soybeans, strawberries, pecans, peaches, sweet potatoes, and hot peppers have proven profitable, though tung nuts are no longer produced for sale.

Louisiana shares with other states the present boom in soybean production. The soybean is a native of Asia. From its seed

Rattooning sugarcane

Sam Hilliard

come oil, flour, and protein-rich meal. The plant is also used for forage and for soil improvement and is planted widely over the state. It is particularly noticeable in the upper Mississippi floodplain of Louisiana, in some instances replacing cotton, and in others growing in newly cleared swamplands. In fact, soybean acreage has shown such a spectacular increase since 1960 that it often is called the "miracle crop." It thrives in a variety of locations with little care; thus its replacement of both cotton and corn is understandable (Fig. 29).

The acreage devoted to traditional agriculture in the state has remained relatively constant at five to six million acres for the past half century. But the shift from cotton and corn to other crops has been important. Whereas soybeans were grown on only a few thousand acres as late as 1955, the 1979 acreage totaled over 3 million acres, far more than any other crop in the state. Both cotton and corn acreages have declined drastically since 1940, but both rice and sugarcane have held on fairly well. It must be kept in mind, though, that acreage is but one measure of a crop's importance. With better fertilization and newer, more productive seed varieties, farmers keep production high even though acreage has declined. For example, the average yield of cotton (pounds of fiber per acre) increased from 175 in 1930 to over 700 in 1979. During the same period corn yields increased from 11 to 54 bushels per acre, sugarcane from 15 tons per acre to 21, and rice from 1,760 to 3,910 pounds per acre. Thus farmers produce much more per acre, making it possible for land to be used for other purposes. Such intensity of production puts pressure on soil resources, making it absolutely essential that farmers continue to fertilize judiciously to avoid soil depletion.

There have been modest developments in the production of certain specialty crops, such as sweet potatoes, strawberries, and hot peppers, but the high cost of labor and competition from other states make the future uncertain. Certain tree crops do well in parts of the state, but nature is not always favorable. Both peaches and pecans have increased in importance. The development of new, disease resistant varieties is encouraging expansion. Some 150 growers accounted for over 5 million dollars in peaches in 1983. Pecans contribute some 11 million dollars to the state's agriculture with a potential for a much larger crop. The development of mechanical pecan shellers has reduced labor costs drastically, but state growers must compete with other, more established pecan producers all along the Gulf Coast from Georgia to Texas.

Of all tree crops in the state, citrus fruits have suffered most from environmental hazards. Only in the southernmost parishes can citrus trees survive for very long without freeze protection, and even there commercial production is limited to especially favored sites. Many years ago the cheniers of southwestern Louisiana as well as parts of Beauregard and St. Tammany parishes were important producers, but the great area of production was along the Mississippi River south of New Orleans, and that is where the greater part of Louisiana's citrus is produced today. Over a thousand acres are devoted to the production of satsumas and oranges with the former being the most widely grown. Despite the best

Burning sugarcane during harvest to remove dead leaves   Sam Hilliard

A modern cotton picker

John Deere Co., Moline, Illinois

efforts of growers the periodic freeze is always a threat. Growers are now trying to recover from the severe freeze of 1982, but if the past is any measure of the future, another freeze will come in 8 to 10 years.

Aside from the changes in crop emphases, Louisiana farms have themselves been transformed. Mechanization makes it possible for one farmer to work much more land than before, and thus farms have grown larger. Farms that were too small to provide adequate income for a family have disappeared. Tenancy, so characteristic of the plantation areas after the Civil War, has all but vanished as tractors replaced mules and sharecroppers left the farm to seek city jobs. By 1969 only a fifth of Louisiana's commercial farms were tenant operated. Four-fifths of them were farmed by their owners. Since each tenant-operated portion of a plantation had been counted as a separate farm, the reduction in tenancy gave a false picture of reduction in the number of farms. Even so, the number of farms continued to decline from a peak in 1930 to about 30,000 farms around 1980. At the

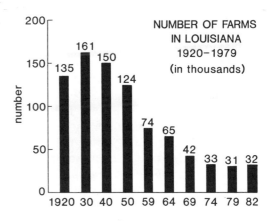

NUMBER OF FARMS IN LOUISIANA 1920–1979 (in thousands)

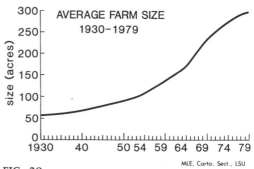

AVERAGE FARM SIZE 1930–1979

MLE, Carto. Sect., LSU

FIG. 30

As the number of farms decreases, the average size goes up. Fewer farmers now work larger acreage.

181

TABLE 6
Agricultural Production Rank in Cash Receipts from Farm Products, 1950–1978

Year	Rank				
	1	2	3	4	5
1950	cotton	rice	sugarcane	cattle	dairy
1953	cotton	rice	cattle	sugarcane	dairy
1956	cotton	rice	cattle	sugarcane	dairy
1959	cotton	cattle	rice	dairy	sugarcane
1962	cotton	cattle	rice	dairy	sugarcane
1965	cattle	rice	cotton	sugarcane	dairy
1970	cattle	cotton	soybeans	rice	dairy
1973	rice	cattle	soybeans	cotton	sugarcane
1975	soybeans	sugarcane	rice	cotton	dairy
1978	soybeans	cattle	rice	cotton	dairy
1983	soybeans	cotton	poultry	cattle	sugarcane

same time, average farm size jumped from 58 acres in 1930 to nearly 300 acres in 1982 (Fig. 30).

Cash income in 1978 amounted to about 1.5 billion dollars with 67 percent coming from the marketing of crops. The remainder came from selling livestock and livestock products. In 1978 soybeans provided the greatest farm income, followed in order by cattle, rice, cotton, and dairying. A glance at the table listing the top five ranking crops from 1950 through 1978 reveals that the number one place has been held by soybeans, rice, cattle, and cotton (see Table 6). We can only wonder what crop will be number one in the year 1990 or the year 2000.

Louisiana ranks high among the states in the production of rice, sugarcane, cotton, and soybeans, but relatively low in other commodities. Factors other than regulations or economic considerations influence the farmer in choosing which crop he will produce. There is also the factor of human values. What do people prefer to do? For example, it is constantly pointed out that Louisiana is exceedingly well situated for the production of hogs for market. This can be a most profitable undertaking. Yet, comparatively few take advantage of the opportunities. Raising hogs somehow lacks prestige. Most farmers prefer to raise beef cattle, even though the return on a greater investment is considerably less.

Agriculture in Louisiana has always depended upon livestock, and improvement over the past 20 or 30 years has been substantial. Cattle and calves have led the advance in livestock production, increasing greatly in recent years. This increase has accompanied practices somewhat different from those of the early days, which was open range on the prairies and in piney-woods areas. Stock is much better bred and better looked after. Also, areas of good soils, such as the Feliciana blufflands and the so-called delta area of northeastern Louisiana, have given great emphasis to cattle production. Sheep and lamb raising reached a peak of importance in the early 1940s in the cutover section of southwestern Louisiana and on the prairies. There has since been a decline in total production. The number of milk cows has sharply declined from a peak in 1954. However, the total milk production is up, indicating better stock and improvements in husbandry. Production of eggs and broilers has risen sharply in recent years. Unexpectedly, eggs and broilers are not produced in the same area. Eggs come mostly from the eastern Florida Parishes and broilers from the hill belt between the Ouachita and Red rivers.

The growing of trees for pulp and lumber is of constantly increasing economic importance, and it largely takes place in areas unsuited for most agriculture—swamps, flatwoods, and hills. Some fourteen million acres of Louisiana land may be considered commercial forest, about two-thirds of it in hardwoods and the rest in pine. Of the commercial forest, about three-fourths is industrially owned. The balance belongs mostly to farmers. A small amount is owned by the state or federal government, and about 20 percent of this is planted in tree farms. Income from forest products is substantial. The sale of pulp and sawtimber brought in nearly half a billion dollars to landowners in 1983, second only to soybeans as a cash producer. More than a

dozen parishes reported forest products as the leading income producer, and in a dozen others forest products ranked second or third. In 1983, forest products amounted to 86 percent of all animal and plant sales in La Salle Parish, and in Winn Parish the figure was 91 percent.

The nature of Louisiana's forests was discussed earlier. From that section we learned that the forests are composed of tree species of variable commercial value. Some trees, such as cypress and longleaf pine, make excellent sawtimber for building purposes while others make good pulp for paper. The commercial forest industry uses a wide variety of trees, but the bulk of both sawtimber and pulpwood comes from pine. Pine accounts for 77 percent of the pulpwood cut in 1975 and 82 percent of all sawtimber. Louisiana's forests grow rapidly, adding more to their bulk each year than is cut. This promises well for the future of forestry. A unique combination of climatic and other basic

A Louisiana sugarhouse with associated buildings

Don Nugent

VALUE OF
AGRICULTURAL COMMODITIES
by Parish
1983

F   forest products
Fr fruits
S   soybeans
R   rice
Ct cotton
Cn sugarcane
L   livestock
D   dairy
P   poultry
H   horses
HG home gardens
N   nursery

S SINGLE CROP DOMINANT

TWO CROPS DOMINANT
$\frac{S}{Ct}$ Primary Crop
     Secondary Crop

THREE CROPS DOMINANT
$\frac{S}{L|F}$ Primary Crop
Secondary Tertiary
Crop   Crop

MLE, Carto. Sect., LSU

MAP 57

The map shows the dominant product by parish, based on the value of agricultural commodities. Note that some are dominated by a single crop but others have two or three that rank closely.

conditions is such as to make Louisiana one of the most favored of all states in which to grow trees.

To sum up the emerging shifts in agricultural emphasis in Louisiana, we may point out a number of trends. First, there is less production of crops for home consumption. People find it easier to buy food in stores than to raise and process it themselves. Farms are becoming larger, more specialized, more mechanized, and are employing less labor. Livestock is expanding more rapidly than field crops. Less and less are the poor lands of the flatwoods and hills given to field crops. Instead, they produce trees and improved livestock. On the other hand, bottomlands are being more intensively and extensively used than ever before. It may be comforting to know that we have great acreages of unused bottomlands that can be pressed into service to meet the increased demand for food which is certainly not far off. Some of the old traditional crops remain important—cotton, rice, sugarcane. The new crop, soybeans, is increasing phenomenally in importance.

One of the most striking characteristics of Louisiana agriculture is its variability from place to place. Owing to a variety of environmental, historical, and cultural factors, each parish concentrates on those commodities it produces best, resulting in a complex of large and small regions that fit together to make up the state's agricultural profile (Map 57).

Despite recent industrial growth, agriculture in Louisiana remains economically important. Food processing is one of Louisiana's leading industries. Some important products of this industry are sugar, rice, sweet potatoes, strawberries, and hot pepper sauce. The pulp and paper industry ranks only slightly behind chemicals in number of employees; the processing of lumber and wood remains high. Despite the proven significance of agriculture in the state's economy, it could be made better with the same investment and effort. Production standards are generally below national averages. The yields of many of our crops could be higher than they are. Currently, cows do not give as much milk as they should, and hens do not meet the expected egg production. Louisiana is blessed with an unbeatable combination of favorable climate, productive soils, and abundant water. We must match this natural endowment with knowledge and skills.

32
Industrial Growth

Louisiana has become industrially important only in the present century. Most of this recent industrial development has been based on the exploitation of the state's natural resources, particularly petroleum, natural gas, sulphur, salt, and forest products. In the previous two centuries, there was some milling of lumber, extraction of salt, refining of sugar, and ginning of cotton, but no more than was the case of every neighboring state. In some instances, Louisiana lagged behind its neighbors, as in the commercial spinning and weaving of textiles, which has never been an important industry in this state.

In the pioneer days industry was largely a personal matter, because each family produced the bulk of the things it needed. Cotton lint was separated from the seed by hand and then spun and woven into cloth from which clothing was made. Houses were made of wood, either logs, posts, or of lumber that was hand sawed on the spot. Bricks were made of local clays by the people using them. Itinerant shoemakers made shoes for the family from hides produced on the place. There were a few things, such as guns, axes, knives, and the like, that could not be produced locally and had to be purchased.

Lumber was one of the first exports from Louisiana, but it amounted to little prior to the late nineteenth century. Sugar processing began about 1795, but the largest refineries, dependent in part on imported brown sugar, came into being after the Civil War. Cotton gins expanded operations to meet local demand. Although processing of cottonseed for oil began in 1835, it was relatively unimportant until after the Civil War. In 1870 there were two cotton mills in Louisiana; in 1894 there were four. But, as already suggested, textile manufacturing in Louisiana was never important. Cleaning and polishing rice became a considerable industry only after the center of production switched from the river to the prairies of southwestern Louisiana late in the nineteenth century.

Even taking into account all the industry involved in processing agricultural products, the total was hardly impressive until the twentieth century. In 1840 the value of manufactured products was only $15,500,000. By 1900 it had increased some eight times to $121,000,000. Lumber led the list by a wide margin. Other items were processed foods, such as bakery goods, candy, flour, and cornmeal. The balance of the list was equally unimpressive: brick, boots and shoes, cordials, fertilizers, moss, cigars and cigarettes, mattresses, and jute bags. There were some offshoots of sawmilling in the form of box factories and producers of staves for cisterns and barrels. More suggestive of manufacturing as commonly understood were iron foundries and carriage and wagon works, but they were of limited importance.

The modern era of industrialization began with the discovery of petroleum in 1901. Major economic growth has come since World War II. As late as 1937, the processing of agricultural products, if grouped together, exceeded industry based on petroleum. In that year lumber, especially hardwood, was next in importance, and pulp and paper, rising in significance, were in the next place. In 1938 the last big sawmill cutting virgin pine closed down operations at Bogalusa. In the meantime, paper and pulpwood, first cut commercially in 1917, were advancing in importance, reaching a value of $300,000,000 in 1954. This total placed Louisiana behind only Washington and Florida in paper and pulpwood production. A recent development is the addition of plywood plants that use a variety of trees, among them pines and cottonwoods.

Petroleum and related production has developed gradually. The first sulphur was produced in 1905. Salt was commercially produced from the Five Islands only after 1920. In 1947 the first big move toward offshore petroleum production was made. Since World War II Louisiana's industrial investment growth has exceeded the national average but has fallen below the southern average rate (Fig. 31). Chiefly stimulated by the petroleum industry, the state's industrial growth increased 100 percent between 1939 and 1953. The petroleum and gas industry increased 953 percent in the same period, and the chemical industry, 574 percent. Even today, chemicals and petroleum products combined exceed in yield the value added by all other types of manufacturing in the state. ("Value added" is an index of manufacturing importance. It is calculated by subtracting the cost of raw materials from the value of the finished product.)

The discovery and extraction of oil and gas is only a small segment of the petroleum industry. Crude oil must be refined to produce the gasoline, fuel, oil, diesel, and lubricants needed, but oil and gas also serve as raw materials for the petrochemical industry. Stimulated by a demand for synthetic rubber during World War II, the petrochemical industry now produces a variety of plastics and synthetic fibers that are used to replace natural materials, such as wood, metals, paper, and cloth. Nearly 200 such chemicals are now produced in Louisiana, for which the raw materials are primarily oil and natural gas. Most such products are sold to other manufacturers who then

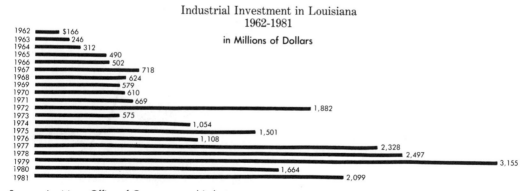

Industrial Investment in Louisiana
1962-1981

in Millions of Dollars

1962	$166
1963	246
1964	312
1965	490
1966	502
1967	718
1968	624
1969	579
1970	610
1971	669
1972	1,882
1973	575
1974	1,054
1975	1,501
1976	1,108
1977	2,328
1978	2,497
1979	3,155
1980	1,664
1981	2,099

Source: Louisiana Office of Commerce and Industry

MLE, Carto. Sect., LSU

FIG. 31

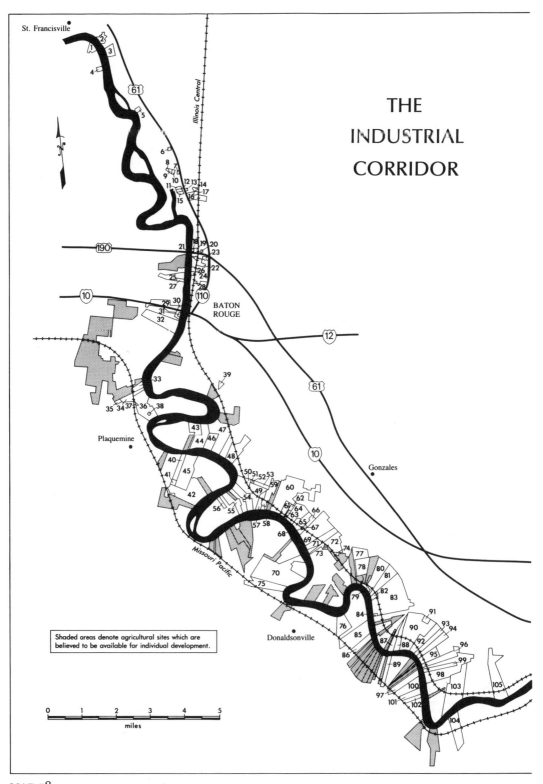

THE
INDUSTRIAL
CORRIDOR

St. Francisville

Illinois Central

61

190

10

110

BATON
ROUGE

12

61

10

Gonzales

Plaquemine

Missouri Pacific

Shaded areas denote agricultural sites which are
believed to be available for individual development.

Donaldsonville

0 1 2 3 4 5
miles

MAP 58

188

1 Cajun Electric	51 Grief Bros.
2 GSU, River Bend	52 Thompson-Hayward Chemical
3 Crown Zellerbach	53 Evergreen Industrial Park
4 Louisiana Coop.	54 Stauffer Chemical, St. Gabriel
5 Georgia Pacific	55 Apex Oil
6 Grant Chemical	56 Sunoco Terminals
7 Acme Brick*	57 American Petrofina
8 Schuylkill Products	58 COS-MAR
9 Reynolds Metals	59 Borg-Warner
10 Union Tank Car	60 Allied Chemical-Union
11 Allied, North Baton Rouge	Texas Petroleum-Arcadian Corp.
12 Louisiana Cellulose Specialities	61 Union Oil, Geismar
13 Exxon Resin	62 Shell Oil, Geismar
14 Stupp Corporation	63 Mobil Oil
15 American Hoechst*	64 Union Oil, Geismar
16 Maryland Tank Farm	65 Borden
17 Exxon Chemical, North Baton Rouge	66 Uniroyal
18 Ideal Cement	67 Rubicon
19 Stauffer Chemical, Baton Rouge	68 Liquid Carbonic
20 Realex Corporation	69 BASF Wyandotte
21 Kaiser Aluminum & Chemical, Baton Rouge	70 Texas Eastern Transmission
22 Ethyl, Baton Rouge	71 Shell Chemical, Geismar
23 Copolymer Rubber & Chemical, Baton Rouge	72 Vulcan Materials
24 Exxon Chemical/Exxon Refinery, Baton Rouge	73 McKesson Chemical
25 Exxon Chemical/Exxon Refinery, Port Allen	74 GSU, Geismar
26 GSU, Baton Rouge	75 Placid Oil, Donaldsonville
27 Placid Oil, Port Allen	76 C.F. Industries
28 Allied Chemical, Baton Rouge	76 Triad Chemical
29 Westport	76 Melchem
30 Port of Baton Rouge	76 First Nitrogen
31 Cargill, Port Allen	77 IT Corp.
32 Sun Plus	78 Olin
33 Occidental Chemical, Addis	79 Burnside Terminal
34 Copolymer Rubber & Chemical, Addis	80 Ormet
35 Sid Richardson Carbon Black	81 Exxon Chemical, Burnside
36 Dow Chemical	82 Dupont, Burnside
37 Air Products, Plaquemine	83 Texaco
38 B.F. Goodrich	84 MO Portland Cement
39 Gulf South Research	85 Agrico
40 Georgia Gulf	86 Gulf Chemical
41 Big 3, Plaquemine	87 Optioned
42 Union Carbide, Plaquemine	88 Zen-Noh Grain
43 Louisiana Chemical Specialties	89 Optioned
44 Hunt International	90 LP&L, Union
45 Allemania Chemical*	91 Ethyl, Union
46 Petro-United	92 Peabody
47 Ethyl R&D	93 Optioned
48 GSU, Willow Glen	94 Skelly Oil
49 Ciba-Geigy	95 Convent Chemical
50 Air Products, St. Gabriel	96 GATX
	97 Koch, St. James
	98 Freeport Chemical
	99 Optioned
	100 LAJET

101 Shell Pipeline
102 Koch, St. James
103 Optioned
104 Getty Oil
105 Optioned
106 Peavey
107 St. James Industrial Park
108 Coral Petroleum
109 Colonial Sugars
110 Kaiser Aluminum & Chemical, Gramercy
111 Clark Oil
112 Liquidchema
113 Nalco
114 Shell Oil, Wallace
115 Marathon Oil
116 Cargill, Garyville
117 Airline Industrial Park
118 Mitsui-Continental Grain
119 Godchaux-Henderson Sugar
120 Dupont, Reserve
121 Bayou Steel
122 Koch Industries, Hahnville
123 LP&L, Hahnville
124 LP&L, Gypsy
125 Occidental Chemical, Hahnville
125 Beker Industries
126 Union Carbide, Hahnville
127 Shell Oil, Hahnville
128 Shell Chemical, Destrehan
129 Optioned
130 Shell Oil, Hahnville
131 Shell Oil, Destrehan
132 GHR Energy
133 Plantation Business Park
134 Big 3, Destrehan
135 ADM Milling
136 St. Charles Grain
137 Bunge
138 Monsanto
139 Optioned
140 International Maytex
141 Farmers Export
142 Riverbend Industrial Park
143 Universal Match
144 American Cyanamid
145 Optioned
146 Catepillar
146 Coca-Cola
146 Continental Can
146 Dan Kelly Warehouse
146 National Foods
146 Sears Roebuck
146 Winn Dixie
147 Elmwood Industrial Park
148 LP&L, Bridge City
149 Continental Can

*No longer operating

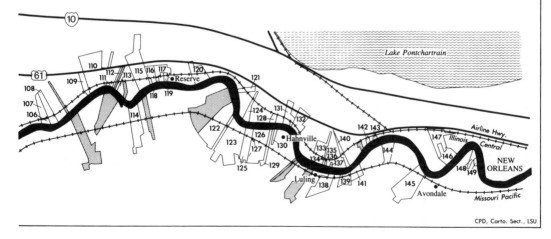

CPD, Carto. Sect., LSU

Louisiana National Bank

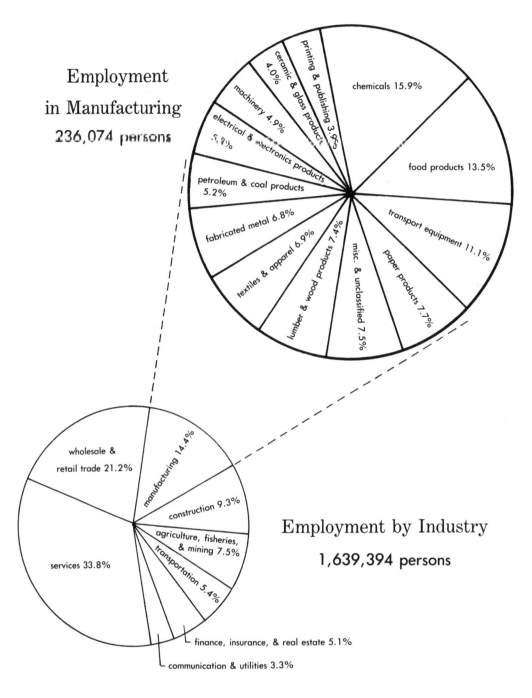

Employment
in Manufacturing
236,074 persons

printing & publishing 3.9%

ceramic & glass products 4.0%

machinery 4.9%

electrical & electronics products 5.8%

chemicals 15.9%

food products 13.5%

petroleum & coal products 5.2%

fabricated metal 6.8%

textiles & apparel 6.9%

lumber & wood products 7.4%

misc. & unclassified 7.5%

transport equipment 11.1%

paper products 7.7%

wholesale & retail trade 21.2%

manufacturing 14.4%

construction 9.3%

agriculture, fisheries, & mining 7.5%

transportation 5.4%

services 33.8%

Employment by Industry
1,639,394 persons

finance, insurance, & real estate 5.1%

communication & utilities 3.3%

FIG. 33
Louisiana employment by industry. The lower circle shows workers in many industries. The top circle is an enlargement of the slice of workers employed in manufacturing to show the relative importance of each manufacturing type.

State Planning Office
Louisiana Statistical Abstract

MLE, Carto. Sect., LSU

190

turn them into consumer goods. Manufacturing of end-products is limited within Louisiana. That is, raw materials or partially processed materials are often sent out of state for manufacture into finished goods. The manufacture of consumer goods lags behind that of other sections of the country.

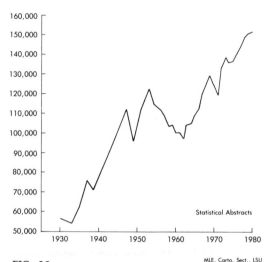

FIG. 32
Increase in production workers from 1930 to 1980

One measure of industrial growth in the state is the number of workers employed in manufacturing (Fig. 32). Employment rose rather sharply through the 1930s and 1940s but declined around 1960; since that time the number of persons employed has increased by half. It would be a mistake to assume that all persons listed as employees are workers on an assembly line. About one-third are employed in services, and one-fifth are employed in wholesale and retail trade. If we examine the group employed in manufacturing only, we see that many types of manufacturing are found in the state (Fig. 33). The chemical industry employs about one out of every eight workers, and if petroleum products are added the figure increases to one worker in five.

There is a strong localization of the chief industrial development in Louisiana. The major area is along the Mississippi River between Baton Rouge and New Orleans, where over 100 corporations have plants that manufacture, process, or transport industrial materials. Additional sites are near Lake Charles; in fact, the Gulf Coast petrochemical industry stretches all the way from Texas to Florida. A secondary but nevertheless important area of recent industrial growth centers on Shreveport, where the number of workers is second only to New Orleans. Geographical factors are prominent in determining the major regions of industrial activity, for industry is attracted largely by the availability of water transport for deepwater vessels. Excellent facilities may be found along the Mississippi below Baton Rouge where ocean-going ships may dock adjacent to the manufacturing facilities. Other attractions include an abundant supply of fresh water, ready access to fuel and raw materials, and a mild winter climate.

33
Population and Urbanization

Louisiana's population growth has been steady since the first settlement around 1700. By the time the state was accepted into the Union, the population was about 75,000. Since that time population has grown to number some 4.2 million in 1980. Most important geographically are matters of where in the state the population settled and the shifts that have taken place, particularly in the twentieth century, during which the cities have grown at the expense of the rural areas. Increased specialization of agriculture and the growth of industry have been responsible for this shift (Fig. 34).

In 1722, when New Orleans was made Louisiana's capital, there were about 5,000 people in the colony. About 300 of these lived in New Orleans. The rest lived in isolated agricultural settlements, chiefly on the Mississippi; the German Coast; Upper Bayou Lafourche; Bayou Manchac; Baton Rouge; Pointe Coupee; and

Natchitoches on the Red River. At the time of the Louisiana Purchase (1803) there were some 50,000 people in what would later become the state, and New Orleans was a city of 10,000. Below New Orleans were Lower Coast plantations and the Isleños of St. Bernard Parish. The St. John District lay along the bayou of that name, extending from the city toward Lake Pontchartrain. Above New Orleans, with the German and Acadian coasts, settlement was fairly solid as far as Bayou Lafourche at Donaldsonville. Still somewhat isolated were the communities of Baton Rouge and Pointe Coupee. West of the Mississippi, settlement pushed down Bayou Lafourche rather solidly for some twenty miles and more sparsely beyond. There were rapidly growing settlements in the Attakapas District along the middle section of Bayou Teche and the Vermilion River, and the Opelousas District of the Upper Teche and prairie

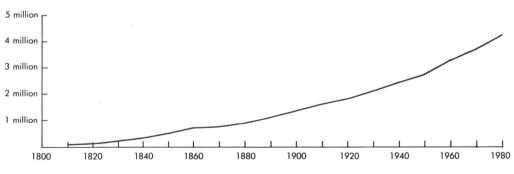

FIG. 34
Population growth from 1810 to 1980

MLE, Carto. Sect., LSU

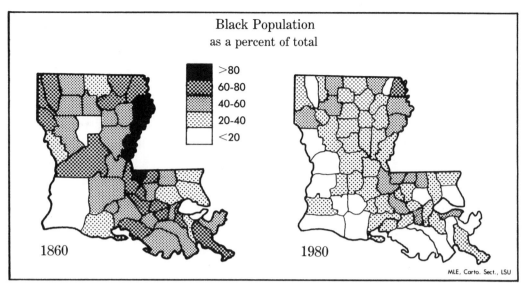

Black Population
as a percent of total

>80
60-80
40-60
20-40
<20

1860

1980

MLE, Carto. Sect., LSU

MAP 59

*Black population. Note the geographical shift
from the river parishes. Remember, however,
that the maps show percentages only.*

borders. Isolated communities were on
the Avoyelles Prairie and at Natchitoches.
The few settlers of British descent were
largely restricted to the Spanish-held Florida Parishes. Note how the settlements
clung to the major streams where fertile,
well-drained soils were found, with the
back country nearly as isolated and wild
as it had ever been.

Following the Louisiana Purchase there
was an influx of people of British descent,
many of whom joined the boom in plantation agriculture producing sugarcane and
cotton. Along the Mississippi, as we have
already seen, plantations were frequently
formed by joining together small holdings. Otherwise, the new plantations occupied areas that had not yet been
settled, such as the Lower Bayou Teche
and Lower Bayou Lafourche. Northward,
cotton plantations pushed slowly up the
Mississippi, into the blufflands to the
east, and up Red River after the removal
of the raft. Some developed in favorable
sections in the northern uplands between
the Red and the Ouachita rivers. The
movement into this latter region began in

the second quarter of the nineteenth century but always with an eye toward waterways as a means of shipping out
cotton. The spread of plantations is
important in one sense because it determined the areas of densest black population. Blacks were brought in in great
numbers to grow plantation crops. They
never were as numerous in other rural
sections as in the plantation parishes;
today many have moved to the cities. In
several parishes blacks made up over 80
percent of the total population in 1860,
but by 1980 only one parish showed
blacks amounting to 60 percent (Map 59).
This redistribution of blacks took place
during the twentieth century with people
moving to both northern and southern
cities. Orleans Parish had only an 8 percent black population in 1860, but today
blacks constitute over 55 percent. Others
have moved to St. Louis, Chicago,
Houston, or even Los Angeles.

By 1810 Louisiana's population was
over 75,000. In 1820 it was about 150,000,
with the marshes, prairies, flatwoods,
hills, and of course swamps largely un-
populated. Although the population increased to about 200,000 in 1830, to
500,000 in 1850, and to 1,000,000 in 1890,
the regional distribution remained about

193

the same. In 1890, in the early stages of far-reaching developments, the marsh, prairies, swamps, and the longleaf flatwoods and hills remained sparsely settled. We have already read of the invasion of the prairies for rice growing and the descent of industrial lumbering on the longleaf areas. Both brought a jump in population. In the pine hills new parishes were created, as well as in the prairies. And there was an increase in dairying. The location of petroleum resources is completely unrelated to the observable qualities by which we selected the natural regions of Louisiana. The increases of population linked to petroleum development cannot, then, be understood in terms of the natural regions in which they occur, for the occurrence of petroleum and natural gas is related to geologic conditions deep beneath the surface.

The new developments underway in the 1890s and the following decade set into motion population growth and change that are still taking place. Briefly, industrialization based largely on natural resources was the new force, and the growth of cities, together with some rural

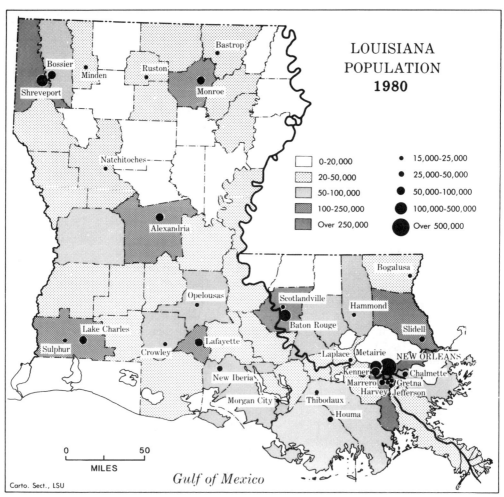

MAP 60

Population in Louisiana. Rural population is shown by various shadings; cities are shown by circles whose size represents population.

TABLE 7
A Century of Urban Growth, 1880–1980

	1880	1900	1920	1940	1960	1970	1980
New Orleans	216,000	287,000	387,000	495,000	628,000	593,000	558,000
Shreveport	8,000	16,000	44,000	98,000	164,000	182,000	206,000
Baton Rouge	7,000	11,000	22,000	35,000	152,000	166,000	219,000
Lake Charles	838	7,000	13,000	21,000	63,000	78,000	75,000
Lafayette	—	3,000	8,000	19,000	40,000	69,000	82,000
Monroe	2,000	5,000	13,000	21,000	63,000	56,000	58,000
Alexandria	2,000	6,000	18,000	27,000	40,000	42,000	52,000

depopulation, was the result. By 1970 Louisiana had over 3,500,000 inhabitants, and today has an estimated 4,400,000. The phenomenal growth has been in the cities, where industrial and service jobs are found. The most striking city growth has occurred since 1940. Today metropolitan New Orleans exceeds 1,000,000; metropolitan Baton Rouge approaches 500,000, and Shreveport nearly 400,000. Baton Rouge serves as a good example of the rapidity of city growth. In 1930 its population was approximately 25,000; in 1940, 35,000; in 1950, 90,000; in 1960, 152,000; and in 1980, 219,000. There is no doubt that until very recently Louisiana was a rural state, with only New Orleans being a true metropolitan center.

The importance of a city is often greater than its population would suggest, because many people live outside the city who commute to jobs within the city. Recognizing this fact, the United States Census Bureau has set up new areas called Standard Metropolitan Statistical Areas (SMSA) that encompass the city and adjoining areas. Louisiana has seven such areas. Altogether, these seven areas account for 2,666,401 people, 63 percent of the state's population (Map 61). This dramatic migration of people into Louisiana's cities has produced a boom in building construction. The seven metropolitan areas have grown in two ways, upward and outward. Upward growth is most spectacular in New Orleans, where the fifty-story One Shell Square is the tallest of a huge cluster of skyscrapers. The downtown areas of the other six metropolitan areas boast their own tall buildings, most of which were constructed since 1975. Such buildings serve to increase the space available for offices, permitting large numbers of people to work downtown. They also reflect local pride by showing an impressive skyline.

To house the millions that live in them, cities have grown outward, forming subdivisions of houses and apartments that extend up to a dozen miles from the city's center. Such subdivisions are clustered around schools and shopping centers and function much the same as small towns did fifty years ago.

In addition to those people living within the metropolitan areas, others often drive into the nearest metropolitan area to conduct business, go shopping, or simply for pleasure. Thus each of the seven has its own sphere of influence, called a hinterland, within which people often travel to the central city.

The turbulent population shifts of modern times were not known in the old days of steady agricultural production. True, a booming river town might decline, but it would be a slow process, not an overnight catastrophe. Perhaps a railroad would keep it going and then a major highway. In the prosperous industrial days of the twentieth century, sudden changes have been frequent. Consider the history of the village of Swartz in Ouachita Parish. Swartz was named for its lumberman founder in 1890. Lumbering operations supported a thriving population until the abrupt cessation of activities in 1907. Swartz became and remained a ghost town until the boom in the Monroe gas field in 1919. Situated in the center of the field, it eventually had twenty-eight carbon black and gasoline plants. Abruptly in 1935 all but one plant moved out. Swartz again is an inconspicuous village.

City growth is in large measure possible because of population inflow from other sections. New Orleans has always drawn extensively from a distance. Other Louisiana cities, in contrast, have drawn largely from the rural sections adjacent to them. Baton Rouge, for example, has drawn blacks from plantation areas of Louisiana and Mississippi, as well as French-Americans from the small farms to the west and south, and British-Americans from the pine flatwoods and hills to the north and east, even into Mississippi. It is thus not surprising that some rural sections have lost population. Other areas might have declined, except for the chance that brought them oil and gas

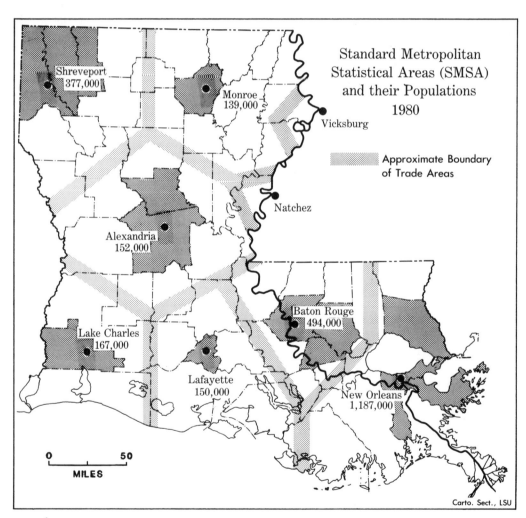

MAP 61
Metropolitan centers and their trade areas

Aerial view of Baton Rouge

Gulf Coast Aerial Mapping Co., Inc., Baton Rouge

fields. Chief losses have been in cutover sections of flatwoods and hills, and where subsistence farming was once widespread. It has also happened where bluffland plantations have turned from cotton to cattle, and in continuing plantation areas where mechanization has reduced the demand for labor.

In our discussion it might appear that the population of Louisiana is composed exclusively of people of French or British descent and blacks. Such is certainly not the case, for Louisiana has important groups of recent European derivation: Italians, Germans, and Irish, not to mention Mexicans, Canadians, and Orientals. Most intriguing and little-known are several distinctive, native-born groups of largely undetermined ancestry. Louisiana must be considered the more interesting for the variety of its peoples.

A "vertical" city. New Orleans has grown up as well as out.

Sam Hilliard

34
Louisiana's Past, Present, and Future

It has been our procedure in this geographical study of Louisiana to observe the works of nature and the works of man as they compose the varied landscapes of the state. We see these works as hills, streams, forests, houses, roads, fields, factories, and the like. We see them as something from the past, belonging to the present, or portending the future. We see them as they are grouped or dispersed, as they are related or unrelated to each other. In short, the things we can see and measure, whatever their sources, are the raw materials with which we, as students of geography, work. Those belonging to the present are easiest to work with; those belonging to the past are often only fragments of the whole; and those belonging to the future we detect from the recognition of trends. Past, present, and future are equally important.

We began our study with nature. To understand nature in Louisiana we must go back over the millions of years during which nature has been in the process of constructing the state. We find that the same natural processes that operated then are operating now. We find that nature changes very slowly as compared with man and that nature has no design for man to follow in occupying the earth. Nevertheless, the natural base is the one on which man must operate. His choice as to what he will do must be conditioned by the presence of the Mississippi River,

the wealth of the land, of the forests, of the sea, and of the salt domes. Without constant reference to the natural base our study of man is certainly not geographic.

The Indians were the first humans to appear in Louisiana. They lived here for thousands of years before Europeans appeared. Their needs—shelter, food, water, communication—were simple and not too far above the animal level. They practiced hunting, gathering, and agriculture. For their purposes they found the bottomlands and the marshes most fruitful. Their effects on the land were so slight or so subtle that we are hardly aware of them.

Some three hundred years ago Europeans arrived in Louisiana to stay. Initially they borrowed freely from the Indians—their foods, crops, routes, and settlement sites. As agriculturists they also quickly recognized the superiority of the bottomlands. They introduced many crop plants foreign to Louisiana's Indians, including indigo, rice, cotton, tobacco, sugarcane, citrus, melons, okra, and peanuts. But there developed two rural landscapes, one French in its cultural tradition and the other Anglo-Saxon. These landscapes differed as to the manner in which land was surveyed, the pattern of settlement, attitudes with regard to the handling of livestock, food preferences, and house types. They show a common plantation system established on the better soils. In an overwhelmingly rural way of life there was but one large city—New Orleans.

Despite the steady growth of population and a slow evolution of technology from steamboats to railroads, the lines remained drawn. The distinctions between French and Anglo-Saxon were largely the same, and life remained quite unchanged until the end of the nineteenth century. Then came a revolution so strong as to bring much greater changes in the twentieth century than had taken place in all the preceding European period in Louisiana. New technological capacity unleashed raw materials that had remained unused since the beginning of time. There were two world wars and other social upheavals to weaken normal human resistance to change.

New engineering skills made possible the wholesale exploitation and utilization of timber and petroleum. The automobile and the airplane brought new concepts in transportation. Roads could go wherever man wished, across swamps and on bridges across the Mississippi. Even the home climate could be modified by electricity. Cities extended themselves, as in the case of New Orleans, over swamps and marshes and across Lake Pontchartrain. As suburbanization from Baton Rouge extended to the east, subsistence farmers let their fields go back to pines, and modified their farmstead buildings to house workers daily commuting to plants in the city. Other rural areas were abandoned entirely, especially in the piney woods areas. Clearly, subsistence farming was out, and commercial agriculture on the good lands had become big business. Little towns died when fast transportation made them competitive with large ones. This took place despite the fact that rural electrification has made country living at least as comfortable as dwelling in a city.

The growth of industry and cities has been a mixed blessing. Pollution of air and water, the growth of slums and attendant evils, and the denial of the very real values of rural living are all on the debit side of the ledger. At the same time, the steamroller effect of the revolution in smoothing out old distinctions, differences, and values has by no means been complete. The property lines of the original surveys are still largely prevalent and assert themselves in either agglomerated or diffused patterns. The courthouse squares of the parish seats remain. Many of the older urban sites retain their importance in modern developments. And today, as with the first agriculture in Louisiana, the productivity of the bottomlands is appreciated. Finally, the Mississippi River remains the prime fact of Louisiana geography.

What of the future? It is difficult to see beyond the trends evident in the last decades. Industry will continue to expand to occupy the Lower Mississippi continuously. With it will continue the expansion of urban centers and their fringes. Agriculture will become even more mechanized and on a larger scale in areas of better soils. Further drainage of swamp and marsh areas for agriculture seems certain. The areas of poor and exhausted or eroded soils will certainly continue to go into forests and grazing land. If the joys of city living begin to pall, rural areas of farm and forest will provide respite.

In this time of awesome change it is difficult to remember that man started with the basic animal need for shelter, food, water, and communication, and that the satisfaction of these needs constituted his first imprint on the land. Nevertheless, man must still satisfy these needs in order to exist. And, these matters in all their elaborations are still the essence of human geography. However much it may be obscured in the modern world, we must continue to seek out the manner in which groups of men live and the imprint that they make on the face of the earth.

Glossary

by Irene S. Bass

Acadians—French refugees from Maritime Canada who came to Louisiana during the second half of the eighteenth century.

agglomerated pattern—placement of houses close together or in villages.

aggregate—cluster of soil particles held together by natural glue.

air current—vertical movement of air.

air mass—great body of air that transfers the atmospheric conditions of one area to another.

alluvial deposit—clay, silt, sand, gravel, or other material carried and laid down by running water.

alluvial valley—a broad valley such as the one occupied by the Mississippi and related streams.

altitude—height of a place, usually with reference to sea level.

anthropologist—one who studies man and his works.

anticline—a fold that is convex upward.

arpent—land measure about 192 feet long, also used as a square measure.

atmosphere—the gaseous envelope surrounding the earth.

backslope—outer slope of the natural levee between the crest and the backswamp.

backswamp—flat, wet area in the floodplain beyond the natural levees.

barrier beach—beach ridge pushed up against the land.

barrier island—beach ridge separated from shore by open water.

bateau—flat-bottomed, sharp-ended boat made of planks.

batture—the slope between the levee crest and the river.

bay gall, or bagol—shallow, moist depression with a cover of bay trees and inkberry bushes.

bayou—a small stream. This name is used chiefly in South Louisiana.

beach ridge—low ridge constituting a beach.

belted coastal plain—coastal plain on which there are two or more parallel cuestas.

bluff lake—a lake lying between the levee backslope and the bluff bounding the alluvial valley.

blufflands—areas of considerable relief generally bordering the alluvial valley.

bousillage—French term for clay and moss filling between the timbers of a house frame.

bowed sediment—normally flat or gently dipping sediment deformed by a force from below.

braided channel—network of channels formed by the splitting of a single channel.

briquette entre poteaux—French term for brick filling between the timbers of a house frame.

canebrake—a thick growth of wild cane.

chenier—former beach ridge now surrounded by marsh.

chenier plain—the western marsh of Louisiana where cheniers are dominant features.

chute—narrow river channel between an island or towhead and the nearest shore.

claypan—impervious soil layer lying a short distance below the surface.

coastline—a series of straight-line segments extending from point to point, eliminating the irregularities of the coast.

commissary—plantation store.

continental climate—climate characterized by seasonal extremes of temperature.

continental shelf—the gently sloping margin of a continent lying beneath the sea.

contour plowing—plowing along a slope, rather than up and down it, to check rain runoff that might wash away soil.

Creole—generally one who was native-born, but of European descent.

crevasse—channel cut through the natural or artificial levee by a distributary during floodstage.

cuesta—ridge of resistant sedimentary rock lying parallel to the coast.

cultch—old shell laid down on oyster grounds as a place of attachment for the young oysters.

culture—the learned ways of thinking and acting transmitted by group members to other group members.

cutbank—the steep face forming the outside bank of a river meander.

cutoff—elimination of a portion of a river's course by the cutting of a new channel.

cyclone family—winds that move counterclockwise in the northern hemisphere around a low-pressure cell.

deadening—area within which the trees have been girdled, causing them to die and creating a clearing for planting.

delta—set of distributary channels through which a river discharges into the sea.

deltaic plain—the eastern section of the Louisiana coast dominated by several systems of old natural levees.

depositional cone—cone-shaped deposit of sediment made by a stream.

differential erosion—the wearing away of rock in accordance with the amount of resistance it offers to erosion.

dispersed pattern—scattered placement of houses or farmsteads.

dissection—the cutting up of a land surface by erosion.

distributary—river branch flowing out of a main stream.

dogtrot house—one building in two separate parts joined by a covered passageway.

dust whirl—a short-lived wind swirling around a small, low-pressure cell; a warm season phenomenon.

economy—manner of gaining a living.

epiphyte—a plant living upon another plant, but getting its nourishment from the air.

equilibrium—the stage a river reaches in which it is neither cutting nor filling its valley on a major scale.

eustasy—a worldwide change in sea level.

extratropical cyclone—very large cyclone, low in wind velocity, moving west to east in the middle latitudes.

fault—fracture of the earth's crust resulting in displacement.

fault escarpment—a steep edge or slope resulting from earth movement.

flatwoods—flat, timbered lands; chiefly pine covered.

flocculation—deposition of suspended clay particles in salt water.

floodplain—the floor of a valley over which a river spreads sediment when it overflows its banks.

Florida Parishes—the part of Louisiana east of the Mississippi and north of the Isle of Orleans.

geology—the study of the history of the formation of the earth by great natural forces such as volcanoes, earthquakes, and deposition of sediments.

glauconite—a green mineral high in iron, commonly occurring in sedimentary rock.

glaze—smooth coating of clear ice that forms when cold rain freezes on contact with surface objects.

graben—depressed section of the earth's crust, bounded by faults.

gradient—degree of steepness of a slope.

gravel—accumulation of waterworn pebbles, usually rounded.

great circle—a circle on the earth's surface whose plane passes through its center. Its arc is the shortest distance between any two points.

gristmill—mill that grinds grain, especially corn.

gut—steep-sided trench eroded in loess soil.

headland—unplowed land at the ends of furrows.

heliophyte—a plant that grows well in full sunlight.

hip roof, or pyramidal roof—roof sloping in four directions.

horseshoe lake—see oxbow.

humid subtropical climate—a climate characterized by warm summers and mild winters, with precipitation well distributed throughout the year.

immature soil—soil deposited too recently to have developed a soil profile.

interglacial period—time period between two advances of the great ice sheets.

interlevee lake—a basin enclosed by distributary channels extending their levees into the open water of the sea.

Isleños—Canary Islanders brought to Louisiana as colonists by the Spaniards about 1730.

isobath—line connecting points having equal depth.

isochrone—line connecting points having equal time duration, such as the same number of days of growing season.

isohyet—line connecting points having equal rainfall.

isostasy—a sinkage of the earth's crust in one place, with a balancing rise in another.

isotherm—line connecting points of equal temperature.

lagoonal lake—coastal lake formed behind cheniers or natural levees.

lapse rate—rate of temperature decrease that occurs with increasing altitude.

latitude—distance on the earth's surface north or south from the equator, measured in degrees along a meridian. The length of a degree of latitude is about seventy land miles.

leaching—removal of soluble elements from soil by percolating water.

league—a distance of three nautical miles, or 3.45 land miles.

lick—a place where salt is found on the surface and is licked by animals.

line settlement—houses closely spaced along a road.

loess—fine depositional material, largely silt, having a high lime content.

longitude—the distance in degrees of a place east or west of the prime meridian.

marais—French word meaning a small, shallow undrained pond in the prairie.

marine climate—a climate with low diurnal and annual temperature variations; reflects nearness to the sea.

marsh—low, wet, treeless, grass-covered area.

mast—nuts such as acorns that accumulate on the forest floor and are eaten by animals.

meander—loop-like bend in the course of a stream; a characteristic of the Mississippi and related streams.

meander belt—the part of a valley bottom across which a stream shifts its channel.

meridian—a north-south line from which longitudes are reckoned.

metes and bounds—name applied to irregular survey system of the colonial English.

midden—an accumulation of refuse around a dwelling place.

middle latitudes—the area between 30°–60° north and south of the equator.

monsoon effect—a situation in which, like the monsoon, the prevailing wind is seaward in winter and landward in summer.

mud flat—low strip of river silt along the seashore.

mudlump—small island near the mouths of the Mississippi, produced by escaping gas.

natural levee—bank or ridge built up along either side of a river by flood-time deposition.

natural resource—a provision of nature of which man can and does make use.

nautical mile, or geographical mile—a distance of 1.15 land miles; generally one minute of latitude.

nogging—material used to fill open spaces between timbers of a house frame.

occupance pattern—the imprint made by a group of people as they live on the land, expressed in the kind and position of such elements as buildings, fields, and streets.

old field—abandoned Indian field.

oxbow—a crescent-shaped lake occupying a cutoff meander.

oxidation—chemical weathering process involving combination with oxygen; commonly leaves a red stain where rocks contain iron.

paling—thin slab placed upright to form a fence.

parallel of latitude—line on a map joining points of the same angular distance north or south of the equator.

parent material—underlying weathered rock material from which true soil is formed.

petit habitant—small farmer of French descent.

pimple mound—small, low, circular or elliptical hillock composed of sand and silt coarser than the surrounding soil.

pirogue—dugout canoe; today often made of plank.

plankton—minute animal and plant life of a body of water.

plastic—capable of being deformed under pressure without breaking.

platin—see *marais.*

Pleistocene—the Ice Age, ending about 10,000 years ago.

point—deposit on the shelving slope on the inside of a meander.

poteaux en terre—logs or posts set vertically in the ground, in the French manner of building a log house.

potsherd—pottery fragment.

prairie—extensive area of tall grass.

quarter boat—a boat that serves as living quarters for a work crew.

raft—timber jam blocking a river channel.

raft lake—water impounded in parts of the main and tributary valleys of Red River, commonly attributed to the Great Raft.

reach—straight stretch of river channel between meanders.

Recent period—approximately the last 10,000 years following the Ice Age.

relict feature—a feature surviving long after a process of change has destroyed features once associated with it.

relief—the difference in elevation between the high and low points of a land surface.

retting—soaking in order to promote the loosening of fibers by bacterial action

ridge-and-swale topography—series of low ridges and intervening low areas on a river point.

rive—to split with a sharp instrument, normally a froe, or cleaving tool.

round lake—shallow lake developed in uniform deposits of the coastal marsh.

salt dome—upthrust salt plug that bow the layers of sediments which it penetrates.

scouring—deepening of a channel by the river current.

section line—boundary line between the mile-square sections into which the land is commonly divided.

sediment—mineral or organic material deposited by water, air, or ice.

sedimentary rock—rock formed by the consolidation of a deposit of sediments.

shoreline—the actual line where land and water meet.

slash-and-burn agriculture—felling and burning trees to create temporary fields.

sleet—frozen rain.

slip—a wheelless scoop for moving earth; pulled by animals.

snake fence, or worm fence—zigzag fence made of interlocking wooden rails.

soil—the outer weathered crust of the earth to which have been added various organic materials.

soil profile—vertical section of soil through all its horizons and extending into the parent material.

solstice—position farthest north and farthest south where the sun is directly overhead. The sun is at 23½° north (Tropic of Cancer) on June 22, and at 23½' south (Tropic of Capricorn) on December 22.

solution lake—small pond associated with salt domes, caused by solution of salt and caving in.

spat—young oyster.

spillway—emergency outlet for river waters at floodstage.

squall line—edge of a cold front along which there are violent, gusty winds.

storm surge—great, rolling swells of water pushed inland by onshore winds.

stringer—(road) timber laid along a road to support cross pieces that form a floor; (mineral) narrow vein of mineral across a rock mass of different material.

structure (of soil)—the arrangement of individual soil particles into aggregates.

subsistence farming—a system of farming that provides essentially all the goods required by the farm family, without any considerable surplus for sale.

swamp—low, wet, forested area.

technological capacity—the degree to which a group has tools to accomplish work efficiently.

tenancy—system of land usage under which land is rented from the owner or is farmed on a share basis with the owner.

terrace—flat surface lying above the present surface of Mississippi River activity.

thalweg—deepest natural channel of a stream.

tidewater—coastal area in which waterways are subject to tidal action; the immediate coastal area.

topography—description of the surface forms of the land.

towhead—small body of land between main river and chute.

trenasse—French word meaning a small canal through the marsh.

tributary—stream flowing into a large stream.

vacherie—French word meaning ranch.

vacuum pan—pan with a vacuum pump that speeds the condensation of sugar by boiling at a low temperature.

value system—a group's notions about the right and wrong ways to do things.

wattle and daub—method of building whereby a wattle, or frame, of poles and interwoven twigs is covered with mud or plaster.

winnowing—the sorting of fine and coarse materials by the sea.

wold—see cuesta.

workshop—an archeological site containing an accumulation of stone chippings.

Index

Acadian Coast: description of, 7
Acadians: in Acadian Coast, 7; in Acadian Country, 7; customs of, 127–28; agriculture of, 178. *See also* French
Agriculture: and climate, 21–25; and soils, 76–77; Indian, 107, 112, 115–16; in French colony, 120–22; Bienville and importance of, 122; of early German farmers, 124; of Anglo-Saxons, 132–34; and population, 141; prairie, 161–65; shifts in, 16, 178–81. *See also* Acadians; Cotton; Rice; Sugarcane
Air, movement of, 19
Air masses: affecting climate, 18–19, 25, 29, 30–31
Alexandria, 20, 27, 149
Alluvial cones, 51
Alluvial valley, 44–52
Amite River: as part of historic waterway, 6
Anglo-Saxons: cultural influence of, 7–8; use of "bagol," 60; house types of, 33; in the prairies, 162; imprint on land, 199; as distinctive culture, 199
Annular drainage. *See* Drainage patterns
Anse la Butte, 172
Atakapas: Indian linguistic group, 110; economy of, 111–12; mentioned, 129
Atchafalaya Basin: description of, 7, 58; as distributary, 45, 48; production of Spanish moss, 99; home of Chitimacha Indians, 112; cypress in, 162; mentioned, 127, 129
Atchafalaya River: De Soto on, 116; as distributary of Mississippi, 45, 48; diversion of, 158–59
Atchafalaya Spillway, 55, 158–59
Atmosphere, elements of, 17
Attakapas District, 192
Avery Island: drainage pattern of, 59; Lithic cultural remains on, 106
Avoyel Indians, 110
Avoyelles Prairie, 51

Bagol. *See* Anglo-Saxons
Balize: as active delta, 54, 56
Barataria, Bayou, 7
Barrier beach, 56
Barrier island, 56
Bateaux: in early commerce, 126–27, 142–43
Baton Rouge: Iberville at site of, 118; founded, 123; oil at, 172, 174, 177; industrial development of, 191; population of, 195; mentioned, 6, 25, 199
Bayou Dan Hills, 38
Bayou Sara, 143, 148
Beach ridge, formation of, 56
Belted coastal plain, formation of, 34–35
Bienville: at English Turn, 120; and agriculture, 122; and land division, 122; establishes New Orleans, 122–23
Biloxi: Iberville at, 117–18; colony moved from, 120; mentioned, 122
Bison: no evidence of, 115; as seen by La Salle, 116; mentioned, 6, 126
Blacks: migration of, 193
Blufflands: as division of terraces, 9–10; forest, 83
Bogalusa, 21, 169
Bonnet Carré Spillway: and flood control, 7, 158
Bottomland soils: as resource for Indians and Europeans, 86
Boulaye: established by French, 120
Boundaries: natural and arbitary, 8–9; of Louisiana, 13–15; disputed, 15; change in, 15
Braided channel. *See* Drainage patterns
British: traders in Mobile Bay, 120; gain Florida Parishes, 126; agricultural practices of, 178. *See also* Anglo-Saxons: imprint on land
Burrwood, 21

Caddoan: Indian linguistic group, 110
Caddo Indians, 69, 112

Cameron, 33

Cameron Beach: formation of cheniers, 65

Campti, 61

Caprock: and preserving ridges, 37; in salt domes, 175

Carbon black: from natural gas, 175

Carpet grass, 81, 85

Cattle: on loessal soils, 75; Anglo Saxon method of raising, 129–31, 132; Spanish method of raising, 130–31, 178; on prairies, 141; mentioned, 7, 179, 182

Chandeleur Islands: as common kind of island, 6; as barrier islands, 56

Chenier: plain, 55–56; formation of, 64–66; mentioned, 7, 22, 31

Chitimacha: Indian linguistic group, 110; economy of, 112

Choctaw Indians, 114, 127

Chutes, formation of, 48

Citrus trees: as commercial crop, 21–22, 180–81; as introduced plant, 84, 125; mentioned, 13

Civil War: importance of Mississippi River to, 141

Clams: as shells for roads, 99; as food of prehistoric Indians, 105, 107; and shell effigy mounds, 108; mentioned, 54

Clay: as stream deposit, 35, 40, 41, 49, 54, 55, 72

Claypan: in prairie soils, 76

Clinton, 21, 148

Coastal Hinge Line, 36, 42

Conservation, function of, 100

Continental climate: effect of relief on, 18, 25, 28; for North Louisiana, 21, 26, 31

Continental shelf: extent of, 56–57; and discovery of jumbo shrimp, 57; and petroleum, 15, 57; mentioned, 41

Contour plowing: practiced by subsistence farmers, 139

Contraband Trail, 121

Corn: growing season of, 23; and agricultural shift, 178–80; mentioned, 126. See also Maize

Cotton: growing season of, 23; on loessal and terrace soils, 75; and plantation systems, 138–39; and agricultural changes, 178–82

Coypu. See Nutria

Crabs, 92, 94

Crawfish, production of, 92, 94

Creole: use of term, 128

Crowley, 162

Crozat, Antoine: granted commercial monopoly, 120

Cuesta. See Wold

Cultural landscape: photograph of, 3

Culture: as modifier of earth's surface, 101–102; of prehistoric Indians, 104–109; of historic Indians, 110–13. See also Geographers; Geography; Occupance patterns

Cutoff, development of, 58

Cyclone family, 29–30

Cypress: forests, 79–81; heartwood, 83; lumbering, 167–68

Delacroix Island: land formation, 6; and Spanish, 130

Delhi, 173

Delta: as natural region, 10; definition of term, 49–50. See also Deltaic lakes; Deltaic systems

Deltaic lakes, formation of, 59–60

Deltaic plain, 56–57

Deltaic systems: of Mississippi River, 53–55

Dendritic. See Drainage patterns

De Pauger, Adrien: and improvement of Mississippi navigation below New Orleans, 122–23, 159

Deposition: as relief builder, 34–39

DeRidder, 35

De Soto, Hernando: explores Louisiana, 115–16

De Vaca, Cabeza, 115

Distributaries: of lowland streams, 58; of Mississippi River, 48, 49, 50, 53, 58

Dolet Hills, 37

Drainage patterns: description of, 58–59; altered by domes, 68

Driskill Mountain, 15, 37

Eads, James: and jetties at Mississippi mouth, 123, 159

Economies, basic, 103

Effigy mounds, 105, 108

English Turn, 120

Erosion: destruction of hill farms, 139; reduced by contour plowing, 139–40; mentioned, 34, 35, 39, 101

Europeans: technological capacity of, 4; imprint on land, 4; first ascent of Red River, 61; alteration of vegetation by, 78; use of bottomland, 86; use of Spanish moss, 99; changes by, 101; first appearance in Louisiana, 110; influence on Caddo Indians, 112; as influenced by Indian culture, 113; introduction of pigs, 116; as permanent settlers, 122. See also British; French; Germans; Spanish

Evaporation: related to water budget, 24–25

Evapotranspiration, 25

False River: seen by Iberville, 118; settlement at, 123; Acadians settle at, 127. *See also* Cutoff

Felicianas: and loessial soil, 6, 75; British enter, 126

Five Islands: as salt domes, 6, 67; as minor feature, 34; origin of, 36; solution lakes on, 60; mentioned, 187

Flatboats, 142

Flatwoods: as division of terraces, 8–9; soils of, 76–77; as forest cover, 81–82; as resources for Indians, 106–107; as commercial forests, 183–84

Floodplain: soils, 72–73; as home of primitive Indians, 106; origin of name, 107; historic Indians on, 111

Florida Parishes: location of, 6; terraces in, 36; present-day forest types in, 38, 84; water supply in, 95–98; gained by British, 127; Anglo-Saxon culture in, 136; retained by Spanish, 137; become part of United States, 137; pine lumbering in, 169; egg production in, 183

Forests: first-bottom hardwood, 79–80; second-bottom hardwood, 79; longleaf pine hills, 81–82; longleaf flatwoods, 81; short-leaf, 82; bluffland or upland hardwood, 83

Frasch process, 175

French: cultural influence of, 4, 7–8, 16; house types of, 132. *See also* Acadians

French Settlement, 14

French West Indies: as influence on plantations, 136, 139

Front: and air masses, 18–19

Frontal winds, 30–31

Fur, production of, 87–90

Geographers: task of, 1–4; physical, 101; cultural, 101–103

Geography, definition of, 1–2

Geologic deposits: conversion to soil, 70

German Coast: description of, 7

Germans: settlement of German Coast, 7, 124; agriculture, 178

Glaciation. *See* Ice Age

Glauconite, 37

Glaze, 25–27

Graben lakes, 51, 60

Grand Canyon of the Mississippi River, 43

Grand Isle: as common kind of island, 6; as barrier island, 56

Gravel: stream sediment, 35, 40–41; as ridge capping, 37; and road surfacing, 99; Indians' use of, 105, 113

Great circle, 12

Great Raft. *See* Raft

Gristmills, 95–97

Growing season: for South Louisiana, 21–23, 25; for North Louisiana, 22–25; as resource, 86

Gulf Coastal Plain: Louisiana within, 15, 34; formation of, 34–35

Gulf of Mexico: effect on climate, 18–19, 28

Hail: kinds and occurrence of, 25–27

Hardwoods: upland, 15. *See also* Blufflands; Forests

Harrisonburg, 37

Harvey, 167

Highways: modern, 149–53; imprint on the land, 150

Hills: as natural region, 89; as relief division, 34–36; soils of, 77; and gravel, 105; as source of salt, 106

Honey Island: braided channels of, 58; mentioned, 6, 14

House types: French and Anglo-Saxon, 132–33

Humidity, 25

Humid subtropical climate: in Louisiana, 19–20, 32

Hurricanes: as destructive storms, 17; description of, 30–33

Hydroelectric power, rise of, 95

Iberville: ascent of Mississippi River, 117–18

Ice age: formation of Mississippi River during, 39; and formation of terraces, 39–43; extent of continental glaciation during, 39; end of, 42–43. *See also* Marais

"I" house: construction of, 133; on upland plantations, 139

Indian mounds, 105, 108–109

Indians: first appearance in Louisiana, 3; as occupants of Mississippi deltaic systems, 53–54; on Chandeleur Islands, 56; their mounds and middens as cheniers, 64; and origin of pimple mounds, 69; alteration of vegetation, 78; use of natural resources, 86; use of Spanish moss, 99; mound building, 105, 108–109; and streams for travel, 105, 111; cultures, 109; linguistic groups, 110–11; imprint on land, 112–13; population figures, 113–14; modern place names, 114

Indigo: destroyed by disease, 136; introduction of, 198. *See also* Agriculture: shifts in

Industrial corridor, 188–89

Industry, development of, 187–91

Interior domes: as source of limestone and

gypsum, 68; surface character of, 68; and salt for Confederacy, 141

Intracoastal Canal: as east-west connection for waterways, 63

Iowa, 162

Ironstone, 37

Irrigation: of prairie rice, 162–64; of strawberries, 97

Islenos: on Delacroix Island, 130

Isle of Orleans: location of, 6; ceded to Spain, 127

Isostasy: and significance of Coastal Hinge Line in formation of terraces, 37, 42

Istrouma: seen by Iberville, 118

Jackson Military Road, 143

Jefferson Island, lakes on, 62. See also Five Islands

Jennings: discovery of petroleum at, 172; mentioned, 162

Johnson grass: introduced, 81, 85

Joliet: descent of Mississippi River, 116

Kaplan, 162

Keelboats: in early transportation, 142–43

Kisatchie Wold: extent of, 6; geological formation of, 35; as hill section, 37; mentioned, 58

Koasati Indians, 114

Koroa Indians, 112

Lafayette, 7

Lafourche, Bayou: habitable levees of, 7; as Mississippi distributary, 45, 48; as deltaic system, 57; water-deficient area, 98; reached by Iberville, 118; first settlement of, 123; Acadians on, 127

Lagoonal lakes, formation of, 60

La Loutre, Bayou, 6. See also Deltaic lakes

Land division: French method of, 122, 161; metes and bounds, 161; and General Land Office, 164

Land-sea contrasts: effect on climate, 17–18

Lapse rate: affects climate, 17–18

La Salle: exploration by, 116–17; territorial claim of, 121

Last Island, 6

Lithic culture stage, 105–106

Live oaks: northern extent of natural growth, 79; mentioned, 31, 99

Livestock. See Cattle

Lockett, Samuel: and natural regions of Louisiana, 10

Loess, 73–76

Longleaf: as division of hill region, 8–9; forest, 81–82; heartwood, 83; present-day extent of, 81–82; pine growth following fire, 113

Louisiana Purchase: change of boundaries, 137; population at time of, 177

Lowlands: as natural region, 8–9, 36

Lumbering: vegetation prior to industrial, 83; early development of, 166–70; imprint on land, 167–68; present importance of, 183, 84

Lutcher, 167

Macon Ridge: as boundary of Tensas Basin, 6; as alluvial cone of Arkansas River, 5, 73

Madisonville, 147

Maize: as Indian crop, 106; mentioned, 125. See also Corn

Mammals, 87–90

Manchac, Bayou: as part of historic waterway, 6; as Mississippi distributary, 45, 48; as boundary of alluvial valley, 49; reached by Iberville, 118; as route to Mississippi, 118, 120; settlement on, 123; as early limit of sugarcane growth, 136

Manchac, Pass: and return trip by Iberville, 119

Marais, 60

Marine climate: cause of, 17–18; for South Louisiana, 21, 31

Marksville: Indian culture, 109

Marksville Prairie, 51

Marsh: as natural region, 8–9; as product of river and sea, 54; as base of chenier formation, 64; soils, 71–72; vegetation, 78–79; as habitat for prehistoric Indians, 105

Marsh Island: as common kind of island, 6; as dividing line between chenier plain and delta plain, 56

Maurepas, Lake: as part of historic waterway, 6, 117–18; as a graben lake, 60

Meander: importance of size of, 6

Meander belt: of Mississippi River, 44–49

Menhaden: as basis of commercial fishery, 91–92

Mermentau River: saltwater intrusion into, 163

Metallic ores: Louisiana deficient in, 86–87

Metes and bounds: as used by Anglo-Saxons, 132

Midwest: influence in Louisiana prairies, 7, 162–63

Minden, 27

Mineral fuels: in production of electricity, 95

Mississippi floodplain: as natural region, 8–10

Mississippi River: in Tensas Basin, 6; its channel as state boundary, 14; as prime factor in state's geography, 15, 181, 182; formation of,

39–41; Grand Canyon of, 43; gradient of, 44; meander belt, 44–49; tributaries and distributaries of, 44, 45, 48–49; deltaic systems of, 54–56; lakes associated with, 59; record of shifting channels, 65–66; fish kills on, 92; soils associated with, 74; as source of surface water, 95; and Indian agriculture in floodplain, 108; exploration of, 15–19; importance during Civil War, 141; control of, 154–60; artificial outlet to Gulf, 160; industrial development along, 188–89
Mississippi Sound: as part of historic waterway, 6, 118
Mobile Bay: colony established, 120; mentioned, 115, 122
Mobilian: Indian language, 110
Monroe, 98, 153
Monsoon effect, 18
Morgan City, 167
Mud flats: deposition of, 55, 65
Mudlumps: formation of, 64, 66, 67
Muskhogean: Indian linguistic group, 110; economy of, 112
Muskrat: as fur producer, 87–90

Nacogdoches Wold, 37
Narváez: explores near mouth of Mississippi, 115
Natchitoches: founded, 120–22; as limit of commercial sugarcane, 137; mentioned, 123
Natchitoches-Nacogdoches Road, 121, 143
Natural landscape: photograph of, 2
Natural regions: basis of, 9–10
Naval stores, 166
Negroes: as slaves of French, 122; mentioned, 193. See also Blacks
New Orleans: significance of location, 11–12; founded, 122–23; early connection by road with Nashville, 143; population, 192–95
North Louisiana; distinctive character of, 7–8; climate of, 25–29; salt domes in, 66–67
Nutria, 89–90

Occupance patterns, 4, 101–102
Old Spanish Trail, 143
Opelousas District, 129, 177
Orleans, Isle of: extent of, 6
Osage orange (bois d'arc): as bow wood, 111
Ouachita hills, 38
Ouachita River, 37–38
Oysters: production of, 92–94; shells for road surface, 99

Passes: of the Mississippi, 49. See also Delta

Patterson, 167
Pearl River: as state boundary, 14; as boundary of Florida Parishes, 6; relation to Honey Island, 6
Pecan Island, 88
Perique, 124, 178
Petits habitants, 127
Petroleum: on continental shelf, 57; development of, 172–75; in association with salt and sulphur, 172; imprint on land by industry, 173–75; offshore drilling, 176–77
Pimple mounds: formation and origin of, 69
Pine: upland, 78; kinds of, 81–83; loblolly on denuded areas, 84; lumbering, 169–70
Pineda: explores coast, 115
Pipelines, 151, 173–77
Pirogues: Indian, 112; mentioned, 142
Plain Dealing, 27, 38
Plaquemine, 167
Plaquemine, Bayou: as Mississippi distributary, 45, 48; reached by Iberville, 118
Platin, 60
Pleistocene. See Ice Age
Plywood, production of, 187
Pogy. See Menhaden
Pointe Coupee, 118
Ponchatoula, 167
Pontchartrain, Lake: as part of historic waterway, 6; as seen by Iberville, 118. See also Graben lakes
Population: prehistoric Indian, 3; growth, 16, 176–80; historic Indian, 114; urban, 195
Port Hudson, 143, 148
Ports: deepwater, 63
Poverty Point: Indian culture and effigy mounds, 108–109
Prairies: description of, 7; as division of terraces, 8–9; soils, 77; vegetation, 78–81; primitive Indians, 106; and line settlements, 141; cattle grazing on, 7, 129; modern settlement of, 156–60; rice growing in, 172
Prairie Terrace: and imprint of Ice Age Mississippi River, 43; near Baton Rouge, 43; remnants of, 51
Providence rice, 163

Quinipissa Indians, 116

Radial drainage. See Drainage patterns
Radiocarbon dating: of Indian remains, 3; and deltaic systems, 53–54
Raft: formation of, 64; removal of, 61, 154; mentioned, 121
Raft lakes: example of, 61; formation of, 61

Railroads, 148–49, 161
Rayne, 162
Red River: size of meanders, 6; alluvial cone, 51; as occupant of Teche channel, 51–52; cutoff lakes associated with, 59; raft lakes associated with, 61; formation of raft, 61; first ascent by Europeans, 61; as part of Mississippi navigation system, 63; soils, 72; Indian agriculture in floodplain, 108; as home of Caddoan Indians, 112; and site of Natchitoches, 120–21; Acadians on, 127
Red River Valley: as natural region, 8–9
Regions: distinguishing characteristics of, 83
Relative humidity, 25
Relief: related to climate, 17; as soil builder, 71; local, 15
Rice: growing season of, 23; as introduced plant, 84, 198; irrigation of, 98, 163; river rice, 123; prairie rice, 162–65
Ride-and-swale topography, 47–48
Rigolets: as part of historic waterway, 6
Rio de las Palmas: on Cantino Map, 115
Rio del Espirito Santo, 116
Roads: early, 121, 129, 143–45; modern, 149; in prairies, 164. See also Highways
Round lakes, formation of, 60

Sabine River: and state boundary controversy, 13–15
Sabine Uplift: as crustal deformation, 35, 37
St. Bernard Delta, 56
St. John, Bayou: and Iberville, 118, 120
Salt: extraction of by Indians, 106; from Five Islands, 175
Salt domes: location and formation of, 66–68. See also Five Islands; Interior domes
Sand: stream deposition of, 41; and road surfacing, 99
Sea level: Ice Age effects upon, 41
Settlement patterns: French, 129; British, 132–33; linear, 132, 135, 141, 161; dispersed, 132, 163; Midwest, 135, 165; sugarcane plantation, 136–37
Shortleaf pine: as division of hill region, 8–9; forests, 82–84
Shreve, Henry: his removal of Great Raft, 61–62; as builder of river steamboat, 147
Shreveport: precipitation, 27; and Great Raft, 61–62; covered road near, 144; and railroad, 148–49
Shrimp: commercial production of, 92–93; and introduction of trawl, 92
Sicily Island, 6
Slash-and-burn agriculture: and Indians, 112–

13; practiced by hill farmers, 134–35
Slavery, introduction of, 122
Slidell, 33
Solvay process, 168
Southern Mississippi Uplift, 36
South Louisiana: distinctive character of, 7–8; climate of, 21–27; salt domes in, 66–67
Soybeans: as new crop, 179–80
Spanish: settlement of Louisiana, 129–31; land grants, 129; cattle raising, 129, 130, 156; league, 130; settlement on Teche, 130. See also Isleños
Spanish moss: gathering and use of, 99
Spillways: Atchafalaya, 158–59; Bonnet Carré, 157
Steamboats: importance of, 146–47; imprint on the land, 153
Strawberries: growing season of, 23; on flatwoods soil, 76; commercial production of, 76–77, 179–80; irrigation of, 98
Subsistence farming: on hill farms, 139–40; and livestock, 178
Sugarcane: growing season of, 22–23; introduced, 84; as substitute for indigo, 136; and plantation system, 36–37; and agricultural shift, 178–79; introduction by Europeans, 198
Sulphur, production of, 175
Sun: angle at New Orleans, 12
Swamp: life in, 7; forest, 79; as home of primitive Indians, 105
Swartz, 196
Sweet potatoes: as subsistence crop, 139; as commercial crop, 180

Tangipahoa Indians, 116
Tchefuncte Indian culture, 108–109
Teche, Bayou: early settling of area, 7; as old Mississippi River channel, 51–52; Acadians on, 127
Tenant farming: adoption on cotton plantations, 139; reduction of, 181
Tensas Basin: as former Mississippi River channel, 51
Tensas Indians, 110–11, 116
Tensas River, 6
Terraces: as natural region, 8–9; as relief division, 36; formation of, 39–43
Terrace soils, 73–75
Terre aux Boeufs, Bayou, 6
Three-corner grass, 78
Time zones, 11
Tobacco: introduced, 126. See also Perique
Tornadoes, description of, 31

Township survey system: in prairies, 162

Transportation: navigable waterways, 62–63; and trade with Illinois country, 126–27; river roads (French period), 127; river roads (Spanish period), 129; military roads, 143; in nineteenth century, 143–44; in twentieth century, 150–51; by air after World War II, 151. *See also Bateaux*; Highways; Keelboats; Pipelines; Railroads; Roads; Steamboats

Tree crops, 183–85

Trellis drainage. *See* Drainage patterns

Tributaries: of upland dendritic streams, 58

Troyville: Indian culture, 108–109

Tung nut, production of, 179

Tunican: Indian linguistic group, 110–11; economy of, 112

Tuscaloosa Trend: as gas producer, 174; map of, 175

Vacherie, 156

Water: as natural resource, 95–99; for irrigation, 98; industrial use, 98; saltwater intrusion, 97; pollution of, 99

Water budget: described, 24–25

Waterfowl: migratory, 87

Water hyacinth, 79, 84, 85

Waterpower, early sources of, 95

Waterways: navigable, 62–63

Wax Lake: as outlet for Atchafalaya Spillway, 55

Welsh, 162

Wine Island, 6

Winnfield, 169

Wold, 35. *See also* Kisatchie Wold; Nacogdoches Wold